SUCCESSFUL
PROPERTY LETTING

Other titles

Computerised Book-keeping

Work from Home

Starting and Running a Sandwich-Coffee Bar

Mastering Book-keeping

Writing a Business Plan

SUCCESSFUL PROPERTY LETTING

HOW TO MAKE MONEY IN BUY-TO-LET

David Lawrenson

A How To Book

ROBINSON

ROBINSON

First published in Great Britain in 2005 by Elliot Right Way Books
Revised edition published in Great Britain in 2015 by Robinson
This revised edition published in Great Britain in 2017 by Robinson

1 3 5 7 9 10 8 6 4 2

Copyright © David Lawrenson, 2005, 2013, 2015, 2017

A CIP catalogue record for this book
is available from the British Library.

ISBN: 978-1-47213-997-9

Typeset in Bembo by SX Composing DTP, Rayleigh, Essex
Printed and bound in Great Britain by CPI Group (UK), Croydon CR0 4YY

www.littlebrown.co.uk

How To Books are published by Robinson, an imprint of Little, Brown Book Group. We welcome proposals from authors who have first-hand experience of their subjects. Please set out the aims of your book, its target market and its suggested contents in an email to Nikki.Read@howtobooks.co.uk.

Dedication

To Dagmar Svehlik, my partner, for her fantastic love and support, to Alex, our son, and to my parents.

Special Thanks

Thanks to all those who have taken time to comment on the good work that we try to do at Letting Focus and to all those who have shared their experiences of residential property investment and letting over the years.

Also, thanks to the Elliot brothers, who, in 2004 showed a unique and insightful faith in the original manuscript. I think their faith was fully rewarded.

Any useful comments on the script or suggestions for future editions are welcome.

About the Author

After university and his MBA at Cass (formerly City University) Business School, David Lawrenson worked in the financial services industry as an internal consultant and project manager whilst moonlighting as a residential landlord.

In 2002, he left to become a full-time property investor. Then in 2005, the first edition of *Successful Property Letting – How to Make Money in Buy-to-Let* came out and became the UK's top-selling property book.

Lawrenson's views on the private rented sector are quoted regularly in national newspapers like *The Times*, *Independent* and *Daily Telegraph* and in many specialist property magazines and on buy-to-let websites.

He is a regular speaker at trade shows and for public and private organisations and trade associations and he runs a thriving consultancy business which helps banks, building societies, investment funds, letting agents, local authorities and housing associations develop and market their products and services for the buy-to-let and landlord markets.

He has advised the London Assembly and spoken at the Council of Mortgage Lenders.

Lawrenson also has a low-cost seminar programme and a one-to-one consultancy service for people wishing to get into buy-to-let for the first time as well as for more experienced landlords and investors. His website and blog are at *www.LettingFocus.com* and he can be contacted at *david@LettingFocus.com*.

He also has a site for tenants at *www.tenants-renting-guide.com* and a new book, *Tenants' Guide to Successful Renting*.

Contents

Preface to the 2017 New Edition   11

1.   An Introduction to Property Investment   15

Why you need this book, 15; A brief history of residential property letting, 16; "Landlord" or "Property Investor", 17; How property differs from other types of investment, 17; When to buy? Good and bad times in the property market, 20; Meet the people who want your money, 21; Is it for you? What kind of person makes a successful landlord?, 22; How much should I put in property?, 26.

2.   Easy as ABC: The Simple Economics of Property Letting   29

Income and capital growth, 29; How to calculate the true income from your property, 29; How to calculate capital growth, 39.

3.   How to Find the Right Property   41

Location, location, location: How to choose the right area, 41; How to choose the right kind of property, 44; Which is best: Leasehold or freehold? What questions should you ask?, 47; Whether to buy a new or old property: Things to consider, 53; How to buy in new developments and off-plan (and avoid the pitfalls), 54; How to buy at auction, 62; Does everything work? Things to check before you buy, 69; How to negotiate successfully, 70; Buying below market value (BMV), 72.

4.   Ready to Buy: Finance and the Legal Stuff   78

*How to arrange your finance, 78; How to make the
conveyancing process work for you, 89.*

5.   Refurbishing and Preparing Your Property   93

*How to deal with builders, 93; How to deal with
architects and surveyors, 97; How to get planning
permission and building regulations approval, 98;
How to decorate and furnish, 99; Legal regulations:
Furnishing, gas safety, electrical, EPCs, HMOs and
disability, 104; Energy Performance Certificates
(EPCs), 106; Licensing and Houses in Multiple
Occupation (HMOs), 107; Disability, 111;
How to get the right insurance cover, 112;
Keeping everyone informed: Telling people who
"need to know", 115.*

6.   How to Get the Tenancy Agreement Correct   117

*The different types of tenancy, 117; The assured shorthold
tenancy (AST) agreement: What's in it?, 120;
What tenants need to know: The emergency and
maintenance "House Guide", 124.*

7.   How to Find a Good Tenant   129

*Letting to friends . . . and why you shouldn't!, 129;
Getting your existing tenants to find new tenants, 130;
Letting to a social housing organisation, 130; Using a letting
agent, 131; How to find a good letting agent, 137;
If you're looking for a tenant yourself, 140;
How to screen potential tenants and take references, 147;
Final steps and what happens on move-in day, 165.*

8.   How to Manage the Tenancy   169

*How to manage the tenants, 169; How to manage housing-
benefit/local-housing-allowance (LHA) tenants, 170; How to
manage a letting agent, 172; How to manage maintenance, 175;
How to manage a problem neighbour, 182; How to end your
tenancy, 184; Other things to do to make sure the end of
tenancy goes smoothly, 186; Tenancy deposit schemes, 193;
How to manage utilities and council tax, 195; How to
manage paperwork, 196; How to keep up to date, 197.*

9.   Difficult Tenants and How to Deal with Them   199

*The sorts of things that can go wrong . . . and how to deal with
them, 199; How to evict a tenant, 202; How to serve a notice,
204; Possession proceedings, 205; How to make a claim for
money owed, 207; Evicting squatters and Rent Act tenants, 210;
Whatever you do, don't harass!, 212; What to do if a tenant dies,
213; What to do if a tenant abandons the property, 213; How to
solve housing benefit/local housing allowance problems, 214.*

10. When it's Time to Sell   218

*What's the best time of year to sell?, 218; How to sell
successfully through an estate agent, 219; Selling at auction,
221; Selling it yourself, 221; Why it pays to be prepared, 223.*

11. Tax   224

*Completing the tax return, 225; All about income tax, 226;
All change for tax relief on interest, 230; All about capital
gains tax (CGT), 232; Tax on UK and European Economic
Area (EEA) Holiday Lets, 239; Tax on other foreign holiday
lets outside the EEA, 240; The rent a room scheme, 241; All
about stamp duty land tax, 241; "SIPPS", Syndicates and
"REITS", 244.*

12. Jet to Let: Diversifying Your Property Portfolio   246

UK and EEA holiday lets, 246; Investing in property abroad, 247; Things you need to know – some other considerations, 251; Where to buy and what to buy abroad, 253; All about taxes on foreign property, 255; Other opportunities, 257.

Appendix 1: A Sample Assured Shorthold Tenancy
                    Agreement   258

Appendix 2: Useful Contacts   269

Index   273

Preface to the 2017 New Edition

First things first, being a landlord is great fun and is still a great way to make money whilst, at the same time, doing something which is useful for other people – giving them a safe and comfortable place to live in.

And this book tells you everything you need to know.

So, welcome to this, the brand new 2017 edition of *Successful Property Letting,* the book which first came out in 2005.

Since the last edition came out in 2015, it has been another busy two years for the residential private rented sector. To reflect this, we have made lots of changes to the text throughout. In fact, we have made changes to almost two thirds of the pages that were in the 2015 edition. And this new 2017 edition is longer, too, packed with more facts and even more information.

There has been the usual array of small changes in legislation, so more things for landlords and letting agents to have to know about and comply with. Interestingly, too, the Scottish and Welsh administrations are increasingly "doing their own thing", necessitating landlords to have to keep up to date with different rules in the different countries of the UK, so landlords need to understand this.

Plus, the market has changed. New opportunities have surfaced, new ways of making money from residential property have emerged. I explain the latest ideas and the new ways of thinking.

And then there was one Mr George Osborne. The former Chancellor seemed to "have it in" for landlords, making a number of changes in the last two years to the tax regime that landlords face. These tax changes, when taken together, have made it just that little bit harder for some of the more highly leveraged buy to let landlords.

Of course, there was also the little matter of Brexit.

Without a doubt, the changes – both fiscal and regulatory – have put some people off the idea of becoming landlords. And some successful experienced landlords have thought twice about expanding their businesses further.

But that is all most of them have done – they just thought twice.

Then they sat down and had a cup of tea, looked at the alternatives and realised that this is still a great business to be in, where the returns are still far higher, but still safer and less risky than can be achieved elsewhere. Being a buy-to-let landlord is certainly a lot less risky than buying shares – and of course, you are in control, not someone else. And you can still borrow to invest in property, which you cannot do with shares and most fund-based investments.

Today, around 18 per cent of all property in the UK is privately let. And it is much higher than that in places like London, where in some boroughs, the private rented sector accounts for around three tenths of all properties. And it is still growing.

Being a landlord provides a lot of satisfaction – and not just for you but for your tenants, too. You are providing somewhere warm, comfortable and secure for someone to live in.

At the same time it remains a great add-on or alternative to a traditional pension. (Interestingly, many people are increasingly taking advantage of pension reforms to take some cash on retirement to invest in buy to let). So, you can see, there is still lots of money and satisfaction to be gained from being a landlord.

If you do it well, you can be your own boss, too. And if you follow the advice in this book, you will find it is really not *that much* work either. Good tenants don't call you in the middle of the night. In fact, in thirty years' letting lots of properties, only one tenant has ever called me outside normal business hours. And that was for a very good reason.

But be warned. There are lots of shark "gurus" out there offering poor advice and risky, madcap schemes to landlords and would-be "investors". They inhabit many property shows and are active online.

Hopefully, once you've read this book, you will know how to avoid them. In fact, once you've read this book, you'll know that most of their advice is nonsense, designed to make themselves rich at your expense.

The book is aimed at new and experienced landlords alike as well as corporate players such as pension funds who wish to understand how the sector works. Even really experienced landlords tell me they learned many useful things from this book.

As ever, in the book, I don't hold back from challenging those who provide products and services to the private rented sector to do better. I'm particularly critical of many letting agents and most of the big banks and building societies, who still fail to understand buy-to-let or to design suitable mortgage products for landlords.

And I'm often critical of government whose polices are too often muddled, contradictory and politically-driven. Too often their policies have made life harder for good landlords and good tenants, whilst at the same time, fail to deal with the small minority of bad landlords and letting agents who are undoubtedly still out there.

You can find more about me at my website for landlords at www.LettingFocus.com. Here, you can join my (still free) quarterly newsletter, read my blogs and find out about my occasional seminars and private one-to-one consultancy advice service. You can email me at david@LettingFocus.com.

If you know tenants who would like some good advice, please direct them to my site for tenants at www.Tenants-Renting-Guide.com and my book, *Tenants Guide to Successful Renting*.

David Lawrenson, April 2017

1

An Introduction to Property Investment

Why you need this book

This book is about how to make a success of property investment through letting residential property. I will tell you what you *really* need to know to make money in the buy-to-let market and talk you right through the residential letting business.

This book will be of interest to people who are thinking of becoming landlords for the first time as well as those with more experience. It will tell you where to buy, what to buy, how to spot locations that are on the up, how to buy at auction, below market value and "off plan", how to arrange finance, how to find good tenants and how to look after them. If you need to do work on your property, it will tell you how to hire builders and architects, how to deal with planning and building regulations and how to furnish and decorate your property.

You'll also learn all you need to know about your legal responsibilities as a landlord, what to do if things go wrong, how to minimise tax on your rental profits and how to buy abroad.

When you've read this book you'll know how to let out property successfully, either by yourself or with the help of an agent whilst keeping your costs and time to a minimum. You'll know what the big risks are, what sort of things to look out for and how to avoid disasters. You'll know how to keep your tenants happy and the rent rolling in!

This book is kept regularly updated to reflect the current conditions in the property market. So, look out for new editions and updates.

A brief history of residential property letting

You've probably heard about people who have made a fortune out of property investment and about a few people who have lost money too. And the news is full of it.

These days, there is always some survey or other on how house prices are moving, how long it's taking to sell properties and how rents are faring.

As a well-known expert in the sector, I'm increasingly targeted by different government departments and other foundations, all wanting to learn more from me about the private rented sector and barely a month goes by without some new report or other emerging – to be opened, read, discussed and dissected before eventually finding a permanent home as a useful doorstop.

However, property hasn't always been the obsession it is today.

In the old days, mortgage loans were even harder to obtain than they are today and loans were small, relative to the value of the properties they financed. The "flexible" labour market, where employers could make people redundant because their companies weren't making *enough* profit hadn't yet been invented.

In the housing shortage after the Second World War, a few nasty landlords emerged who overcharged and used intimidation tactics against their tenants. One landlord, a certain Mr Rachman, led to the word "Rachmanism" becoming forever associated with particularly unpleasant landlord practices.

In response, the Government typically overreacted and passed laws that set up what were called Rent Act tenancies. These gave tenants a protected low rent but it became difficult if not impossible for landlords to get their property back. Faced with low returns and little flexibility huge numbers of landlords simply withdrew from the market, resulting in the proportion of properties in the private rented sector falling from 50 per cent in 1945 to less than 10 per cent by the mid 1980s and a shortage of homes to let. Ultimately, this started to harm the economy because people found they couldn't move to jobs in other areas because there were so few homes available to rent.

Finally the Government saw sense and in 1988 and 1996 passed two Housing Acts which made it much easier and quicker for landlords to reclaim possession of their property at the end of a letting. The buy-to-let mortgage followed and the proportion of UK housing stock that is privately rented has since grown rapidly to nearly 20 per cent (and it is much higher in some urban areas).

"Landlord" or "Property Investor"

The word "landlord" has some negative connotations and I suppose this goes back to the medieval times of Lords and Serfs but it was made worse by the activities of Rachman. In general, though, successful landlords these days are ones who look after their tenants and treat them with respect. As a result, the negative associations of the word "landlord" are dying away too, so I'll stick with it throughout this book.

How property differs from other types of investment

With property, unlike many other kinds of investments, you're the one in control, not some anonymous fund manager in the City. You can walk past your property and actually see your investment so you are immediately more connected to it. I wouldn't go around hugging the walls of your property while the tenants are there, but I'm sure you understand what I mean when I say you can start to love property!

Property also provides something we all need – shelter – so there should always be demand for it. With property, you can sell it whenever you want, which you can't do with a pension. Unlike a pension, you can also bequeath it to your heirs when you die and you aren't forced to use most of it to buy an annuity either. (It's worth noting here that changes to pension rules announced in the 2014 budget allow retirees to access some of their pension as a cash sum. This will mean some of these retirees will decide to invest in property letting.)

At this point I'll admit to being cannier at investing in property than I am in the stock market. More than once I've bought a share, only to see the price collapse. I find this somewhat baffling because surely, if the Report and Accounts of a company have been read by a good many clever people (including highly paid fund managers) and the company shares are, say, one pound, then how they can fall to a penny over the course of just one year (or even less time) is a mystery. Of course, in the stock market, the risk is that the products or services of a company can go out of fashion, be replaced by new technology or simply end up being managed by people who lose all the company's money before getting a big pay-off for doing so! The problems don't stop with individual shares either. The audit and regulatory bodies have clearly failed to protect people from endowment and pension mis-selling. Add to this the split capital trusts scandal and PPI mis-selling and it's easy to see why property is now seen as a good way of providing a reliable secondary income or a retirement fund.

The fact is that with property, if you do your homework and check out the location and the local tenant market, you'll know a lot more than you can ever learn about any company in any published source.

If you combine letting property with a day job, you'll have the satisfaction of knowing that if a "new broom" boss arrives and decides your face no longer fits you'll still have the income and capital from your property to fall back on. This can give a great sense of security.

If you're a full-time landlord and you do things right, you'll have an income stream that's reliable and you can choose how and when you work. Want a lie in? Then have one. You're the boss!

Now that everyone and his dog are talking about property it's easy to imagine that the market is being swamped with too many developers and too many properties to rent. And as salary to mortgage multiples become more stretched, the fear is that house price rises may level out or fall a bit.

However, if we step back and look at the big picture, we can see that an increasing population and a shortage of houses, including "social housing", are still forcing prices up. The growing population is driven partly by internal growth but also increasingly by immigration. Also, divorce and ageing means that people are tending to live in smaller units with the number of one-person homes growing markedly. At the same time there has been a recent big increase in the number of families who rent from private landlords, partly because renting is a lot more flexible than being burdened with a mortgage when un-employment hits. There has also been an increase in people renting in retirement too, who often prefer bungalows and other properties with easy access. Housing supply has failed to keep up with these changes and demand for housing, especially in London and the South-East, is outstripping supply.

It is clear that the UK needs a massive house-building pro-gramme to close the gap. The hopes of the Government to meet housing demand by streamlining the planning system have worked only partially and in recent years tough credit conditions have made it hard for builders to get funds to build and borrowers to get mortgages.

This suggests that a big fall in property prices like the one between 1989 and 1994 is unlikely – and whilst first-time buyers are clearly more stretched today, houses are still affordable in many areas, especially for those lucky first-time buyers able to rely on help from their parents.

In the rental market, the trends to more job flexibility, temp-orary workers, more students, more migrant workers, an ageing population, less council/social housing and increasing divorce rates are all factors that should lead to increasing demand for rental accommodation. If there is no significant growth in the number of houses built, then the outlook for rents should be up too.

Changes in government tax policy may also boost property. To encourage more rented housing, the Government has brought in a new form of tax-efficient property fund based on so called "real estate investment trusts" or "REITS" which have proved popular in other countries.

And with a diminishing stock of council housing the Government is paying an increasingly hefty housing benefit bill – a lot of which ends up with private landlords and which has become a huge political football.

When to buy? Good and bad times in the property market

There are undoubtedly some times that are better than others in the property market. However, even in bad times there are still opportunities for the experienced property investor. Let's take a look at a time that is probably regarded as pretty dire: in 2008, following the banking crises, inflation-adjusted house prices peaked over most of the UK and started a decline that went on for about five years.

Nevertheless, there have been many areas and certain types of property that didn't fall in value at all. This was usually due to local factors – a new road, tube, railway, airport or employment opportunities. Compare Middlesbrough with Hackney in London. In Middlesbrough, in the ten years to 2014 average house prices went up by one fifth. In Hackney they went up six fold.

Meanwhile, rents have actually gone up in most places since 2008, especially in London, so if you got the right property in the right place, 2008 was still a good time to invest for many.

The skill of the property investor and landlord is in identifying these local opportunities and acting on them. To do this you need local knowledge and I shall say more about how to do this in Chapter 3. Property does indeed have risks but, if you do your homework, these risks are manageable. To some extent risks with property are reduced because the market has a natural compensating mechanism in which any weakness in house prices is counterbalanced by strength in rents. Let me explain.

When economic conditions are bad and house prices fall, as they did in 2008 and 2009 due to the effects of a tightening of mortgage availability, worried first-time buyers tend to stay on the sidelines and rent – with some hoping to buy at cheaper prices later. This tends to push up rents. At the same time, nervousness among some home owners and inexperienced landlords (and harsh credit conditions) may lead them to sell their properties and also rent instead. This can have the effect of reducing the number of properties available to rent at the same time as further increasing demand for rented accommodation. The higher demand for rentals thus pushes up rents and compensates for falls in house prices. Indeed, this was the picture in much of the UK between 2008 and 2013, a period of falling house prices in many areas but fast-rising rents.

Conversely, when house prices rise and look set to rise further, first-time buyers (who might otherwise have rented but are fearful of missing the boat) enter the market to buy property and the opposite effect happens. With less demand for rented accommodation, rents may tend to be static or fall but the price of property should go up.

Meet the people who want your money

As interest in property as an investment has grown, so too has the number of players involved in the business. There are mortgage and bridging lenders, crowd funders, mortgage brokers, surveyors, solicitors, letting agents, freeholders, managing agents, developers, property syndicates, buying agents, consultants, and last, but not least, the taxman. The thing they have in common is: they all want your money!

There are even people who give seminars on letting property, where they aim to teach you all you need to know in a weekend in exchange for a few hundred (or even tens of thousands) of pounds and the opportunity to join their investment club, where you're supposed to be able to get big discounts off new developments or access to great below-market-value deals from overstretched home owners. Then there are buying agents who'll purchase and kit out investment property for you.

The standard of performance and value for money of many of these players is variable (and some are little better than cowboys) and I'll comment further on each of them throughout the book. I'll also tell you how to get the best out of them, where you can find good advisers and how you can minimise the amount of money that you pay them.

For now it is worth your being aware that some aspects of residential property investment advice are not regulated which makes property a very attractive area of business to the charlatan looking to separate naïve investors from their savings. You have been warned.

Is it for you? What kind of person makes a successful landlord?

The sort of person who makes a good landlord is someone who is sceptical and enquiring and has good people and communication skills. They are usually good administrators and, above all, they really love the property business and are prepared to take some risks.

Successful landlords question everything they hear and are prepared to do their own research. So if a developer or a consultant at a seminar tells them that his new development of 10,000 identikit flats in Liverpool is going to be a fantastic investment, they don't take this at face value.

If a director of a big bank says the housing market is going to grow rapidly, then be aware he has a vested interest in saying this, i.e. to sell more mortgages. Just because he is Chief Executive of an FTSE 100 company and earns more in a week than you make in a year doesn't mean you should listen to him. Similarly, if an investment bank says house prices will collapse, ask yourself could they just be saying that in order to persuade people to invest in stock-market based funds instead?

Be sceptical of what you learn at consultants' seminars. Most people say they learned nothing that they couldn't learn from reading a book. Generally they just got a hard sell to invest in new developments, the idea being that the syndicate uses investors' money to win supposedly big discounts on new-build properties, source non-existent "below market value" stock, buy "soon-to-be refurbed" properties on "no go" estates or meet joint venture funding partners. Probably the biggest long-term losers from the many "property education" charlatans are the many novice investors who bought off-plan new-build identikit flats on big developments from syndicates mainly, though not entirely, in inner cities in the English North and Midlands from 1999 to 2005, who saw the values of their properties collapse and the flats hard to let out.

So beware. You can do well in property but it's simply not the case that you can make a million or "go on a journey" to find the holy grail of "financial freedom" in just a few years without taking what to most people are unacceptably large risks. People who say you can do this are talking nonsense.

A lot of new-build off-plan schemes these days are for developments abroad. The consultant or developer may even pay the cost of the airfare and transport to the development and use high-pressure selling techniques with lots of free drink to get otherwise intelligent people to part with their money.

The hard fact is that you must be prepared to do some work. Not a lot of work, but some work nevertheless! Listen to what people say, but do your own research too before committing to anything. Keep in mind that currently there is no protection from the regulatory authorities for people who invest in property directly. So be careful.

It helps to be good with people as you'll need to form good relationships with your tenants and anyone who does work for you. I don't mean that you should be their best mate. Far from it! But you must be professional and courteous as well as firm and fair.

When dealing with tenants, there is no point being mean and arguing over small things or small amounts of money. As in life, if you treat tenants with respect they'll repay you in kind. The same applies for tradesmen. Pay them promptly because, if you don't, you can't expect them to rush out when you really need them.

It's important to be a clear communicator. Prospective tenants must know exactly what they're getting with the property they'll be renting. They must understand when the contract starts and what their responsibilities are under the tenancy agreement. If you use letting agents, they should understand what you expect of them too, as they will be acting for you, and representing you as your agent. The same applies to builders and decorators. You cannot be too clear, so confirm everything in writing!

It helps to be organised and have a good filing system to keep track of income, costs and repairs. Things should be fixed quickly and phone calls returned as soon as possible. You don't need to do the actual work yourself or be particularly practical. I'm not, but I know just enough to avoid getting ripped off by tradesmen.

Case study

Some years ago, more than one thousand people suffered massive losses after being duped by a property investment company promising "guaranteed" annual returns of 15 per cent. The investors, who included accountants, lawyers and doctors, handed over five- and six-figure sums after being seduced by the company's brochures. The firm used adverts in publications such as the *Financial Times* to tell investors they could make a fortune buying cheap properties in the north of England, which the company would refurbish and let out to "social housing" tenants. The company would supervise all the refurbishment, find the tenants and even collect the rent. Investors would sit back and wait for the money to roll in. If only life were so simple. The company pulled in more than £100 million but much of the refurbishment work was never carried out and the tenants never materialised. It turned out that investors had bought derelict, boarded-up houses that were worth far less than they had paid for them. Some were uninhabitable and worth less than £2,000. The firm was eventually closed down by the Government. Most of the investors were from the south-east of England and had been persuaded that the North was "bursting with investment opportunities within the social housing sector". Amazingly, most of the investors hadn't visited the areas or seen the properties at all.

Finally, you must like property. So, if houses bore you stiff, you're probably better off doing something else. I freely admit to being an addict and, like any successful landlord, I find it impossible to walk past an estate agency without looking in the window at house prices, rental levels, etc. You should be the same.

Follow the commandments set out below and you'll make a success of property investment:

1. You must buy the right type of property at the right time at a good (i.e. low) price in the right location – which means a place where the local economy will strengthen and capital values and rents will increase in the future, not fall.
2. You must do all you can to minimise vacant periods when the property isn't let.
3. You must take care vetting tenants to avoid having a bad one. If you use a letting agent, you must check to make sure he is really doing this properly.
4. You must fix things promptly and cost-effectively.
5. You must be good at dealing with administration – in particular, you must keep account of all your income and costs and have a proper filing system.
6. You must be able to spot when someone isn't being straight with you.
7. You must get the mortgage or other financing deal that is best for you and which meets your short- and long-term plans for the property.

I'll explain how to get these things right in the course of the book.

How much should I put in property?

At a recent speaking engagement I was asked, "How much should I put into property investments?"

Unless you're a highly diversified property investor in terms of the number, type and locations of properties you own, I would caution against having more than, say, 50 per cent of your money in property. However, there is no ideal percentage. How much you invest in property is whatever amount you feel comfortable with, which depends on your own attitude to risk.

It's possible to invest in the UK housing market through collective or unitised funds, including crowdfunding arrangements or through other funds that track house prices. This will give you some exposure but it won't make any real money because, if you are to have real success, you've got to get involved yourself, not give it to a fund manager who may turn out to be useless and will certainly charge a hefty annual fee. We have seen some pretty hefty layers of multiple fees on many property funds that claim great headline gross rents, especially in the current flavour of the month – student lettings. If you must invest in such schemes, for goodness sake read the prospectus carefully and be aware that resale marketability might be very limited and/or only possible through the promoter. Exit fees can be very high too.

Investing in property outside a fund (which is what this book is about) is not without risks either. The biggest risk in property is a downturn in the economy - either the national economy or in the local economy. National economic downturns can have the effect of making house prices and rents fall, increasing interest rates, increasing tenant default and cutting or reversing the flow of inward migration into the UK – thus reducing the pressure on housing. Another big risk is that the Government could change the way residential property investment is taxed, making it less attractive compared to other investment types. There is also a threat from big City funds and big property companies which have started to invest in the private rented sector by building huge new purpose developments exclusively for private rental – thus increasing the competition for private landlords. Some City funds use me as a consultant in this area so I know there is genuine interest, though up to now most have kept their money in their wallets and investment has been limited so far. (It's also my view that many of these players may struggle to compete with the more efficient "private" landlord.)

At the moment, most of your running costs, including the interest on loans to buy properties to let, are deductible costs for tax purposes. This is, of course, one of the greatest attractions of buy-to-let as it means someone else is paying off your mortgage. Another great attraction is the simple fact you can *actually get a loan to buy property to let* – try asking your bank for a long-term loan to buy shares in the stock market and see how far you get!

This book is about managing these and other risks and making profit at the same time. Some risk, however, will always remain – that's the price of the big rewards. If you don't like risk at all you should put this book down now and keep your money in the building society where you will be lucky if your cash keeps pace with inflation.

Any comments or suggestions on this book are appreciated. Please feel free to mail me. You can contact me by email via my website www.LettingFocus.com where I also provide buy-to-let advice and consultancy for organisations and individuals as well as writing a blog and reviewing discounted products for landlords.

Note
To avoid saying "he" and "him" instead of the clumsy phrases "he/she" and "him/her", I simply use "he"/"him" to refer to both men and women.

2

Easy as ABC: The Simple Economics of Property Letting

Income and capital growth

How do you make money out of property investment? Well, it's quite easy. You can make it by the property going up in price (what is called capital growth) and you can make it by earning more in rent than you spend in costs (i.e. income).

Sounds simple doesn't it? The problem is that a lot of people make the mistake of overlooking **all** the costs of their investment and completely forget to account for things like running costs, the cost of their own time and the cost of using their own money. Property programmes on TV make these same mistakes too.

Many people who are new to investing in property seem to forget to budget for the cost of maintaining their investment properties at all or, if they do, they proceed in the mistaken belief that the costs of maintaining a property which is let out will cost no more than maintaining their own property. It won't!

How to calculate the true income from your property

When people talk about property, they often talk about the "property yield". And yet, this term often means different things to different people, so when you are talking about yield, even if you know what it means, it's always useful to check that the other person has the same understanding.

So, what is yield? Yield is just another way of expressing the "income" on something relative to the value invested in it (or its current value). Very simply it's just the total amount of rent, less the running costs of the property, divided by the total value invested in the property including buying costs. So if your annual rent is, say, £18,000 a year, the running costs are £2,000 per year and the total value of the property is £250,000, then the "yield" is calculated as:

Yield = Total Rent minus Running Costs/Current Value of Property

In this case it is:

£18,000 − £2,000 running costs/£250,000 =

£16,000/£250,000 = 0.064

or, expressed as a percentage, 6.4 per cent − quite a decent yield!

Generally, it's that simple, but even with something so simple there are some potential snakes in the grass as I shall explain.

Step 1: Estimating the rent and allowing for voids

If you haven't yet bought a property, how do you work out what the rent will be? Well, you could look online to see what rents are being charged for *equivalent* properties. Unfortunately, this may lead you to believe you can get a higher rent than is achievable for a *permanently let property with no voids*.

I'll explain. For my properties, the rents I achieve are typically 5 to 15 per cent less than those being asked by other landlords and letting agents for the same type of property. This is not because I am a bad businessman. (Well, I hope not.) It's because I set my rents so my properties are always fully let whereas my competitors don't. I know this, because sometimes I pose as a tenant and go and look at other properties. (It's always good to check out the competition!) Six times out of ten, the previous tenants have left and the properties are standing empty and burning up their owners' money.

I don't doubt that sometimes other landlords and letting agents do eventually let their properties. Very often though, they'll have had to drop the rent. Even where they achieve high rents they may have been forced to agree improvements such as redecorating or buying new furniture which will hit their profit.

The period of time a property is not let, the "void period" in landlord's jargon, is extremely costly. In the example above, the annual rental was £18,000 or £1,500 per month. If the property is unlet for a month, then the annual rent falls from £18,000 to £16,500 and the effect on the yield would be to reduce it by 0.6 per cent.

In fact, the situation is worse because, with an unlet property, running costs are likely to be higher because you *may* have to pay for council tax and utilities too. Also, if the property is furnished and empty, your insurance premium could well go up as well.

You may get lucky and get a tenant to pay top dollar with no gap between tenants. Your super new tenant might not even demand a new bed or cooker for his top dollar rent! But he'll probably find out soon enough he's paying a premium rent and chances are he will become more demanding and ask more of you! He may be more likely to leave after a short period and you'll have the costs of re-marketing to bear.

If instead, you offer to let at a rent just below the market average, you'll have more tenant demand and be able to cherry-pick the best tenants and those who can move in just after your previous tenants move out. You'll have no void period, you won't need to throw in extras to get the new tenant and you'll have someone who is happy and will stay longer.

This isn't about being a "nice landlord". It's just good business, because those voids, additional things thrown in "free" to attract a premium-rate tenant and, most of all, your time have to be paid for somehow!

Step 2: Work out your running costs

The running costs of renting out property include interest on money borrowed, letting agency fees (where a letting agent is used), ground rent and service charges (where the property is leasehold), insurance premiums, replacement of fixtures and furnishings, general maintenance including an annual gas inspection (where gas appliances are present), Energy Performance Certificates, tenants' deposit protection, advertising, legal expenses, membership of landlord organisations, phone calls, travel costs and the cost of your time. Apart from the cost of your own time, all these costs can be deducted from rental income for tax purposes.

Letting agency fees

These are typically about one month's rent plus VAT for finding a tenant including doing reference checks, signing agreements, dealing with utilities and doing the check-in. Landlords with large portfolios may get lower charges than this though fees in London could be higher. Typically, agencies deduct fees from the tenant's first month's rent and deposit and before any residual money is paid over to the landlord. Also, some agents try to re-charge the fee each time a property is re-let to the same tenant, so watch out for this. If the agent provides management services too, you'll need to add another 3 to 8 per cent plus VAT. Chapter 7 has some good advice on how to negotiate these costs down.

Ground rent and service charges

If your property is leasehold you'll have to pay ground rent and service charges. Obviously, the cost varies enormously between properties and locations; however, it's nearly always charged in advance. For flats, a cost for some element of buildings insurance is usually contained within the service charge.

Insurance premiums

Buildings insurance premiums vary depending mainly on the size of property and its location. Buildings insurance is something you really must have and you should budget for up to about 3 per cent of the rent for it. Where the property is furnished, contents insurance is also a must. Allow for between 1 and 3 per cent of the rent depending on the level of furnishing.

Some landlords take out separate cover against a tenant defaulting on the rent and the cost of doing this is typically 2 to 4 per cent of the rent. In addition, you can also take out insurance against things going wrong with plumbing, drains, gas, electrical appliances or whatever or you could get a good plumber and save on this cost.

Replacement fixtures and fittings

Build in an allowance for replacing furnishings. How much furniture you provide will depend on the type of market you're pitching at. In Chapter 5 I'll explain how to figure out, before you even buy a property, how much furnishing (if any) you need to provide. Allow for the fact that furnishings, whether white goods like washing machines or soft furnishings like sofas and beds, will wear out faster in a let property than in your own home. You need to budget for buying good hard-wearing models that will last. Do not buy cheap rubbish.

General maintenance

In a let property more things need maintaining more often than they do in a private home. The main things that go wrong are boilers, pipes, overflows, drains and the like. Gas appliances must be checked by a registered gas engineer so you should add an additional £60 to the annual running costs for each gas appliance in the property.

Advertising

If you don't use an agent, you will need to advertise for tenants. In many media you can advertise for tenants for free. However, if your property is more up-market, you may have to pay to advertise in the sort of publications or websites that your intended tenants read. You can get your property advertised on all the main portals like Rightmove and Zoopla by going through specialist online landlord letting sites for under £100 per property. See the useful links at LettingFocus.com.

Legal and other regulatory expenses

If you follow the instructions in Chapter 7 and properly reference check potential tenants, you'll be very unlucky to get a tenant who doesn't pay his rent and needs to be evicted. However, if that does happen, the good news is you won't need to employ a solicitor or lawyer. Lawyers earn quite enough money already and you can do it all on your own without having to use their services. I'll explain how to in Chapter 9. The bad news is it takes about four to six months to get rid of a really bad tenant so it's wise to budget for about half a month's rent per year to cover the cost of unpaid rent of a bad tenant, just in case.

Other regulatory type costs include an Energy Performance Certificate (once every ten years and costing about £75 for a small flat), tenancy deposit protection in an insured scheme (about £30), landlords' registration (Scotland and Wales only at present) and HMO or other landlords licensing fees (if applicable). These are all covered later in the book.

Landlords' organisations

For less than £100 a year, you can join a landlords' organisation and get all the news including any legal updates, helplines in case things go wrong, local meetings, access to up-to-date tenancy agreements, discounts on websites which advertise property, and money off buildings insurance, tenancy deposit schemes, energy performance certificates and building materials. Two of the biggest are the National Landlords Association and the Residential Landlords Association. (See Appendix 2 for a list of the main associations.) And check out my own blog at www LettingFocus.com for occasional offers.

Personal costs

Allow for the cost of your own time plus incidental expenses such as phone calls, travel costs, stationery and cleaning materials.

Step 3: Calculate how much your total investment will be

If you are considering whether to invest in a property, your investment will be more than just the basic cost of the property. You should also include *all costs associated with the purchase*, including mortgage fees, survey and legal costs. In addition, include any development, decoration costs and repairs you must do before you first let it out. If you are furnishing the property, you should include these costs too.

Also don't forget to count the cost of the money invested in the property from the time you bought it to when you first let it. This will be whatever interest your total investment could have earned elsewhere for the time from completion to first let as well as whatever interest your deposit money could have earned from exchange to completion.

In the previous example, where we were buying a property for £250,000, your total investment may look something like the details shown below.

So, the total cost or value of your investment is £256,937, a full 2.77 per cent more than the £250,000 basic cost of the property. Remember the calculation:

Yield = Total Rent minus Running Costs/Current Value of Property

When evaluating this example as a property investment, the figure that should go in the bottom half of the equation is £256,937 because this is the total investment that you, the buyer, will have to make.

Basic Cost of Property:	**£250,000**
Add	
Mortgage arrangement fee	£500
Solicitor's costs and expenses (including basic stamp duty land tax)	£3,350
Survey fee	£300
Cost of basic redecoration	£500
Cost of very basic furnishings	£1,000
Subtotal	£255,650
Cost of money from completion to first let, say one month on £255,650 @ 5%	£1,065
Cost of utilities and council tax up to first let	£150
Cost of deposit from exchange to completion, say 21 days on a £25,000 deposit @ 5%	£72
Total	**£256,937**

In 2016, Chancellor George Osborne introduced an extra levy of 3 per cent stamp duty on all second or further property purchases. It remains to be seen if this will stay in place. Some have argued for it to be scrapped, at least for new builds. For now it remains in place, so factor it into your calculations.

There are a few things you need to watch out for. You'll hear some developers talk about very high and attractive yields on investment properties. Be careful, because when developers talk about yields some may be simply dividing the gross rent by the basic cost of the property. In other words, they ignore running costs and voids completely and don't take any account of the transaction and set-up costs you'll have to bear. By doing this, they make the yield seem much higher than it actually is.

Even worse, many investors and every property TV show I've ever seen fail to account for the opportunity cost of using the investors' own money. Let me explain.

In the example above I took as my starting point the £250,000 basic cost of the property. Few in the buy-to-let mortgage market are going to lend 100 per cent of the value of the property – 70 per cent is normally the maximum that's advanced, with the investor finding the remaining 30 per cent. In this example, you would need to put down £75,500 (30 per cent of £250,000) of your own money in order to buy this property, with the mortgage company putting up £175,000.

Some developers then simply divide the rent by the value of the mortgage loan. As this is much smaller than the total value of your investment, it again produces a much higher yield. It's possible to see how big a difference this makes. In our example, if you just take the basic £18,000 gross rent and divide this by the mortgage loan of £175,000, you get a "yield" of 0.103 or 10.3 per cent!

However, if you subtract from your £18,000 gross rent an allowance for a one month void each year of £1,500 as well as annual running costs of £2,000 and then divide this by your total investment cost of £256,937, you get what we could call a "true net yield" of about 0.056 or 5.6 per cent. £18,000 less £3,500 (£1,500 + £2,000)/£256,937 = 0.056 or, expressed as a percentage, 5.6 per cent.

This true net yield is obviously very much smaller than the 10.3 per cent figure some would have you believe! Also, bear in mind in this example, if you used an agent to find a tenant, and if a major refurb is needed, your total running costs are likely to be higher.

As long as the true net yield is greater than whatever the cost of borrowed money is to you, then you're making money on renting. In our example, the true net yield is 5.6 per cent and if the cost of mortgage money is 5 per cent, we are 0.6 per cent to the good. Put another way, 0.6 per cent of the value invested in the property (£256,937) is about £1,542, so this is what we are making in net income from the property.

Of course, if mortgage interest rates go up above 5.6 per cent, then, in this example at least, we will be making no money in net income at all. However, over time, if you have bought wisely you would expect rents to rise, thus increasing the income from a property in the future.

Still, you should be looking to get a much higher yield and a better starting income than the one quoted in this example – which I have simply used to illustrate how you must be realistic on costs.

The fact is that you cannot bank on higher rents coming through or increases in property value (and you cannot live on the latter, either), so you should look to get a better starting net yield than 5.6 per cent whenever you can.

If you are investing in property you need to allow for the possibility that interest rates can go up and you must make sure that you can afford to meet interest repayments.

The key messages of this discussion about yields are:

- Be very sceptical about what anyone tells you about the rents they think they can achieve for a property – especially if they want to sell you a property or let it for you.
- Be realistic about *all* your costs – both the running costs and the transaction and set-up costs of a property investment.
- Be aware of the impact of interest rate increases on your cash flow.
- Be aware that many people misunderstand or mislead when they talk about yield. Do your own sums!

How to calculate capital growth

Of course, the other way that properties make money over time is by going up in value, or "capital growth". Fortunately, calculating this is easy. It's simply the difference between the value of the property when you buy it and the value when it's sold less the total costs incurred in buying and selling.

In the example above, the total buying cost (including mortgage cost, solicitor's, survey, furnishing and all pre-letting costs) is £256,937. In the same way, when a property is sold, it's important not to forget to include solicitor's costs, selling agent fees, costs in making the property ready to sell and the cost of utilities and lost rent from the day your last tenant leaves until completion.

Often, a property that has been let for a long time can look tired so, when the final letting ends, it's worth spending some money to make it look attractive to a potential buyer. I will discuss in Chapter 5 how to get the property to look its best. Don't forget to allow for this cost.

Don't forget about tax either. Most income on residential property is subject to income tax, and capital growth may be subject to capital gains tax. For more on taxes see Chapter 11. Many people today invest in properties where the starting net yield is quite small, as in the example given. These people are hoping for better rents in the future, lower borrowing costs and good capital growth. But is this wise?

Well, it all depends. It is certainly a bit risky. But if you've done your homework, and follow my advice in Chapter 3, you'll have a good idea of whether future rents will be higher and if the property is going to go up in price. I think such a strategy can work, but some degree of caution and a long time horizon are required.

Of course, yield and capital growth go together like a horse and cart. If the price of a property shoots up over time (high capital growth) but the rental income from the property stayed the same, then the yield must have gone down. If the yield goes low enough, then it's always worth thinking about selling and doing something else with the money, like investing in another area or even just putting it in the bank. If you put it in the bank though, you'll miss out on any further capital growth there might be in the property. (Property tends to be a much better hedge against inflation than money on deposit in the bank!) Also, if you sell, you'll have to consider possible capital gains tax complications. Again, for more on tax see Chapter 11.

So, good professional landlords are always evaluating their property investments, looking at their potential, working out the best time to buy and sell and the best types of property to invest in. It is this that is the subject of the next chapter.

3

How to Find the Right Property

Location, location, location: How to choose the right area

I became a property millionaire mainly by focusing on buying into the right locations before they got discovered by others.

Location is extremely important when buying any property, and even more so when buying property as an investment. If you are buying to let, remember you aren't going to be living in it, your tenants are. So, if your idea of a superb location is somewhere on the moors, miles from main roads and public transport, you'll need to think again because such a location is very unlikely to appeal to many tenants.

Buying a property to suit themselves rather than their tenants is a common mistake that inexperienced landlords make. And it extends to the way they furnish their properties too, in that they tend to put in furnishings they like, which are often too expensive for tenants, when "clean, simple and durable" is what usually works best (the exception being very upmarket lets where high quality will be expected).

The ideal property for letting is one that will give a good rent and will have potential to go up in price too, in other words good income (or yield) and good capital growth. To achieve good yield we need to find areas (and types of properties within those areas) where there are lots of people looking to rent but not enough rented accommodation available of the type tenants are looking for. For the price of the property to go up, the area (and type of accommodation) must become more attractive to both home owners and tenants over time.

The papers are full of tips for which areas are going to do well. Some of these will be good tips. However, if a journalist is writing about an area, it has probably "come up" quite a bit already and you may have missed out on being there at the beginning. "Ah," you think, "if only we had bought in London's Shoreditch before all the young and happening new-media people moved in. If only we had spotted that second-home owners were driving the rapid growth of property prices in coastal towns. If only!"

Well, if you missed out on these opportunities you shouldn't punish yourself too much. Being in at the very start of an area's regeneration is the property investment equivalent of buying tech stocks – you could be lucky or you could be very unlucky. The fact is that these areas were once real wastelands and, to get in at the start, you would have been banking on a lot of things happening together. You would have been hoping that all those big office developments would really happen, that the government would really build that transport link and the council would put in those major improvements to the environment and schools.

Experienced property investors with large property portfolios are able to risk investing in such "frontier" areas. But it is risky. If you're more inexperienced, look to find areas that not only have existing *potential,* but where future improvements are *really* coming – not just promised. In other words, that area of derelict land close by *really will* be built on and bring two thousand jobs and the green light *really has* been given for the diggers to move in and start work on the new tram link.

To get this information try to get up to date with what is going on in the local area. Good sources of information are the local council planning departments, planning magazines, local newspapers, libraries and estate agents. Appendix 2 gives details of good websites containing local information. Many of these, such as Rightmove, have dedicated sold-prices sections which can be an excellent tool to use in your negotiations. Other simple tools like Google Street View will allow you to quickly compare one street with another without even visiting the area.

If you know that a local haulage site is going to become attractive housing, then the value of neighbouring property should go up too. So, talk to local people. They'll tell you all about local schools, crime and the efficiency of the council. Look around at different times of day and at night. Do the streets become rat-runs at rush hour? Is it a no-go area full of drunken hooligans at night? Is it under a flight path or next to a busy depot that starts at 4 a.m.? Is it close to a sports stadium with all the problems of parking and rubbish on match day? What is the maximum price of other properties in the street as this may set a ceiling on re-sale value, which is important if you are thinking of doing a major refurb to add value.

Try to imagine what the area will look like in the future and think about the risk of over-supply. What plans are there for other housing developments? Your new two-bedroom flat with a canal view might be in high demand in a newly attractive city centre when there are only two hundred other two-beds. What about where there are twenty thousand two-bed flats all competing with yours for a finite number of tenants? The supply of student accommodation, in particular, can change rapidly, especially where a big operator such as Unite suddenly builds a huge purpose-built block. Your market can disappear rapidly.

Once you have found an area with good potential, develop good relationships with estate agents and treat them with professional respect so they call you when they have a property that suits your needs.

To let well the property must be close to local transport. Most tenants will rely on it at some time and few tenants are prepared to walk more than half a mile to the nearest station or bus stop; and the route should be well lit and safe. Property further away will achieve lower rents and take longer to let. Tenants also like to be close to shops, bars, restaurants and, if they have children, good local schools. With more up-market lets, being close to an international school can make a significant difference.

How to choose the right kind of property

Once you've spotted a good area, you have to buy the kind of property that meets tenant demand in that location. There's no point buying a big family house if there's little demand for big family houses to rent!

Suppose you buy a big property and your target market is visiting families from overseas who want to be close to the local American school. You need to ask: Is this really a big enough market? How many families are there looking for properties like this in this area? Will the school be there forever? If not, would other families rent it? Could you let it to student sharers instead?

Letting agents know what kind of property is most in demand in an area. They'll tell you what sort of properties let easily and what they are most short of. Advice from agents who only do lettings (i.e. don't sell houses) is best because what they tell you won't be biased by any desire to sell a similar property to you.

Talk to letting agents

In 2003/4, the UK saw a big increase in the number of migrant workers – particularly from the new EU countries in eastern Europe. Government statistics didn't initially show the true number (and probably still don't) and the media only picked up on it about two years after the first big influx but letting agents were well aware of it as soon as it happened. One letting agent told me that people from Lithuania and Poland made up about 60 per cent of his tenants. These groups have given a huge boost to private letting across the UK.

Get a feel for what lets quickly by tracking how long properties stay on the market before being let. If they stick on the market for too long, either the desired rent is too high or the demand from tenants is too weak. If they let quickly, similar properties priced at the same level will also let quickly. Suppose you have identified a strong demand for two-bed properties. What kind of two-bedroom property is best? You could go for a house or flat, leasehold or freehold, purpose-built or conversion. Think about if there are permissions and space to add another room and "add value"? How does an ex-council property sound? Which is better – a new-build or an older property? Very often, within a specific location, you may not have a choice.

Some investors talk about "buying for yield" or "buying for income", meaning the property has a relatively low price, will give a good rental income but probably won't go up in price too much. The classic "income" or "yield" properties are flats above shops which are often priced low because lots of owner occupiers don't want to live above a shop and mortgage lenders are not keen on such properties, but, as long as it's attractive, safe, close to transport, etc, then it will probably rent quite well. In my opinion, such a property could give good yield and capital growth together because there is no reason why such a property shouldn't also go up in price, especially if there is a large pool of potential landlord buyers locally. True, it will be slightly less marketable to first-time buyers, but it will still sell to other landlords and other buyers who do not need a mortgage.

Buying above a shop

If you buy above a shop, check whether the type of shop can change under the terms of the lease. A flat above a shoe shop is more saleable and rentable than one above a kebab shop!

Yields on ex-council houses are also good. Such properties can usually be bought at prices below other equivalent-sized ones. Provided that the area itself is safe and the property attractive, they tend to rent well. Many tenants like the fact that most council flats often have larger room sizes, better sound proofing and greater storage space than conversions and modern purpose-built blocks and they are therefore prepared to pay more in rent for them. Good capital growth is often achieved especially in developments where there is a high (and increasing) proportion of owners relative to council tenants. Service charges also tend to be lower because the local authority is *usually* not out to rip off the leaseholders. However, be aware that some mortgage companies will not lend on certain types of ex-council properties.

The lowest net yields (and hard to get mortgages on) tend to be on flats in older "mansion type" blocks. The effect of all that free hot water, porters and lift maintenance will be felt in high service charges, which will dramatically hit your net yield. Until recent years it was the case that smaller properties generally yielded more than larger ones. However, as more families have started to rent, this has pushed up rental yields on houses above that achievable on flats in many areas. For the same reason, prices of houses have also risen faster than flats in most areas ever since 2001.

This shows how you need to keep up to date with demographic changes and housing supply. (Local authorities usually have a wealth of information on predicted demographic trends.) Alternatively, if you want to buy lots of property you could cover your bets by building a portfolio of different types of properties!

Parking facilities will be relevant where tenants or their visitors have cars. If the property has no parking space it needs to be easy and safe to park in the street. Tenants also like bright airy properties so, if it's summer, think about what the property will be like in winter. If all the windows face north it could be cold and dark. Watch out too for basement or ground-floor flats: these may be harder to rent out (and later sell) than flats on the first floor because of security concerns and because they're often gloomy and have damp issues! Some people won't rent above the second floor if there is no lift.

If you're interested in a particular road or area, register your interest with the local estate agents or auction houses who can contact you as soon as property comes to market. You could try privately leafleting houses in the street(s) you are most keen on, however be aware that some people would still prefer to use an estate agent to manage their sale, rather than sell direct.

If you see a derelict property you like, find out who owns it from the Land Registry website (see Appendix 2). If this fails, the neighbours or local shop owners might know who is looking after it and you could approach them. If the owner has died, the heirs might be interested in selling privately.

Which is best: Leasehold or freehold? What questions should you ask?

Where you own the freehold, you own the land on which the property sits too. If you have a flat, however, it's probably leasehold, and you are effectively buying the right to occupy space between the bricks in your part of the property, including, possibly, part of the garden.

I said "right to occupy," but really you effectively own it. In a typical lease of say ninety-nine years, you usually have the right, for a fee, to extend the lease or join with other leaseholders to buy the freehold or obtain the right to manage.

The lease document will contain a list of obligations on you (the leaseholder) and the owner of the building (the freeholder). The freeholder (or his managing agent) will charge you ground rent and service charges, and it's normally his responsibility to look after the maintenance of the building, arranging the buildings insurance, etc.

If everyone involved did what they were supposed to do, it would all work well. Leaseholders wouldn't annoy other leaseholders and they would pay their ground rent and charges on time. The freeholder would properly maintain the property, insure the building, not rip off the leaseholders by overcharging on insurance and other services and do everything to ensure things ran smoothly.

Where it works well, there are financial benefits for the flat-owning leaseholder in that the cost of exterior decoration, buildings insurance and garden maintenance will be less than they might otherwise be in an equivalent-size freehold property.

It can, and often does, work like this. Millions of people are leaseholders and, in cities, living in flats is often the only option for the first-time buyer. However, nearly every newspaper will have a column in their property supplement where frustrated leaseholders (and some freeholders) seek advice from the paper's solicitor on how to solve some problem or other with the working of their lease. Their questions are usually about how to get a freeholder or managing agent to do something they should be doing anyway, how to stop other leaseholders from doing things they shouldn't, how to extend a lease, buy the freehold or take over the management.

The fact is there are quite a few flats – especially conversions – where the building is managed badly. Typical problems are noise, crumbling exteriors, filthy common areas and rip-off charging for services provided. Given that the law on leasehold has changed frequently in the last twenty or so years suggests it needed fixing. Things today are better than they were, but for many leaseholders there are still problems.

Although lots of leaseholders have problems with the management of their block, with other leaseholders or with the freeholder, many take no action because they know that, if they did, they would then be legally required to tell potential buyers as part of the pre-contract sale enquiries. So, if you're buying a leasehold property, you need to be particularly careful. Here are some tips.

Before even putting in an offer, find out how many years are left to run on the lease and what the ground rent/service charges are. If the lease has fewer than seventy five-years left to run, many mortgage companies won't offer a mortgage. Extending a lease or buying the freehold gets considerably more expensive from when the lease has fewer than eighty years left due to something called "marriage value". Since short-lease properties are hard to sell, because of the difficulty in getting a mortgage, you'll need to pay to extend the lease sooner than with a longer lease. A short lease should be reflected in a lower asking price of the property and the cost of extending a lease or buying a freehold will depend on location, the flat's value, the amount of ground rent and the number of years outstanding on the lease.

To widen his market to include buyers who are reliant on mortgage financing, a seller may have to offer to extend the lease whether he wants to or not. The short lease is his problem, so use that fact in your negotiations, especially if you are a cash buyer.

Get a copy of the leasehold title from the land registry. This costs just £3 and can be done immediately online and will provide information on the lease term remaining and amount of ground rent. Obtain a copy of the lease document as soon as possible. Check it carefully and have your legal adviser do likewise. Are there proper provisions and arrangements for collecting ground rent and service charges? Is it clear who is responsible for the maintenance and redecoration of communal hallways, exterior walls and gardens? Is there a planned schedule for doing this? When was it last done? What state are the communal areas, bin stores, gardens and exterior in? Are communal areas used as a dumping ground for rubbish? Do the doorbells and entry buzzers work? Is it clear who is responsible for arranging the buildings insurance? Are there any restrictions or charges levied where the property is let out? (There are some leases that completely ban lettings.) Are there likely to be major building or repair costs in the future? How involved are residents? (If there is already a management company to run the services with active participant directors, this is a big plus point.) Is the managing agent a member of the Association of Residential Managing Agents (see Appendix 2)? If it's a new-build, but a similar block has already been completed, talk to residents living there. What do they say? Are they plagued by noise or rude and inconsiderate neighbours? What is security like? What is the attitude of other residents to security? What is the ratio of owner occupiers to tenants? (The more owner occupiers the better.)

Even if the flat has a share of the freehold or there is a "tripartite residential management company" (i.e. there is a freeholder, a leasehold company and a managing agent appointed by the company), how the place is actually being run will *still* matter. So try ringing doorbells of neighbouring flats and ask the neighbours how things are managed in practice. If you find that there is a resident management company but that everything is run by a sort of Captain Mainwaring-type figure who brooks no dissent, keeps poor or inadequate records, is unresponsive or nasty and does not let anyone else do anything, this can be a bad thing. Ideally, responsibilities should be shared out between directors and good records kept so someone can pick up the reins, if required.

Many people don't understand the difference between a resident management company and the managing agents they appoint. Their roles are distinct and separate – the agent works for the company. Too often the roles can get blurred and the block managing agents can get too chummy with the company directors.

With a flat, it's particularly important to visit at different times of the day and night, and especially when people in an upstairs property are in. Many flats with stripped wood flooring are unbearably noisy. (This is a particular problem with older and "badly done" conversions from the 1980s.) Find out before you buy!

Where a flat has joint share of the freehold, the freeholder's responsibility will be shared with others. Someone (and it may be you) has to arrange for moneys to be collected, insurance arranged and redecoration carried out. Where your flat alone owns the freehold, it will be you doing this – and it can be quite a chore.

The trouble with communal hallways

When buying a flat with a communal hallway, try to check out what sort of people live in the block and what the arrangements are for access and delivery of post. With communal hallways you sometimes get people leaving rubbish bags, bikes, mattresses, etc. (If you suffer from this, go through the rubbish and see if you can identify the culprits, then get the managing agent to send them a warning letter.)

Other problems with communal hallways are lack of security – some people let anyone in and regularly leave communal doors unlocked. If post is left in insecure communal areas it can be pilfered and people can even find that they have had their identities stolen.

Be careful too, when buying a newly built leasehold flat in a new development. Some developers can underestimate what the service charges will be (for example, service charges to cover the swimming pool or gym), so make sure you do your homework. Ask yourself whether the additional rent will be sufficient to cover adequately the cost of the gym, etc, which you'll be paying for in service charges.

Recent changes in the law have brought in another option called "commonhold". This allows leaseholders, provided that certain qualifying criteria are met, to take over the management of their blocks without buying the freehold or proving that the freeholder is at fault, by simply serving the appropriate notice on the landlord. There will be a responsibility to file annual accounts so a commitment to make self-management work is crucial. As agreement from each person's mortgage company is also needed to convert to commonhold, unsurprisingly the rate of take-up has been abysmal.

Unfortunately, it's beyond the scope of this book to look in detail at leasehold or how to solve specific leasehold problems. In fact it would require another book! If you have problems with a leasehold property see the Leasehold Advisory Service website (see Appendix 2) which provides a wealth of advice for free and also get in touch with the other support organisations such as News On the Block that help flat owners.

At the end of this discussion, I'd say that although I have both freehold and leasehold properties, I much prefer the greater simplicity of my freehold houses. I like running my own show and think that, despite recent changes in the law, it's still difficult and expensive to enforce your rights as a flat owner when things are not working as they should. I'd rather that it's down to me to decide when the exterior needs redecorating and which company should insure it without reference to anyone else. Maybe that's just me being a grumpy sod?

Another factor which has always directed me more to freehold is is that nobody is making more land. Councils can give permission for "building up" and give the go ahead to skyscrapers galore, but they cannot find new land! So in towns and cities, where residential land is scarce, a freehold property with a garden is more likely than a flat to go up in price.

Despite this, it must be said that leaseholds can be good investments, and hassle free – provided that everyone involved meets their responsibilities in the lease contract in full. It's up to you to check this is the case *before* you buy.

My very annoying freeholder

Every year or so, the particularly rapacious freehold company of one of my London leasehold flats writes to me and says: "Mr Lawrenson, It has come to our attention that your flat is being let out. As you know, as a leaseholder this requires approval from us. Please fill in the form attached and send it to us along with the requisite cheque for £300."

My response letter reads as follows: "Dear Sir, Thank you for your letter. I'd be grateful if you would kindly point out where in the lease terms and conditions it refers to the need for a leaseholder to (a) inform you of a subletting and (b) pay you £300 for this service. Please send me a cheque for £40.60, this being the cost of my time to write this letter and the cost of a first-class stamp."

Needless to say, that is the last I hear from the freeholder for a year or so. Are they making a genuine mistake or are they just trying to extract money where it's not due? Probably not as they are famous on the Internet for this kind of stunt. It is just one of the hassles of being a leasehold flat owner!

Whether to buy a new or old property: Things to consider

In the lettings market, it doesn't really matter whether the property is new or old. Some tenants prefer old properties, some new, but what they *all* like is space.

Brand-new properties can be problematic because they sometimes have lots of snags, things that need fixing that you only become aware of after moving in. In fact, one of the biggest buying agents has said he'd never buy a newly built property for this reason!

Many new properties these days seem to have quite small rooms and little storage space. Some developers and agents try to cover this up by dressing out their show houses with the tiniest furniture, televisions, refrigerators and dishwashers. If you're thinking of buying new, watch out for this trick.

If buying on a new development, check out what building work will be going on nearby as lots of noise will upset your tenants. If you know that the waste ground opposite will be a building site for a while, be honest and tell your prospective tenant upfront.

If buying an older property look closely. Don't be afraid to look for signs of damp or mould under carpets and behind cupboards and consider getting a fuller survey than the standard "valuation report" that mortgage lenders tend to use. But use your judgment here – if the property looks in good condition and there are no visible signs of anything wrong structurally, you might just be OK with a basic valuation report. If you do go for a fuller survey, ask the surveyor specifically to check anything that particularly worries you and get a builder in so you can budget for building costs. Watch out too if you are thinking of developing or extending an older listed property as it may be impossible to get planning permission.

How to buy in new developments and off-plan (and avoid the pitfalls)

In recent years there has been a newly rediscovered desire to live in the centre of towns. The attractions are obvious. After a long tiring day you can just walk from the office to home in a few minutes without a long stressful commute. Builders have been busy putting up apartments in city and town centres throughout the land to meet the demand. Wine bars and restaurants have followed to make living in the middle of things more and more attractive.

In some cases, the developer may have finished an identical existing block, so you'll know what your property will look like. In other cases, your property may be the first to be built.

Either way, if it's not been built yet, you're buying "off-plan". Most developers ask for a small initial non-refundable goodwill deposit, with the balance of the deposit – typically 5 or 10 per cent or £10,000 per unit – payable a few weeks later. Negotiate hard on the goodwill deposit because at this stage you may not know all the facts, like whether a huge ugly Tesco is going to be built just opposite! The attraction is that once you've paid all the deposit it will be some time before you have to pay the balance on the property. However, even where your intention is to sell on before completion, you must still ensure that you can get a mortgage, just in case you can't sell on for whatever reason.

In a rising market, it's easy to see how people can make money out of buying new-build properties. Suppose you're buying a flat that is valued at £200,000, and the deposit is 5 per cent – i.e. £10,000. Suppose also, after twelve months when the property is nearly completed, it's risen in value by 10 per cent. The new valuation should come in at £220,000, so you'll now have £30,000 equity in the property. (Your £10,000 plus a £20,000 gain in value.) You could sell the property on to a cash buyer, and your only outlay will be the £10,000 initial deposit plus interest, legal and agency fees for selling the property. There may be some liability for capital gains tax unless you can convince the Revenue that you should be classified as a property trader, in which case income tax will be payable instead.

Get a good solicitor

If you are buying off-plan and selling on before completion, find a good solicitor who understands the principle of back-to-back sales. But be aware that if you have to go to completion, most lenders will currently not lend to another potential buyer if the property is sold on within 6 months. (This is also a consideration for anyone doing refurbishments with a view to selling on.)

There are of course a few pitfalls with this, the most obvious one being that prices won't increase by 10 per cent and another that you actually paid too much for the property in the first place.

How does new-build and off-plan work? A lot of the developer's costs are upfront – he's got to get planning permission and then fund all the initial building and marketing. To do this he needs to raise cash as soon as possible. The problem is that many people won't buy until they can actually see something – and it may be some time until the show apartment is ready. Fortunately, for the developer there are a lot of investors who will take the risk of buying upfront and off-plan. This is particularly attractive to the developer if he can sell multiple units to a single buyer. The development is therefore often marketed to investors through buying clubs/syndicates who buy on behalf of individual investors, through buying agents/finders as well as through estate agents.

The buyer club, syndicate or agent is supposed to negotiate with the developer to get big discounts on a number of properties in a development on behalf of its members in exchange for a fixed fee levied on its members – typically 1 to 2 per cent. If you join a buying club or syndicate, the key is to satisfy yourself that the deal is sound and that you have got a genuine discount off the true value of the property. If you've got a discount off the price of an overpriced property, you don't have a good discount at all! Some developers can overvalue their developments, so do your homework to ascertain the market price.

To ensure that you've got a good discount get an *independent* valuation from an independent valuer, not one who is linked to or recommended by a buying syndicate or a developer. Bear in mind that the valuation of a new-build is quite imprecise, as there may be little similar property to compare with. Even where there are comparables, each development will have its own specification, making it difficult to compare. Don't be afraid to quiz the valuer on how he arrived at the valuation. It's thought that most valuers don't want to disrupt the sales process and will pass anything within 5 per cent of the true value as a fair asking price!

Will you get a mortgage?

As a result of past bad experiences of fraud and the over-valuing of new-build property, many mortgage companies now refuse to lend on new-build or even anything less than two years old and all now require higher deposits for new-build properties. Others set limits to the number of buy-to-let mortgages that they'll offer on a single development so watch out for this if you hope to buy multiple units in the same block.

With new-builds, it's even more essential that you check out how many properties will be built locally in the next few years. Many inexperienced investors have found out that their property is just one of thousands of others, all competing for that same buyer or tenant. As a result, the capital growth and rental return performance of many new-build inner-city flats has been poor, especially true over the years from 2000 to 2008 when a large glut of new-builds hit the market.

If there is a block of derelict land opposite, get your solicitor to check out with the local authority Planning Department what will be going in on that site – don't take the developer's assurances on this.

Will your development be a tenants' ghetto? Where too many properties in a single development are sold to investors the price of the properties may fall in time. Most people, tenants included, want to live in blocks where there is some degree of permanence not one full of potentially transient tenants. In my consultancy work advising private clients I have seen many examples of blocks where more than a third of the units were let out and because absentee landlords were not around to push the freeholder, the blocks, car parks and gardens had descended into a dreadful state with no one around to fix the snags. So find out who is buying by looking online to see how it is being marketed. If it is being heavily promoted overseas, you can expect it will be heavily tenanted.

Check out the service charges carefully. Some developers can be highly optimistic about how low service charges will be. If no properties have been completed yet, I'd add 50 per cent onto the service charges the developer quotes. If some blocks have already been completed and occupied for a few months, add on a third. You can get an idea of what service charges are locally by asking a local independent letting agent. Better still, if some of the development has already been completed, don't be afraid to knock on a few doors and ask the residents if they are happy with the service they're getting for the charges they pay. If there is a gym, pool or car park, you could stop and ask people there.

Find out what car parking will be provided. Will your target market need parking spaces? If it's not available and parking is on the street, how safe is it? Many new off-plan developments are in trendy inner-city areas which have what many property journalists call an air of "grittiness" to them. Basically, this means they aren't the sort of places you'd like your granny to walk around in at night and a smart car is likely to be a target. If it's too rough, many people will be put off renting there.

Check out the local lettings market carefully with independent letting agents to find out what the property should let for and use tools like the Rightmove Price Comparison Report. Take away 15 per cent from the rent an agent says can be achieved to get an idea of a rental figure that will ensure the property is let quickly, and allow a month before you get the place let.

Some buying agents and syndicates will offer to do the furnishing, letting and management for you too. See if you can do this part of the work cheaper or more effectively by arranging it elsewhere or doing it yourself. You usually will!

Despite all these concerns, you can still do well buying new-build and/or off-plan. Indeed, some investors who "got in" back in the early days of inner-city development have made a fortune. These people know their market well. They fully research the area and have a good picture of all new upcoming developments locally so they know to avoid areas where there will be an oversupply of properties. They also know all about planned regeneration schemes and new infrastructure.

They buy at times when the developer is most likely to give good discounts, which is often a few months before the developer's year-end or mid-term results, when the developer needs every sale it can get to show good results to the City. Buying at first release is also good – some developers will offer good deals to help their financing. At the end of a development, the developer may also give good discounts in order to hand over to the management company and cut site security costs. Most developers are publicly quoted companies and it's easy to find when their year end is.

Many developers offer sweeteners like guaranteeing the rent for a year or two or paying the stamp duty land tax. This makes good marketing copy but it often hides the fact that the property itself is overpriced. Also, where a developer guarantees to pay rent, the development is a sure fire bet to end up mostly let out to tenants. Watch out too because guaranteed rental yields are worked out on just the basic cost of the property – i.e. with no added carpets, furniture or transaction costs.

Experienced investors will be able to disassemble these sweeteners. They'll know if the rent guarantee is worth having and usually prefer to negotiate on the basic price with all the sweeteners stripped out. You should do the same.

Many new development schemes these days are what are called "mixed tenure" developments, meaning there'll be a mix of "affordable [i.e. social] housing" and private property. Where this is so, check exactly what sort of affordable housing it will be. If it's a "shared ownership" where people will be part mortgaged and part renting from a social housing organisation, this is better than where they are fully renting. Where it's a shared ownership scheme, the owners will have at least a 25 per cent stake in the property and will look after it as well as full owners. I would be wary of buying where the social housing residents had no ownership or were not "key workers".

Check floor plans

As part of the legal process, obtain the floor plan for the property you are buying. Check size, dimensions, layout and outlook and compare with the show flat. Is it as good?

Finally, a word about buying agents and property syndicates. One reason people use them is to save time. The idea is that they'll find good deals for you so you'll save shoe leather. This is partly true. However, you must do at least *some* of your own research too. Satisfy yourself that the property is a good investment and it's in a good location. Ask questions! Many buying agents and property syndicates are very good. Some aren't. Ask how long they've been in business, what references they can give you, how experienced the directors are, what guarantees there are, whether they are robust and what would happen if they went bust. (Usually you will lose your money!) Check out their accounts at Companies House (see Appendix 2). If you don't understand accounts, get someone who does to look over them for you. What does it say about them on the Internet? Do they have an open forum where past investors are free to post comments?

In my view the better buying syndicates are those where they have actually used their *own money* to buy property in bulk from a developer and then sell on. At least you'll know they've put their own neck on the line financially. Others are just "introducers" who are using your money and that of other people to negotiate a good deal from developers on bulk purchase.

Whatever you do, don't be pressurised to sign up on the day to get a special deal. There are many deals out there. Don't waste lots of money going to seminars or pay upfront before exchange of contracts. Be especially wary where a syndicate wants you to use its own mortgage firm, valuer or solicitor.

Since syndicates are inevitably made up nearly entirely of people looking to sell on before completion or to let out, where a syndicate is buying multiple units in a new development there will be a lot of competition from other landlords for tenants. Rents will be much lower as a result.

If a syndicate claims that it can get a discount on a new-build property, find out if the developer will sell direct. If he does, ask what discount he would give you. How does that compare with what the syndicate or agency claims it could get? Finally, remember that much of the activity of buying agents, clubs and syndicates are not regulated and there is currently no recourse to a professional body. The glossy brochure may promise a profit, but it's not a guarantee.

More tips for buying off-plan and new-build

When buying new property use a developer that is a member of a recognised guarantee scheme. With some of these it can mean that if during the course of construction the developer goes out of business, the deposit paid by the buyer (up to 10 per cent of the agreed price) will be refunded. Also, during the first two years the developer should pay the cost of putting right damage or defects if these arise from a failure to follow the Scheme's building requirements.

If there are lots of things wrong with your new-build, consider employing a professional snagging company. Get an idea of the sturdiness of the construction by jumping up and down in the middle of the room. If pictures fall off the walls, take that as a bad sign! If possible, get a friend to go into the flat upstairs and make some noise. Can you hear every footstep?

If you want to buy quickly, see if the developer will agree to a deposit back clause in the event the property isn't ready in a certain timescale.

If you want to sell on the property before completion, check that the developer will allow you to do this. Some off-plan buyers find that once they have bought the property their friendly property developer is totally uninterested in how the block will be managed in the future. In some cases, no managing agent has been appointed at all; in other cases, he is impossible to contact. See the section on "Lease or Freehold" above for the list of questions you should ask about this before you buy.

How to buy at auction

Buying at auction has become more popular in recent years and many properties sold this way are bought as investments, either to rent out or do up and sell on. You can get a good bargain at auction (though sometimes properties sold at auction often sell for even more than they would have achieved at an estate agent) but you need to know what you are doing.

Auctions tend to be a particularly good way to buy when property markets are depressed as there are more repossessions for sale and mortgage finance is harder to obtain. And repos-sessions and bankrupt stock together with probate and public owned buildings usually have to be sold at auction to ensure transparency for vendors.

If you're serious about buying at auction go to a few as a spectator first before getting involved yourself. Forthcoming auctions are advertised in local newspapers, the Internet, at the site managed by the Essential Information Group, or in the

Estates Gazette magazine. Prices at auctions may seem low, but often there is a good reason. The properties may be in poor condition, have subsidence, be blighted by proposed road developments, have been occupied by squatters, have sitting "Rent Act" tenants or have defects in the legal title. Or they may just be unique and hard to value.

Others may have nothing wrong with them at all other than possibly being in a mess. This is usually the case with ex-government housing, those being sold by executors after the death of the owner, repossessions and "distressed sales" where a property is being sold on behalf of people who have overstretched themselves.

The benefit of buying at auction is that you can get the property you want quickly, without lots of negotiation. Once the gavel goes down, that's it! Provided that you are the highest bidder and your bid has matched the vendor's minimum price, the so called "reserve price", then it's yours and the vendor cannot back out of the deal, at least not without suffering severe financial loss.

As well as the auction price, you have to pay the auction house fee (which is usually referred to as a "premium") of around one and a half percent of the price, with a fixed minimum £s amount, plus an admin fee of typically around £150.

It sounds simple and it is! The drawback is that, to be on the safe side, the buyer ought to have the property surveyed, or at least checked over, funds ready and the bulk of the legal checks done *before* the auction. This all costs money, of course, but means if defects turn up and it wasn't worth what it sold for, then at least you will have avoided buying something that may have ended up being a nightmare. As with all property purchases it's really a case of "buyer beware"; if you don't check the property out carefully first and you find that it's falling to bits after you bought it, it's your problem.

Tips for auctions

Some auctions quote a "guide price". It's not the same as the "reserve price" but it's a good indication. Typically, if the guide price is £75,000 to £85,000, the reserve price is probably around £80,000. The reserve price should be within a ten per cent range of the guide price. Guide prices may change before the auction if there has been strong interest so look out for this. And check auctioneers terms and conditions as they can and do change between auctions.

Ensure you have your deposit with you. Normally this is 10 per cent of the price. Auctions won't take cash due to money laundering regulations. Check beforehand what form of payment and ID is acceptable.

If you go with your partner, sit together. It's been known for a husband and wife sitting in different corners to bid against each other!

Try entering the bidding late and if you are confident enough and when things are flagging, ask to change bid increments to unsettle other bidders.

Be aware that the auctioneer's staff can "force the bidding" by bidding up to one increment below the reserve price without identifying themselves. It's called "off the wall" or "imaginary" bidding and it's perfectly legal. So sit at the back or at the side to spot if this is going on.

Also, to get things moving they may say things like, "Well bid" especially if someone has just overpaid. It's all part of the auction game.

As soon as you buy, you're responsible for the insurance. Phone your insurer straightaway and get it covered. (Get quotes before the auction and remember that many insurers will charge more, won't insure at all or restrict cover where there is subsidence.)

If the vendor is in a different part of the country from the solicitor it might be a probate sale and often the vendors will accept low prices in order to "move on" quickly, plus there will be fewer bidders.

Repossessions should have the words "for sale by mortgagee in possession" in the details. These are often left in a mess but if structurally sound can be bargains.

If buying with existing tenants in place, check what sort of tenants they are. (You could try knocking the door at a time other than the viewing day). Assured Tenants or Assured Shorthold Tenants might be OK but "Rent Act" tenants should be treated with caution as the rent will be fixed at a low level and it will be virtually impossible to get them out. See Chapter 6 for more on the different types of tenancy contracts.

If you are a regular buyer it's worth developing a good relationship with the auction house as they can keep you posted on new properties you might be interested in.

You can bid online these days. It can be less intimidating, but you may lose a sense of how things are going from actually being in the room, as well as not being able to spot "off the wall bidding".

Some experts think that the best bargains are to be had early in the catalogue (before the room "heats up") or very late in the catalogue (when other bidders may have left).

Make sure to remove any "for sale by auction" boards as soon after the auction as possible, as these boards are a particular invitation to squatters and drug addicts. And liaise with the auctioneer to get access the next day so you ensure the place is properly secured. If the vendor agrees, you might also want to put in temporary fixes too to prevent deterioration, especially if it is winter.

How do you prepare for an auction? Ask for the package compiled by the auctioneer which should be available about three or four weeks before the auction and be ready to move fast. The pack will have details on each property and the memorandum of agreement which is equivalent to the contract, the title documentation, the searches, whether there are any outstanding planning or environment issues, etc, and replies to general enquiries. Have this checked over by a friendly conveyancer. (If you are serious about buying at auctions, you should look to get a special price from a good specialist auction-experienced conveyancer for this sort of work). Look out also for any special conditions. For example, it may say that the buyer has to pay the vendor's legal fees or other admin costs or that you have to complete in fourteen days instead of the usual twenty-eight. If you want to get planning consent after purchase, assess if this is feasible before you go any further. Also, check that planning consent and buildings regulations approval was obtained for the purpose the building is being used for now.

Then go and view it. Many have to be seen at block viewings, so you'll get to see possible fellow bidders. Always take a torch as often there will be no electric power, especially in repossessed properties. Also, take a step ladder, spirit level, tape measure (if you plan any refurbs) and binoculars to assess the state of roofs, guttering and chimney stacks. Also, look at roofs and chimney stacks from inside. You'll need to wear old clothes for mucky attics. A screwdriver to unscrew the loft hatch may come in handy.

Once you've found a property you like, recheck with your conveyancer that it's free from legal problems, in particular, that there is no problem with legal title. For flats, badly worded leases are often a problem, so have this checked carefully and re-read the section on leasehold, earlier in this chapter.

Since many properties sold at auction have structural problems, it may be wise to get a fairly thorough survey done, though this of course costs money if you don't win the bid – and most experienced property people therefore take the risk of relying on their own assessment and knowledge of refurbishing buildings instead. Alternatively, you might persuade a surveyor or builder to give you a verbal opinion, off the record, for a reduced fee.

If it has subsidence you will struggle to get buildings insurance which will also make it unmortgageable until the problem is rectified.

If it needs lots of work, carefully budget for it with a good builder, though there will be a cost for a formal written quote if you want him to view more than one property on spec. Try to get fixed quotes (not estimates) and obtain a proper specification of the works to be done and what materials will be used (and ensure these are included in the cost). I'll say more about this in Chapter 5.

Before the auction, work out the maximum price you're prepared to bid. If you're the highest bidder and the reserve has been met, you must sign the contract in the auction room and pay a 10 per cent deposit.

You usually must complete twenty-eight days later, so your solicitor needs to move quickly and get all legal documents ready. If you don't complete, you lose not only your deposit but, if the property has to be re-auctioned and it ends up fetching less than you have paid, you'll be liable for the difference plus the sellers' costs! So use a conveyancer who understands the auction process and can work fast. Sadly, many high-street conveyancers are just not up to the job.

On the day, arrive early, check the "addendum" and recheck the legal pack in case any special conditions have been added (and also check that the property has not been withdrawn on the day – most annoying, but it can happen!).

Auctions are very fast-paced events and each property sells very quickly, so keep cool and stick to your maximum price. Don't go above it! Some auctions will have a reserve price stated as well as the guide price. The auctioneer may say something like, "This property will sell today" or "It's in the room", which is "auction room speak" meaning that the reserve price has been reached and the highest bidder will get it. If he says, "We are not there yet" this means the reserve price has not been met.

You may be able to cut out the auction process entirely because if the sales details quote "unless previously sold" you should be able to approach the auction house and make a bid in advance of the auction. This will be conveyed to the owner who may accept it and you may even get longer than 28 days to complete. You'll still need to move fast and ensure that the finance is ready and that the conveyancing can be done quickly.

If the property hasn't met its reserve, the auctioneer will tell you the reserve and advise if he has the vendor's authority to sell at the reserve price for up to twenty-four hours after the auction. Many pro investors actively pursue a strategy of snapping up bargains from desperate vendors where the property failed to reach the reserve price – this is sometimes known as "hawking". Pre- and post-auction offers will not be accepted if the vendor is the government or another public body. Mortgage companies will not accept post-auction offers either.

Because of the time constraints many auction buyers who are not paying cash have to use bridging loans. The interest rate on these is far higher than on a mortgage and the loan to value is usually limited to under 60 per cent. If you take a bridging loan, make sure you have an exit strategy and the property will be mortgageable once any necessary works have been completed. For more on bridging loans see Chapter 4.

Most repossessions are marketed by estate agents before they go to auction, so find out which agents are handling them in your area as you can often get a better deal than you can "in the room" where you are competing with hundreds of other bidders. Agents are obliged by mortgage lenders to keep marketing the "repo" cases even after your offer has been accepted (so move fast), though in my experience, many make as little effort as possible if they are convinced you are a sound buyer. Look out for the formal public notices of offers received in local newspapers as you may be able to out-bid the offered price.

For repossessions, exchange and completion are often required on the same date, which is not a bad thing as it reduces the risk that a former disgruntled owner (or a squatter) could try to get in and damage the place. It is always good advice to check over the property before an auction or just before exchange of contracts to make sure everything is as it was when you put your offer in. Have loads of "Gone away, return to sender" stickers prepared to put on the mountains of post for strangers that will inevitably be there when you get entry and which will keep coming through the post for a few months. And always change the locks immediately – good practice on any house you buy.

Though auctions feel formal, the personal touch still counts. For example, it might be possible to speak to the vendor if he's in the room and if he's willing to talk, you might get useful information from him. Also, if you get interest in your post-auction offer but a competing bidder is sniffing around, make sure your money can arrive in the vendor's account faster than the other guy can. Money talks!

Does everything work? Things to check before you buy

Apart from your survey, you need to check the basics, such as whether the central heating, cooker and shower work properly, what the standard of plumbing and wiring is like, where access to the drains and mains fuse boxes are, the state of the roof and chimneys (take binoculars!), whether the windows open properly, etc. If you have any concerns or are unable to check yourself, get a suitable professional to check for you.

Things to look for

Check where the water stop valve, manhole and electricity fuse board are – they may be in another property. If they're not somewhere accessible, it will cause problems when things go wrong. For example, a manhole cover is often covered with lawns or cement, but it's usually the point where blockages often occur. Try to get the vendor to make these things accessible before you proceed. If the vendor doesn't know where they are, the appropriate local utility company will be able to tell you.

How to negotiate successfully

If you've done your research, you'll know what the property is worth (and what you can receive in rent from a tenant). When you make an offer, allow for the vendor to come back with a counter offer by ensuring that your first offer is some way below your maximum.

If you're buying through estate agents, use them to help your negotiation. They are supposed to work for the vendor and get the best (i.e. highest) price. However, he also wants to earn his fee, so is also keen to shift the property too, so if you probe in the right way they'll usually tell you lots about the vendor's circumstances and what price he'll accept. For example, "The vendor is desperate to sell to meet his divorce costs/kids' school fees/new life and wife in Thailand and he will probably accept X." If the agent isn't very forthcoming, ask questions. Sometimes, junior staffers play it straight, giving little away to buyers. If this is the case, see if you can get more out of the branch manager.

If you're buying direct (i.e. with no agent) you will have to negotiate direct with the vendor. This can be tough, especially when you've put in an offer well below asking price. Keep it professional, it's only money!

How hard you negotiate depends on how much you want it

and how desperate the vendor is to sell. As an investor you can make some pretty hard offers and walk away if they don't come off. Remember: you're buying it as an investment not to live there! Eventually, someone will be keen enough to sell and will accept a low offer – this is especially true in times of economic crises when people are suffering financially.

If your negotiation gets stuck try asking the vendor to make some improvement or repair something broken in exchange for meeting his desired price. If you don't need to sell property to finance this one, keep reminding him that you can move more quickly than someone who is stuck in a chain.

The house market is seasonal with lots of buyers out in late spring and in early autumn too. If you want to buy property cheaply, it's probably best to avoid these times.

If you're a cash buyer and not dependent on getting a mortgage, then use this in your negotiating position too. By all means show them bank or stock portfolio statements to prove you have the money in cash waiting to go. By not having to wait for a mortgage offer, you can cut the conveyancing process by at least two weeks. If the seller wants to move quickly, this will give you a significant advantage over other potential buyers. If buying through an estate agent you could tell them that you will consider putting the letting work through their letting side, if you get the property for the price you want. If you are doing it up and re-selling it, you could promise the agent they will get the sale instruction. You cannot offer bribes, but the old adage "You scratch my back, I'll scratch yours" does work very effectively.

In a busy market a vendor might ask potential purchasers to put in "sealed bids" (rather like the "offers over" system in Scotland). However, the vendor doesn't have to accept the highest offer, so it's still worth reminding him that you aren't in a chain/ are a cash buyer, so can move faster than other bidders or fit in with his timescales. In general though, as a property investor, you should avoid sealed bid situations in favour of finding willing sellers and building relationships with good estate agents so they eventually start calling you when a good deal comes along.

Buying below market value (BMV)

At property investor shows, seminars on how to buy property below market value (BMV) are now very much the flavour of the times with four or five operators running seminars.

Of course, any sensible property investor will always strive to buy cheaply. After all, the advantage you have as an investor is that if the vendor won't play ball, you can just walk away and wait until the next deal comes along. And clever investors have long recognised that to get really good value you have to find a "motivated" or "distressed seller" – someone who is motivated to sell to you at a good price for whatever reason.

And this strategy really just boils down to buying from someone who needs to sell fast – often this means someone who is facing one or more of the three Ds – death, debt and divorce.

All good BMV practitioners have a system to generate a flow of "leads" coming in and a way of finding that special someone who will sell his property cheaply. They also use a number of techniques to drive potentially motivated sellers to them. One of these techniques is leafleting. This involves printing thousands of leaflets and having them dropped through letter boxes in the area you are interested in buying in. The message of these leaflets will be simple. "Do You Own Your Own Home? Do you need to Sell Quickly? Contact 0800 XXX XXX." Another way is to advertise on the Internet – many of the two million sites that are returned when you key in "sell my property fast" are targeted at people who may be motivated sellers. Other techniques may even involve taking out adverts in the local press or radio.

It's all a lot of work, so some big players in the "below–market–

value business" have now set up their own national network of "sourcers" of BMV property and call centres to field enquiries and filter out the genuine "distressed seller". They then sell these "hot leads" to investors who may then be charged for each lead that comes onto his patch.

Once he has found a potentially motivated seller, the investor will then usually call him and try to qualify him over the phone before arranging a meeting and setting up a deal to buy the property from him quickly for at least 20 per cent below its true value. But be warned, this end of the business can result in you seeing some pretty distressing people and sad situations, so it's not for everyone. Also, many areas are now awash with leafletters and other folks in search of BMVs. But that said, many of these competitors will let vendors down, so if you don't get the deal first time, it is worth following up a few weeks or a month later. Some leafletters find that putting their adverts in takeaways, hairdressers and newsagents works well too.

There were many below-market buyers who used to use bridging finance to get the deal done without using any of their own money. Here's how it worked. The investor found a property worth say £200,000 but the owners wanted a quick sale and would sell for only £160,000. The investor raised a bridging loan for the £160,000 and completed the purchase.

At the same time, he applied for a remortgage supported by a valuation for £200,000 on which he applied for a mortgage of, say, £170,000 (85 per cent). This gave him "instant equity" to pay towards purchase costs, the cost of the bridging loan and the cost of his time finding the deal. This was, of course, very attractive to would-be investors who perhaps think property investment is a get-rich-quick scheme and want to get into it but don't have any deposit to put down. However, the credit crunch of 2008 forced mortgage lenders to stop doing "next-day remortgages" and it remains to be seen if they will ever restart lending on these terms. Lenders today will generally not remortgage unless at least six months ownership has expired (which is also a problem for refurbishers looking to add value and sell on). Also, lenders have become wary of clever financial deals for novice investors and are now checking ever more carefully to see that there is real value in the property.

Some critics say the only people who are making any money out of BMV are the marketers of the schemes as they stand to gain from the seminars, from the supply of quality leads from their marketing and from the bridging loan finance too.

I think this is a bit unfair because it is possible to make money buying below market value, though it is not easy because it is very hard work to sift through thousands of leads in search of a good below-market-value deal and then to close the deal.

Some BMV solutions involved the vendor selling to an investor and then renting back the property from them – often called "Sale and Rent Back" (or SARB). This had the neat advantage that it allowed the seller to continue living in his home with no adverse marks on his credit file. This drew criticisms from an ethical standpoint and many people see below-market-value investors as preying on people's misfortune and giving them little back in return. For example, where a distressed seller sells and rents back under an assured shorthold tenancy (the only type of tenancy a buy-to-let mortgage would allow) the seller-turned-tenant has no long-term security of tenure after six months.

But BMV fans point out that many indebted people leave it too late and their circumstances are better served by a below-market-value operator because it means they can stay in their home rather than face being repossessed by their mortgage company. And from the sellers' point of view they won't have to pay estate agency fees and may also come out with some cash to hopefully get their lives back on track.

However, tales of people being ripped off by SARB operators

on the sale price of their home and then being evicted once they were tenants were all too common, so legislation was passed which now requires operators to be authorised by the regulators. They now need to give "distressed sellers" more information about the true value of their property and their future rights as tenants. The new rules make SARB deals a lot harder to do and the compliance requirements are too much for many operators.

At www.LettingFocus.com, I advise many people on the pros and cons of BMV deals. Whether you think BMV is right for you will depend on how much time you can devote to this and your attitude to the ethical issues involved.

In summary, finding and then persuading people to sell their property at say 20 per cent below market value is a time-consuming business. You need to be very patient and persuasive, and you need a team of sharp solicitors and mortgage brokers who understand clever financial deals and can act very fast. But, in my opinion, unless you plan to be a full-time property investor you may do better by focusing on those geographic areas set to reap the benefits of regeneration or transport improvements – and then playing hard ball to buy property at least 10 per cent below asking price from local estate agents or at auction.

Finally, some last bits of advice. First, if you are after BMV deals and wish to pay a sourcing company for access to "hot leads", make sure you check out the company's past performance very carefully and find out how financially robust they are.

Second, it is illegal to offer a bribe or inducement to an agent who is acting for a seller to give a buyer priority access to properties for sale and the agent must declare any conflict of interest to his client. Third, if you fail to declare the true price you are paying for a property on your mortgage application and if you "forget" to declare any discounts or side offers, you have just committed mortgage fraud and you could end up being a guest in one of Her Majesty's high-walled establishments.

Fourth, "the financial freedom through property" lobby have now moved on to promote other schemes. Property (or Purchase) Lease Options, Exchange with Delayed Completion (EDC), Flips for Free, and Joint Venture deals are the current flavours of the year. Some of these techniques are designed to allow an investor to gain control of the cash flow and capital gains from a property without having to part with the 20 per cent deposit the lenders now expect buyers to invest. In some cases the investor does not even become the full legal owner – as in the much hyped and now much discredited "Rent to Rent" schemes.

Joint venture schemes now come under the regulatory authority's radar too, so investors seeking partners must now be very careful about how they promote their ideas. Promoters of joint venture financing should note that the FCA requires compliance with "PS 13/3" which deals with the "retail distribution of unregulated collective investment schemes". There are huge fines for those who don't comply. Shared-equity joint venture property schemes are very much in vogue now, partly driven by changes to the way mortgage interest can be deducted for tax purposes. Using other people's spare cash to assist with property financing has never been more popular. Before entering into a joint venture agreement, have the contract checked over by a solicitor. Many such deals are arranged via crowdfunding companies, who often run deals where the participants can provide either equity or loan finance for the same project.

All these methods have their merits and also their drawbacks but all potentially increase risk (including the risk that you may not get good "legal title") and all come with added legal costs for you (costs which the scheme proponent's pet conveyancer will normally be the beneficiary!).

Some types of property lease option agreement seem to

me to be particulary bad deals for the other party (increasing the risk that your tenant-buyer feels he's been ripped off) and there are also risks that some of these types of schemes will be challenged in court and deemed unenforceable. Tread very carefully indeed. You have been warned.

Ask the Council

Try asking your local authority about empty homes that are on their list and about properties that have received planning permission applications or approvals. The council may also maintain a list of HMOs. These lists may contains gems – people who, for a variety of reasons, are willing to sell for an attractive price. Also, the council may be looking to sell off empty property too. Get the heads up on these too, before they are listed at auction.

4

Ready to Buy: Finance and the Legal Stuff

Now you've found your property, you just need to ensure that your finance is all ready and you know what legal documents you and your conveyancer will need to check. This chapter will guide you through the finance maze and help you get the best from your conveyancer.

How to arrange your finance

Today, I do an increasing amount of consultancy with mortgage companies to help them improve their buy-to-let products and generally things are improving, albeit very slowly.

But there are some things that bug me about mortgage companies – whether they are banks, building societies or other finance providers.

Firstly, they rarely reward loyalty or experience. Only a few of the more forward-thinking lenders have products in place that meet the needs of the larger "portfolio" landlord. Worse still, a few lenders refuse to lend to landlords with years of experience, millions of pounds in equity in their portfolios and small loan exposures just because they cannot show a minimal income from a non-landlording day job or because they have more than a certain arbitrary number of properties already. These lenders view someone with no landlord experience but *with* a day job as a lower risk (even though that job could be terminated tomorrow). This is, of course, great for new-entrant landlords but it is infuriating for the more experienced operator.

Secondly, the tariff of ancillary charges that lenders levy for running a mortgage account gets ever longer and more punitive. "Writing a letter to you, that will cost you £50 sir." "Closing your mortgage, that will be £300 sir." If you are shopping for a new mortgage, ask the lender for their tariff of charges. If they're unjustified, go elsewhere and write and tell the lender's top boss why. Just don't expect a meaningful reply.

Thirdly, they never seem to have enough staff. It doesn't matter how quiet the housing market is, some lenders seem not to have enough staff to answer the phone, arrange a valuation or process your application in a reasonable period of time, which rules them out if you plan to buy at auction or directly from a vendor who wants a fast sale.

Fourthly, a lot of the blanket restrictions some lenders have in place are illogical – examples are "no lets to benefit tenants", "no lets allowed in selective licensing areas" and "tenancy agreements must have fixed terms less than 12 months" – and are based on a lack of understanding of how the private rented sector actually works. (At LettingFocus, in our corporate consultancy, we advise government and lenders on why such blanket restrictions are often nonsensical and our work has forced some lenders to change their policies.)

Not all banks and building societies provide mortgages for landlords. However, there are plenty of lenders out there who do and many of these have specialist units. Obviously you don't need to restrict your choice of lender to the one who provided financing for your own home and you don't even need to be a home owner yourself or even to have had a mortgage, though it does help and an increasing number of lenders now require it. (Following the Mortgage Market Review, many lenders now impose special criteria for first-time landlords who don't already own a property, whilst others apply blanket bans).

Most *sensible* lenders are not too interested in whether your non-rental income is at a certain level, but they *are* interested in the potential rent on the property. As a general rule, you'll need to put in at least 25 to 30 per cent of the property valuation from your own funds – this is often referred to as the "deposit". When the credit crunch eases off, you might, once again, be able to get a higher loan to value than 70 to 75 per cent but you'll always pay a higher interest rate and arrangement fee if the loan to value is over 60 per cent.

If you're struggling to get the loan on your own, see if a co-mortgage is possible, where up to four people can be on one mortgage and covered by a legal "deed of trust". Make sure you trust your co-owners because each of you will be jointly and severally liable for the whole mortgage!

Most lenders charge ever higher application fees for buy-to-let mortgages. Very irritating! These fees can be a flat rate or percentage-based and can sometimes be added to the mortgage itself, which means you pay interest on the fee you have paid to them to lend you the money in the first place.

In addition to the usual valuation, the lender will normally ask the surveyor to report what rent he thinks the property can achieve. The lenders will want the rent to be at least 1.45 times greater than the interest payments on the mortgage loan. So if your mortgage interest will be £1,000 per month, they would expect rental income to be 1.45 x £1,000, i.e. £1,450 per month. This "rent to interest" restriction is often calculated on the "follow on" or "reversion mortgage interest rate" or some other nominated rate – a nasty "trick in the tail" - which often results in the amount of loan offered coming in at well below what you had hoped for. So watch out for this. Landlords with four or more let properties will now have to provide asset liability and cash flow statements.

If the survey values the property below what you've offered, go back and renegotiate with the vendor. However, if you've negotiated well already, you may not get much more off. If the survey is OK, then the mortgage should be approved and the legal process leading to contract exchange and completion can start.

There are many types of mortgage available, the main choice being between fixed and variable rate ones. Fixed mortgages have the interest rate fixed for a limited period, usually one, three or five years. (Fixes for the entire life of the loan have proved unpopular in the UK.) After the fixed period, the rate reverts to the standard mortgage variable rate. A variant of the fixed mortgage is the "cap and collar" where the interest rate is fixed, for a time at least, between a lower and higher interest rate. The advantage of fixed-rate products is that you'll know what your interest payments are going to be for the period of the fix, which can be quite reassuring.

Tips for arranging a mortgage and keeping a good credit rating

You usually have to pay the mortgage company to arrange a survey. They choose the surveyor and make additional profit by paying the surveyor less than you paid to them. However, there are some lenders that let you arrange your own survey. If so, you'll pay less than you would where the lender arranges it.

Even if you're a cash buyer it's still probably worth getting a survey if you're buying in an area with a history of subsidence or if the property is in poor condition. If you have real concerns, go for a fuller structural survey rather than the more basic "valuation report".

Avoid making too many formal applications for mortgages with different lenders and even mortgage comparison sites (if they run formal credit searches) as these all show up on your credit file, potentially worsening your credit rating.

Keeping your credit rating good is something you need to be very focussed on. Get on the electoral roll. Never miss

---

a payment on a utility bill, credit card or any other form of payment arrangement, especially a mortgage. Any CCJs on your file or payment default will mean a straight decline from most lenders. Also, don't be "too cute" in billing lots of maintenance costs on your tax return in a short period of time, because if your declared rental profit is too low, many lenders will be put off. If you are self-employed get your SA302 assessment downloaded as soon as it is available each year. Check your credit report with one provider on a regular basis and if it's wrong have a "Notice of Correction" added. Avoid being associated with multiple addresses as your main home. Never "max out" to your credit cards limits. Pay credit card bills off in full each month, cancel unused credit cards and overdraft facilities, close unused bank accounts and have any unconnected parties removed.

Finally, it's possible to be "too clean": If you run a very basic bank account with no credit facility, don't apply for a credit card and just use a Pay As You Go mobile, this may not establish a sufficiently decent credit record.

Even after you've done all the right things, you may still get rejected by one or more lenders, even if you have the maximum credit score available, simply because you don't fit a particular lender's criteria.

Variable-rate mortgages go up and down depending on prevailing interest rates. Discounted mortgages are a type of variable rate where there is some discount off the standard variable mortgage rate for a period of one, three or five years. After that, they also revert to the standard mortgage rate.

Watch out for early redemption penalties on fixed and discounted mortgages. These penalise borrowers who end the mortgage early, even if only moving to another mortgage with the same company. The penalty period often applies even after the fixed or discounted period has ended. So, for example, you might have a discount for a period of two years, but be penalised if you come out any time up to three or five years. Penalties can be quite high, so avoid products with penalties (and those with high arrangement fees) if you think you may wish to close the mortgage early, perhaps because your plan is to sell it within a short timescale.

My own preference is for "base-rate tracker mortgages" (in fact I have never taken out any mortgage where the mortgage rate does not revert to tracking the Bank of England base rate for the rest of the mortgage life). With these, there is a guarantee that the mortgage rate will never be more than a set amount above the central bank (Bank of England) base rate. If the rate is a standard variable rate and not linked to the central bank rate, the mortgage company will be free to set any rate it likes and call that "the standard variable rate". This might be uncompetitive and, if you're tied in, you may be stuck on a very uncompetitive rate indeed. (In 2016, a long running court action by landlords and actively supported by me forced the West Bromwich Building Society to stop reneging on a tracker rate mortgage and pay back £27.5m in overcharged interest to thousands of borrowers. Further actions against Bank of Ireland and Skipton Building Society who, it is claimed, did similar things are likely to follow. Please contact me if you might be affected).

The other consideration is whether to go for an interest only or a repayment mortgage. With a repayment one, some of your payments go to pay off the loan outstanding, whereas with interest-only mortgages, you just pay off the interest, leaving the amount borrowed the same. Which is best for you will depend upon your long-term objectives and cash-flow position. Sadly, some mortgage lenders no longer offer interest-only mortgages. Others impose age limits by which the mortgage must be paid off, though most of the smarter lenders such as Paragon and TMW consider applications for buy-to-let loans up to a far later age than would be the case for a residential mortgage.

Many professional landlords opt for interest only because interest on an investment property is currently deductible from rental income for tax. The problem with repayment mortgages is that the more you pay off from the capital, the lower the loan outstanding and interest become, so the more you'll potentially make on which you'll have to pay tax.

Mortgage brokers

In periods when mortgage finance is not constrained by credit crunches, mortgage lenders may have special discounted products that are only available through mortgage brokers so it might be worth considering approaching a broker. They advertise on the Internet and in local phone directories. Bear in mind though that they will usually charge a fee, which may cancel out any saving you make on the mortgage.

Mortgage brokers are especially useful for the self-employed or people who may have difficulty proving their income – in which case you may be offered a "self-certificated mortgage". They also know their way around each lender's criteria, so this may save you time if your circumstances or your proposed property are unusual in any way. And they will know which lenders can process applications quickly – useful for anyone running to a tight deadline. This also will save you from making multiple failed applications with different lenders and potentially hurting your own credit rating.

Care needs to be taken not to have too much borrowing because, even with careful planning, things still go wrong – tenants can be hard to find, rents or house prices could fall, interest rates rise and unexpected costs can crop up. Therefore keep borrowing reasonable. (I suggest to my clients to always work out what level of interest rate would put them in a nil cash flow situation – a rather scary situation to be in, because buy-to-let lenders, unlike residential loan providers, do not exercise much restraint before they seize a property, if you, the borrower fails to pay your mortgage.)

Check if your mortgage allows you to make one-off capital payments or to take out additional mortgage funds without having charges imposed on you for doing so. Check, too, that all payments you make are applied to reduce the mortgage loan and interest payments immediately.

The better mortgage lenders can make additional advances on one property based on equity they know you have in another property, without going through the hassle of needing a new valuation. This is obviously very convenient.

You may also be able to borrow money based on capital in your own home if you have one, or on another investment property. And this can be very tax efficient. Again, check the lender's fees for doing this. The interest rate may be lower if you have a good existing banking relationship with your existing lender (but don't bank on it).

Finally, if you want to let out your own home, you must ask your mortgage lender's and insurer's permission first. Even if they don't normally operate buy-to-let mortgages, they will usually be prepared to consider your request and "consent to let" although sadly, most now impose a higher mortgage rate and charge additional fees for this.

Each company has its own criteria, setting out what it will give a mortgage on and who they will lend to based on the applicant's past credit history. Also, some lenders will not lend on new-builds, anything slightly out of the ordinary, such as a flat above a shop, in a big tower block or an ex-council house. Some don't lend on houses in multiple occupation, and those that do rarely go over 60 per cent loan to value. Others will (bizarrely) not lend to landlords with more than three let properties. The message is: shop around.

Mortgages for Houses in Multiple Occupation (HMOs)
Standard buy-to-let mortgages usually restrict the number of tenants to no more than four sharers. If there are five or more, you'll need an HMO mortgage. Most standard buy to let lenders don't allow external locks on internal room doors as they don't like landlords letting "by the room" on different tenancies or licences, which is more the norm in HMOs - a feature which also increases fire risk. They also tend to not like it if there is more than one kitchen. If you are offering bedsits, your best bet for funding might be a commercial loan rather than an HMO mortgage.

Always make sure you are not in breach of the lender's rules and that the type of insurance is right for the way the property is actually being let. If the property were to burn down and your mortgage and /or insurance were invalidated by the way you were letting, you could be facing a painful and costly experience! That said, many landlords do "play the risks" and get away with it, arguing that as long as the mortgage is being paid, the lender will not worry!

"No go" situations for almost all mortgage lenders include flats with leases of less than eighty years remaining, derelict and unsecure properties, properties with no working kitchen and bathroom, those in very high flood-risk areas, properties where there has been non-compliance with building regs, where there are unclear boundaries, where Japanese knotweed is present, freehold flats, properties worth under £50K (or £85K in London) and those where a non-assured shorthold tenant is in occupation.

Post the 2008 credit crunch, the margins that mortgage lenders want over bank base rates for lending you money have widened considerably. In 2007 it was possible, for a mortgage fee of just £500, to get a buy-to-let mortgage with a margin over Bank of England base rate as low as 0.69 per cent *for life*. It could be a long time before such rates reappear.

For bigger players, such as portfolio landlords and refur-bishers/developers, the commercial lending arms of banks may be worth considering as an alternative. Rates tend to be linked to LIBOR and can be more expensive, though the flexibility to move on a deal fast by using the loan facility can be advantageous. Another option for the already wealthy will be to use a private bank for loan finance. Again, LIBOR rates tend to apply and you will have to deposit typically a minimum of £500K of assets with the bank's asset management service, for which a chunky management fee will no doubt apply.

In recent years, there has been a big growth in "limited company buy-to-let mortgages". This is because limited companies are not (so far) affected by the changes to tax relief on interest on loans brought in by George Osborne in 2016. Whether it is financially beneficial for a landlord to go for one of these mortgages will depend on their circumstances. Landlords considering doing this should take qualified tax advice.

Development Finance

Development finance is short-term funding for the purpose of developing property either from the ground up or where existing buildings require substantial change – it can cover anything from a big extension for a house, to a small office to residential conversion and all the way right up to a plot of 100 new homes. Minimum loan size is usually £500K. Lenders will only consider experienced developers and this type of funding is easier to obtain if the lender has other active development sites locally and if planning permissions are already in place. Some developers will use bridging finance to get the plot bought and then seek development finance once planning permission has been obtained. Interest rates

---

are lower than bridging loans but exit fees are higher because the lender takes a percentage of the Gross Development Value (GDV). Exit fees are usually 1 to 1.5 per cent of the GDV and most loans are for twelve to twenty-four months duration and typically repaid inside twenty months. The lender will usually want to be involved with contractors and architects on the project. Maximum LTV is usually around 60 per cent of end value, though in good times 75 per cent of end value is possible.

Expect to provide lenders with a detailed business plan, a development appraisal, your CV setting out your previous experience and an asset and liability statement. Allow at least two months to get the funding and expect to provide a lot of paperwork. Some development finance is available for loans of just £200K, but interest rates and fees will be much higher.

Bridging Finance

Bridging finance is short-term finance (normally for less than six months) and is used by professional investor landlords who want to move quickly to take advantage of a private property deal and for those buying at auction, where speed is also of the essence. Bridges are also useful where a traditional mortgage lender will not lend, for example where the property does not have a kitchen or bathroom, requires some other major refurb or where planning consent is not yet in place. Bridges also appeal to those who aim to sell a property on quickly.

Here are some things to bear in mind: 1) Loan to value is typically limited to less than 65 per cent and interest rates are much higher than on a buy-to-let mortgage. 2) Check what the upfront and exit fees are. Exit fees can be particularly high. 3) Bridging companies always offer the best rates in more prosperous areas where the property could be easily re-sold, in the event the bridge user defaults. 4) Mortgage lenders will generally only allow you to re-mortgage where you have owned the property for at least six months – so you will normally be on the bridge for half a year. It is really important to make sure the solicitors speedily register the property at the Land Registry because this is what the mortgage company will look at when assessing if you've owned it for six months. 5) "Open" or "closed" bridges are available. (Closed bridges are where you have a mortgage decision in principle; open is where you don't and are therefore more expensive.) 6) Normally, you can get a decision on a bridge in forty-eight hours and the cash within seven days. 7) Some experts think conveyancers linked to bridging firms can "drag their feet" on legal work so you end up paying more in interest on the bridging loan. So watch for this. 8) Read the bridging loan Ts and Cs carefully. 9) Ask a mortgage broker for details of what's available. 10) In 2017, some bridging loans became available which have a term up to 15 months. 11) Lower interest rates tend to apply when arrangement fees are higher, the LTV is lower, the loan is a decent size and the property is in an excellent location, for example in Central London. 12) About 80 per cent of bridging loans go over deadline, costing borrowers greatly. The main causes are failing to correctly judge how long it takes to get planning permission, (always risky), and to complete building or refurb works.

How to make the conveyancing process work for you

Once you've got your mortgage offer you can start the legal process leading up to completion and ownership of the property – what is called "conveyancing".

In England and Wales it can typically take up to about ten to fourteen weeks from when the offer has been accepted to when completion takes place. If you aren't relying on a mortgage, and can start the conveyancing process quickly, you should be able to shave at least two weeks off that.

In Scotland the process of buying and selling a property will be faster because contracts become legally binding once an offer is received and accepted.

Lots of people complain about conveyancers. Common gripes are that they're too slow, they ignore deadlines set by clients, they don't provide updates and don't return phone calls. Here are some tips to help you find a good one.

Ask friends and family and look for firms advertising on the Internet.

Get quotes from a number of firms and be prepared to negotiate on fees. Ask about their quality of service and read what it says about them online. Ask if they have service standards to return phone calls within a specific period of time. The average conveyancer's heart will skip a beat at this as service standards and conveyancing firms aren't natural bedfellows!

Ask who will actually be handling your file and providing you with updates and how often. They will automatically say something like, "The partner, Mr X, will be handling your account personally." In reality, what happens in practice is that your file is delegated to a junior member of staff with the partner or other manager only checking the file at the end of the process and your initial call will be the first and last time that the partner actually speaks to you.

Ensure that you get a fixed fee, one that can't go up if things turn out to be more complicated than expected.

Get a written quote and make sure that everything is included, so that when comparing quotes, you know you are comparing like with like.

Local firms recommended by estate agents always seem too expensive to me. (My view is that is often because there is a commission to the agent for the referral hidden in the fee.)

If you can use a local firm then this may help if time is of the essence and you need to drop off or pick up documents. However, my experience of the average high-street conveyancer has been very mixed and I have generally had better experiences with larger outfits that I have found online.

So what do conveyancers do as part of the house purchase process? Here is a very quick guide.

They'll look at the title deeds to check that the person you are buying from (and their mortgage company if applicable) is registered as the owner at the Land Registry. They'll check the questionnaire the seller has completed on the property about such things as if there have been any disputes, who pays to fix things like boundary walls, if there are any restrictions to access, whether the gas, water, drains, electricity and phones are connected, what access is granted, whether any building work has been done and if so was planning consent obtained, whether there has ever been a change of use or alteration (e.g. to a conversion) and whether it has been approved and whether there are any guarantees that come with the property.

The questions will also ask if full vacant possession will be granted. (It is possible to buy a property with an existing tenant *in situ*, but you would need to ensure that the tenancy agreement with the tenant allowed you to gain possession when you want to. For more on tenancy agreements see Chapter 6.) Where the property is leasehold, a separate form will be sent asking further questions about service charges and the like.

If you're buying, you need to check the answers carefully. If it's leasehold, look at the most recent accounts from the managing agent of the freeholder to see what costs have been incurred in the past. Look into whether there are any upcoming major works planned and what the cost will be.

The conveyancer will also check the local authority search information supplied. However, this won't tell you about planned developments a mile away. It's up to you to find this out from your own research of the area including your own checks with the Town Hall's Planning Department and other local estate agents.

Once everything is in place, the conveyancer will send a draft contract which basically states who is selling what to whom. The buyer hands over a deposit, usually 10 per cent of the value of the property. Contracts are then exchanged (normally via a phone call) which means you must complete on the purchase. If you don't, you lose your deposit and will be liable for the seller's costs too.

Both buyer and seller should be sent a completion statement. For the buyer it will show the balance to be paid, including all costs and legal fees. Check it carefully against your initial quote. In particular, check if the conveyancer has deducted any amount you've already paid upfront from his final fee as I've found that most conveyancing solicitors are very adept at forgetting to do this. The buyer will be asked to have the money cleared and in his solicitor's account on completion day.

Your solicitor should ensure the Energy Performance Certificate is available before exchange of contracts.

If you are buying at auction, from a "motivated seller" or in any other situation where you have to move fast or else lose the deal, you'll want a conveyancer who is sharp and can move much faster than the average twelve weeks. Shop around online and look beyond the high street for this kind of specialist conveyancer.

5

Refurbishing and Preparing Your Property

How to deal with builders

If the property you bought requires some work to get it up to standard, you may need to employ a builder. If you're tempted to do difficult jobs yourself, remember that most jobs will take longer for you to do than they would a professional. As a property investor, when you have a big mortgage and no rent coming in, time really is money, so even if you can get it done cheaper doing it yourself, once you factor in the extra time taken you may not be really saving at all.

How to find a good builder? Start with recommendations. If you have friends who have had a job done on time and to a good standard, go and see it yourself. If it's a specific job such as roofing, check if the roofer is a member of the trade body for that profession. Most trade bodies have a website or a phone number listed in local phone directories. Check with the trade body to see what guarantees (if any) a company's membership really gives you.

Find out how long the company has been in business and ask for proof that they possess the necessary public and employer liability insurance. Request references for previous work. Never agree to pay by the hour and always insist on a quote not an estimate. An estimate is nothing more than a rough guess of what the job might cost whereas a quote should be fixed and break down the work involved into distinct parts.

Prepare a detailed specification of the works you want done and be as specific as possible. Leave nothing to chance! Be clear whether it will be you or the builder who will pay for materials. If it's a big job obtain at least three quotes and ask each company to provide a description of materials and their cost. For big jobs, the quote should be itemised for each stage of the project.

Taking legal action against a tradesman

I've only once taken court action against a tradesman. It was against an electrician and as the amount was under £10,000 I went through the small claims court. NICEIC, their trade body, supported me in my claim. I won and the electrician had to refund my money plus the cost of the small claims action and, as he did not pay initially, the cost of the bailiff who was sent to enforce judgment. Claims over £10,000 can't go through the small claims court, so, it's even more essential on big jobs for you to check a tradesman's insurance and to have a proper contract.

Check the builder's availability and avoid those who'll be juggling your job alongside too many others. However, bear in mind, if they can't start right away, that might indicate they are in demand because they're good! So, if you want to buy a property which needs building work, get the builder in to quote as soon as possible, and well before exchange of contracts if it's going to be a big job. If you are buying a property, the builder must commit to start soon after completion day.

Assess how professional they were when they came to look at the job. Did they make lots of notes? Do you think you can get on with them? Did they treat you and your property with professional respect? Then go through each written quote in detail. Did they provide a breakdown of materials' cost and quote for everything in the job spec? Did they explain any technical jargon? Did they provide insurance certificates and agree to provide reference sites for other work? Did they commit to be available and say how long the job would take? Did they say who will supervise the work?

Are they planning to subcontract work? If so, how well do they know the people they'll be subbing to? It might be that they don't have, say, a good kitchen fitter on their books and therefore decline to quote for this part. This is not necessarily a negative thing or a problem. Provided that the part they can't do is self-contained, or at the end of the job and not interdependent with other work, it might be worth employing a separate tradesman. Get references and quotes for any other tradesman you employ directly.

Don't just go for the cheapest quote but take account of everything. On a big job try to retain 5 to 10 per cent of the total cost for "snagging"; this to be payable one month after the job has been completed if there is nothing wrong. Retaining a small amount like this will ensure they come around promptly to fix any defects.

Agree a timescale in writing and don't be afraid of imposing penalties in the contract if they're late. However, you must accept delay if it's you who changes your mind. Builders make lots of money from the extra things you think of as the job progresses because once on the job they can control the price of the extras. That's another reason to be completely clear and have a detailed specification at the outset. So don't change your mind or add things in later!

You should both sign the quote or have a special contract drawn up. If the builder finds unforeseen problems along the way, then it's usually his problem as he should have checked out everything first. In some cases, however, it might have been impossible to have anticipated the problem. If in doubt or in dispute with your builder you could ask an *independent* surveyor for his opinion or request the contractor's trade body investigate and adjudicate. It's worth putting in your contract something like "claims for unforeseeable work will not be entertained, where the work could reasonably have been anticipated".

Don't cheat HMRC by paying in cash, as you'll have less come back if the job isn't done properly. A large builder (with a turnover of approximately £70,000 plus) will be registered for VAT, so at least you'll know that it is a large outfit. Smaller builders may keep under the VAT limit by asking you to pay for building materials and subcontractors' costs directly. There is nothing wrong with this, but remember to keep all receipts. Note that VAT will already have been charged on the building materials supplied, so there is no need to pay it twice. If you are a serious refurbisher, consider getting your own trade account with building materials suppliers – it will help cash flow and good discounts are possible.

If it's necessary don't forget to get planning permission and comply with building regulations (see below). Also, never pay until the agreed stage of the work has been completed, the only exception to this being where perishable or made-to-measure materials are needed.

Of course, you don't want builders to rip you off, but you do want them to be hungry for work from you, next time. So, allow your contractors to make a fair profit and a small mark-up on materials they source. And pay promptly too!

If you are regularly buying and improving property you should start to have a good idea of costs for standard works – this is especially true if you are buying regularly at auction as you cannot expect a builder to keep coming out to quote for properties you may never end up actually buying anyway. In general, it is easier to calculate fit-out costs for a completely stripped out property. Many investors do this and focus on adding capital and rental value above the cost of works by adding rooms or by extending or changing the layout. Turning a lounge into a bedroom and replacing a kitchen and small room with a kitchen-diner is very popular with HMO experts. It is easier to calculate fit-out costs for a completely stripped-out property.

Building Tips
- Get units of a standard size – this especially applies to ovens and showers.
- Avoid any over-fancy fittings as replacement parts can be hard to find.
- Ensure shower cubicles are raised so that there is an access point, or better still avoid shower cubicles altogether.

How to deal with architects and surveyors

If the job is too big or complicated, then consider employing an architect. Contact the Royal Institute of British Architects for help finding a suitable architect. If structural changes are proposed then you'll also need a structural surveyor, so get in touch with the Royal Institution of Chartered Surveyors. Contact details for both of these organisations are given in Appendix 2. If your work involves a wall shared with a neighbour, you'll need to get him to sign up to a party wall agreement.

Seek recommendations from friends and talk to a number of architects. Ask for references, examples of previous work and fees. As for builders, agree a cost for the whole job not a by-the-hour payment, and clearly set out what they'll do for you and whether they'll also project manage the work.

Where you are planning major works, a quantity surveyor might be worth employing. He can produce a "schedule of works" which is basically a detailed spec for the work. He can help you choose the right builder, compare quotes and set out payment stages. The builder should agree and sign a copy of the schedule of works. A building surveyor might be required to ensure that your builder has done the work to the right standards in accordance with current building regulations.

Finally, if you are considering buying a property which has evidence of subsidence, it might be worth getting it checked over by a structural engineer. He can also advise on the consequences of making structural alterations.

How to get planning permission and building regulations approval

Depending on what you're doing, you may need to apply for planning permission. If so, phone the council for the planning forms and submit your plans and your fee. Tell the neighbours about your plans and try to get their agreement before you apply because the council will contact them anyway.

An architect or a planning consultant can handle the process of getting planning permission for you and meet the planning department too. He can also give an expert view of what would be acceptable to the planning department before you even apply. A simple alteration or extension should be passed (or not) within eight weeks but it will depend on your local office. (Some councils fail to take action against developers and businesses who ignore planning conditions. However, as a property investor, you'll one day hope to sell, so you have to be in compliance.)

Work must adhere to building regulations. The Buildings Regulations Officer at the local council planning office can send you their guidelines and application forms appropriate to the work you are carrying out. Once you've submitted the forms, a Buildings Officer will then visit to make sure the site complies with the guidelines.

If employing a builder, check that he has submitted the application forms because Buildings Officers have the power to shut down unsafe sites.

Once the work is completed, a Buildings Regulations Approval Certificate will be issued. Keep it safe along with planning consent forms as you'll need them when you come to sell.

Finally, don't get carried away. Always think carefully whether the work you are planning to do really will add enough value to pay for itself in terms of higher rental potential and/or capital gains. Investments for capital gains may be best kept on hold until such time as you come to sell, as costs of capital improvements cannot be deducted until the property is sold and the gain is crystallised.

How to decorate and furnish

The key thing to remember is that you aren't going to live there, your tenants are! You must avoid overspending and take care to buy things that are hard-wearing, easily cleaned, functional and long-lasting. Try to give the impression of a light, bright, spacious and airy property with a minimum of clutter. This can be done by using light curtains, mirrors, wall and table lights, plants and candles.

To add a bit of "wow" factor, it's also worth putting in a few other things too when trying to let (or sell) a property! If you don't want them there when the tenants move in, you can always store them. You are selling a lifestyle and your job is to help people visualise that lifestyle within your property.

Even if you are advertising a property as "unfurnished", when doing a viewing have just enough stuff to make the place look homely. Here are some tips.

Curtains should be machine washable but alternatively consider using light roller blinds and Hessian or muslin fabrics. Curtain poles can also look good and aren't too expensive. For some reason, tenants are very good at breaking curtain tracks so always put in high-quality curtain tracking. Make windows look wider by extending the track well beyond the frame on both sides.

Mirrors can be used to reflect light and give the impression of more space. If your ceiling is low, pictures can be used to attract the eye away from it. However, don't put too many pictures in or it will make a room feel small.

Lighting is useful for creating the right look. In sitting rooms and bedrooms standard lamps, table lamps and down lights are better than overheads at creating a softer feel while spotlights are best in kitchens. Candles, burning oils, fresh flowers, soft music, a nice rug, a laid table and fresh coffee brewing won't do your chances of letting any harm.

For carpets, use colours and designs that are light but which won't show every mark. Have a large doormat, preferably a fitted one, put in. An alternative to carpeting is to use hardwood or laminate flooring with a few soft rugs thrown in to create a sense of warmth. However, wooden floors need sanding every three years and laminates aren't particularly hard-wearing. Also, if you're letting a flat, check that wooden or laminate floors are allowed under the lease and don't put them in if they will create a lot of noise for the flat downstairs. In the bathroom, ceramic tiles and linoleum are more water-resistant, hygienic and hard-wearing than hardwood flooring or carpets.

Novice landlords are often tempted to overspend in the kitchen and bathroom. Keep it simple unless your target tenant market is very "high end". Buy mid-priced white goods with five-year guarantees, especially for anything that uses water. If they break within five years then you can replace but at least it is covered for that period. Don't buy top-of-the-range units for mid-range type lets as tenants will often not look after it properly, but never buy cheap either. Use stainless steel sinks with a tiled splashback to prevent walls getting grubby and mouldy. Roller blinds are better than slatted blinds which tend to get greasy and are hard to clean. When kitchen units get tatty, use new doors rather than buying a whole unit. Put a few classy cooking bottles and some Jamie Oliver books in the kitchen to spell good cooking.

In the bathroom, light-coloured suites are best and, again, make sure there are tiled splashbacks. Reduce condensation by having an extractor fan fitted and avoid wallpaper, which will peel if the room is not aired properly. Use gloss paints in the bathroom as these are more waterproof or use lots of tiling as it looks good and is easy to clean. Large tiles can quickly cover a large area. Break up tiles with a border tile halfway up the wall and, again, use mirrors to increase the sense of space. Bathroom wall lights add a nice effect but will have to be properly enclosed. Tiles should be regrouted every two years and both bath and tiles should be properly sealed to avoid leaks.

Showers are one of the main causes of landlord call-outs, because they leak. Unfortunately, tenants, especially foreign ones, like them. Get a good quality hard-wearing power shower and hope for the best. Change shower curtains after every let as they get grubby quickly and, if you can, install a glass screen, but make sure it stops all the water escaping! Toilets should be low level with a wooden loo seat. Finally, add some style to your bath and shower rooms with some quality shampoo bottles in the bathroom and put in some matching towels.

If you have more than one property try to stick to the same paint colour and sitting room suites in all of them. Touching up the colours in any one property can then be done with the same paint. Stick to neutral colours and remember that vinyl silk is easier to wash down than emulsion.

Don't forget the outside too. Remember, the first thing to do is to get people inside by making the property look nice from outside. Letting and estate agents call this "kerb appeal". Consider having some hanging baskets outside, buy a quality front door and keep it smart and repainted, polish up brass fittings and letter boxes and tidy the front garden. Keep unsightly dustbins out of sight. If the outside street is a mass of graffiti and abandoned cars, get onto the local authority to clean it up!

Gardens should be low maintenance because most tenants aren't interested in looking after plants and weeding. So no fast-growing hedges and bushes. Leave tools to maintain gardens and include garden maintenance as a condition in your tenancy contract, and include it on your inventory, but don't expect tenants to do much more than tidying it up just before they move out. When showing a property in the summer it's worth having a small fold-away table, a few chairs and even a parasol in the garden. It will help build that lifestyle picture. Provide a washing line so tenants can dry clothes outside, thus reducing condensation and the possibility of mould growth.

What you put into the property by way of other furnishings will depend on your target market. Some tenants will prefer you to supply white goods (i.e. fridge-freezer, washing machine and cooker), some will also expect to see beds, sofas, wardrobes and chests of drawers, and others will prefer everything right down to kitchen utensils, a TV and video. In the old days, whether or not you furnished the property affected how easy it was to repossess it at the end of the tenancy but this rule no longer applies. How you furnish it, indeed whether you furnish it at all, depends simply upon the type of tenant you want to attract.

As well as asking a letting agent for advice, you could track existing properties advertised at Rightmove to gauge what level of furnishings leads to fast lets. With my properties, I usually provide just basic white goods and sometimes also sofas, chairs, beds and tables. However, if I think the tenant is going to be good, pay a high rent and stay for a long time, I'll include other things too. If tenants are scarce, I'm more inclined to be flexible and meet their requirements as there isn't any sense in a good tenant walking away for the want of a wardrobe! However, I try to avoid providing too much stuff, because it all needs to be maintained and insured and, if the next tenant doesn't want it, you then have to store it.

Doing viewings on a property that is already let

As soon as an existing tenant gives notice to leave, you should be planning viewings for new prospective tenants, so include a clause in your tenancy contract that allows you to conduct viewings with prospective tenants in the last month of the tenancy. This will help prevent void periods.

Unfortunately, you can't insist that the old tenants keep the place in a tidy and clean condition whilst they live there. However, I've had many tenants who were so tidy and had such good taste, the property looked better with all their stuff in it than when they had left. When it's like this, it's easy to re-let it. If you get on well with your old tenants, they won't mind you bringing along little tricks like fresh flowers and bottles of balsamic vinegar to help re-let it!

But some tenants live in a mess and this is a problem when you need to do viewings with prospective tenants. Piles of clothes everywhere and yesterday's pizza lying on the floor won't impress anybody or help them visualise what it could be like. If your existing tenants are like this, there isn't really much you can do – you can't withhold part of their deposit (unless they fail to clean up when they leave). Try appealing to their better nature, get to the viewings very early to tidy up a bit or even offer them a cash incentive if you let it fast and there is less than a week's void between them moving out and the new tenants moving in.

Where the place is really bad, and you cannot incentivise or encourage a clean-up then it's probably worth waiting until the existing tenants have gone before remarketing it. You can then go in and make it look good!

Finally, don't forget always to notify existing tenants of times when you'll be doing viewings. Don't turn up unannounced.

Fully furnished lets where everything from china to cups are provided tend to be more the norm in up-market properties rented to top executives, often on short-term contracts. In some of these cleaning and laundry may need to be provided too. These types of lets are often more like "serviced apartments" and need to compete with hotels in terms of standard of furnishings and décor.

Remember, providing lots of furnishing means more cost and work. As well as more contents insurance cover there will be a higher deposit too because the more there is, the more that can be damaged. The more mechanical and electrical items provided, the more that can break down too adding to costs in terms of time and money spent fixing or replacing them.

All furniture should comply with the soft furnishing regulations (see below). If you provide beds, don't buy cheap ones because tenants will soon complain that they are uncomfortable. Ideally, buy quality beds with storage space underneath (although if your tenant is a Feng Shui fan he won't store anything under the bed – bad vibes apparently). Avoid putting in furniture that's too big for the room as it will make the room feel small. Furniture should be in darker colours to avoid showing up every mark. Washable loose covers should be used on soft furnishings. Finally, never leave anything of sentimental value.

Legal regulations: Furnishing, gas safety, electrical, EPCs, HMOs and disability

There are a number of specific legal regulations that affect properties that are let out.

Soft furnishings

All soft furnishings must comply with the Furniture and Furnishings (Fire) (Safety) Regulations 1988 which say they must be fire-safety compliant. Things that must comply are beds (including headboards and mattresses), sofas, garden furniture which could be used internally, cushions, pillows, loose and stretch covers for furniture. Look for the fire-safety label stating it meets the requirements of the 1988 Safety Regulations. Things that are exempt are bed linen, loose covers for mattresses, pillow cases, curtains and carpets or furniture made before 1950.

Gas

The Gas Safety (Installation and Use) Regulations 1998 say landlords must ensure that gas appliances, fittings and flues provided for tenants' use are safe. Installation, maintenance and annual safety checks must be carried out by a Gas Safe Registered Installer for each gas appliance/flue. Provided that everything is OK, the engineer will give you a CP12 Landlord's Gas Safety Certificate showing that everything is satisfactory. You have to give a copy to your tenant when any letting starts and have a new check done each year. Keep a copy for yourself.

Carbon monoxide detectors must be fitted in all privately let properties that use a carbon based heating system.

Before allowing anyone to do any work on gas in your property, ask to see his Gas Safe Registered Installer identification (ID) card and check his membership is valid at the Gas Safe website.

Electrical

In Scotland, all property must be inspected by a competent and registered electrician when you start to let it and then every five years. For the rest of the UK, whilst there is currently no legal requirement to have regular safety checks on electrical equipment, it's a criminal offence to "fail to ensure that the electrical system and appliances are safe" (Electrical Equipment

Safety Regulations 1994.) So it's wise to have electrical equipment and wiring checked before the first letting starts and have periodic checks done by a qualified electrician. Depending on the work that's been done you should obtain either a Domestic Electrical Installation Certificate or a Minor Works Certificate. Use a NICEIC-registered electrician or one from the Electrical Contractors Association (ECA), see Appendix 2, and keep a record of all safety checks and certificates obtained.

All appliances have to be in working order and operating instructions and safety warning notices supplied. Particular attention should be paid to second-hand equipment, so always have these checked. In properties built after June 1992 and in houses classified as licensable HMOs (see below), there must be mains-wired smoke detectors on each floor. All HMOs should also have a full electrical safety check done at least every five years.

Any significant electrical work (for example, installing an electric shower or kitchen appliance) must be carried out by a "competent" person.

Energy Performance Certificates (EPCs)

Though they are currently available to view for free for any property online, it is now a legal requirement that all tenants must be given a copy of the Energy Performance Certificate. These cost under £100 for a small property, last for ten years and show how energy efficient the property is. As long as it was less than ten years ago you can use the one you were given when you bought the property, though if you have improved energy efficiency significantly since you bought it, getting a new one done should pay off as it will show a better score for energy efficiency. The energy rating must be shown on all adverts used to let the property.

The Government's Green Deal funding scheme allowed energy improvements to be made by having the costs paid for by the person paying the energy utility bills (normally the tenant) as long as the fuel savings more than outweighed the cost. The Green Deal and other related energy saving schemes the Government has launched have been poorly marketed, hard to find out about, lacking in funding and of generally poor value. Take-up by landlords has been very low. As a result, the Government has stopped funding for the time being. Properties with the lowest energy ratings, F and G, cannot be let after April 2018, so landlords with these will have to invest in energy efficiency improvements well before then.

However, if third party consents are not available or where the improvements are not cost effective, or where the improvements would reduce the value of the building by more than 5 per cent, the landlord is exempted and can still let an F or G rated property.

Finally, it's worth noting that the plethora of information that's freely and publicly available in an EPC is useful for refurbishers to help build a picture of a property and to quickly establish what's needed to bring it up to an energy efficient standard.

Licensing and Houses in Multiple Occupation (HMOs)

In broad terms, where three or more people occupy a property but don't form a single household, usually because they are not related, the property is classified by the Government as a "House in Multiple Occupation" or HMO. An HMO can be a flat or a house and it does not matter if there is a single or multiple tenancy agreements within the one property.

In England and Wales, landlords with HMOs of three storeys or more *and* with five or more tenants have to get a licence. HMO licences impose tough management standards (and hence higher costs) to ensure that properties comply with fire and electrical safety standards and are not occupied by too many people; even the kind of person who can be a landlord for such a property is regulated.

For smaller HMOs the management standards (the Houses in Multiple Occupation (England) Regulations 2006 since you asked!) amount to little more than what good landlords should be doing anyway, with the main additional requirement being to have an electrical inspection carried out every five years.

However, it's potentially much tougher on licensable HMOs because of onerous rules relating to the number of washbasins. These say that for licensable HMOs, where there are five or more occupiers, there must be one separate toilet (which should also have a hand washbasin) and at least one separate bathroom for every five occupiers. Also, if there are five or more occupiers, the local authority can require that each "unit of living accommodation" also has a washbasin or sink.

Any licensable HMO will also have to be inspected for health and safety hazards under the Housing Health and Safety Rating System (HHSRS) within five years of an HMO licence being granted. A similar set-up to the HHSRS exists in Scotland and Northern Ireland.

Part of the HHSRS assessment is to consider overcrowding, because this can trigger hazards such as fire, poor hygiene and dampness. HHSRS decisions about overcrowding will take account of the age and relationship of the occupiers and whether the property is divided into bedsits or is a single shared house. The law says that no persons over the age of ten should share a room if not of the same sex and not living together as husband and wife.

It's worth noting that local authorities can "additionally extend" HMO licensing in their area (or part of it) to HMOs with fewer than three levels or five tenants if they think there is a need. And if there is a local problem with anti-social behaviour or low housing demand, then ALL privately let properties can be licensed under what's known as a "selective licencing" scheme. Councils are jumping over each other to introduce selective licensing at the moment, in the often mistaken belief that this will somehow rid them of rogue landlords. To find out if your property may be in an area where extended or additional licensing is being applied or is under consideration, check with your council's Environmental Health Officer or the Private Housing Department.

Fees for a licence vary greatly from around £50 in some local authorities up to £1,500 in others and last five years. Penalties for not getting a licence are severe – fines of up to £20,000 can be applied for landlords who don't register; you will not be able to issue a Section 21 Notice and rent paid whilst you were unlicensed may be clawed back.

In Scotland and Northern Ireland *all* HMOs have to be licensed – i.e. mandatory licensing is not restricted to just those HMOs with three or more levels and five or more tenants; it applies to all HMOs. England and Wales may follow suit in 2017 or 2018.

In Scotland, landlords of properties that are not HMOs must also be registered in a separate scheme. There is a small minimum fee and there are additional fees for each local authority where you have a property and for each property that is let. The Scottish registration scheme costs millions of pounds to set up and administer and yet has seen only a handful of rogue landlords brought to justice.

Many mortgage lenders are not comfortable with HMOs at all and will not offer loans on them, while others restrict loan amounts to 60 or 65 per cent loan to value or will only grant mortgages for HMOs to more experienced landlords. One lender has also recently stopped lending in areas where selective licensing schemes have been introduced. In Wales, a registration and licensing scheme called RentSmart Wales requires all landlords to be on a register and for the manager of the property to be licensed. Landlords who find and/or manage tenants themselves, (i.e. without an agent), must now undertake a days' training to get a licence and to ensure they are "aware of their rights and responsibilities".

More experienced landlords sometimes like the potentially higher rents that HMOs can bring and actively seek out HMO properties, especially where there is a large student population combined with a lack of college or other purpose-built student accommodation. But be warned, managing an HMO is harder work than managing a standard let – there is much more wear and tear, tenant changeovers are more frequent and you may even be asked to umpire sharers' disputes (which you should point blank refuse to do – you are a landlord not a parent!). Also, the supply of student accommodation can change rapidly if a new large set of student accommodation blocks are built.

Most letting agents do not handle lettings by the room in HMOs, so that should tell you something about how much work this end of the business can be.

Conversion of a property to and from HMO status may require planning permission under new "Article 4 rules" – this varies by council and size of HMO so check with your local authority. However, where you have six or more people sharing a property you will always need to get planning permission.

Separately, some councils have bought in landlord accreditation schemes. Generally these are optional to join and have struggled to generate landlord or tenant interest due to poor marketing and lack of landlord benefits. The most high profile of these (but still struggling) is the one in London, where the mayor has sought to also push the "London Rental Standard" which is linked in to the accreditation scheme there.

What is the HHSRS?

HHSRS rules cover an exhaustive range of health and safety measures and can be brought into play for any HMO, including non-licensable ones. They cover minimum space requirements, natural light, ventilation, secure means of escape in the event of fire, the number of and location of toilets, bathrooms and showers, food prep space, storage facilities for food and the location of kitchen and bathroom facilities in relation to where rooms are.

Many HMO advocates often get caught out by these rules. For example, it might be very tricky space-wise to physically install two showers in a building or it might prove very costly to uprate the electricity board, increase the water capacity or install a more powerful boiler. Also, neighbours may complain about noise if what used to be an upstairs bedroom is turned into a living room to be used by many people or if parking suddenly becomes a problem.

With HMOs all that glistens is not necessarily buy-to-let gold and high gross yields can turn into a lot of hassle and cost.

Disability

The law defines disability as any mental or physical impediment that adversely affects someone's ability to carry out normal day-to-day activities. The disability has to be "long term", which means it has to be expected to last for over a year. Things like cancer, HIV and multiple sclerosis are included within this definition.

Landlords should make "reasonable adjustments" to their property if asked unless they have "reasonable grounds" for refusing. The reasonableness test involves questioning if any change is really going to help the disabled person, and disruption to others has to be taken into account too.

So, whilst you are expected to provide a large-print tenancy agreement for the partially sighted person, amend a parking policy to allow for an essential motor vehicle or allow a guide dog, you would not need to change or alter any physical feature which is a part of the design or construction of the building.

Failure to comply with the rules could in the worst case lead to court proceedings, claims for damages and if the property is an HMO, the loss of an HMO licence.

Minor adaptations costing less than £1,000 may be provided freely by the local housing department in England and grants from other bodies and charities may also be available.

How to get the right insurance cover

As soon as you exchange contracts to buy a property, the building must be insured up to the rebuild cost (which is not the same as the market value). If you're getting a mortgage, your lender will insist that this insurance is in place, will usually ask to see proof of the policy and be noted as an "interested party". For flats, the insurance will normally be arranged by the freeholder.

The more specialist buy-to-let mortgage companies and most landlords' associations have specialist buildings' insurance policies for landlords. Other sources are letting agents and commercial insurance brokers.

Typically, the policies include a small amount of contents cover which is good if you're only providing a limited amount of furnishings and don't need a separate contents policy. Cover for loss of rent, temporary accommodation and storage of furniture following fire or water damage should be provided too. Replacement locks should be covered as standard as should accidental damage to buildings.

Most specialist landlord policies will include cover for public and employer's liability up to at least five million pounds. You must make sure this risk is covered because even if you just pay a friend to do a job for you, he could become an employee in law! Also useful, (though few insurers now offer it), is a 24–7 emergency assistance feature, especially one which covers the cost of a call out to deal with an emergency. These are really worth getting because the insurer will send out its emergency tradesmen to do an initial fix, with the cost covered up to a certain amount. This will save you having to buy a separate emergency cover policy which is usually expensive for what it is. If your insurance has emergency assistance, ask about service standards because, if you have a flood, you want the problem dealt with the same day, not next week!

Check the policy exclusions. Some policies won't cover students, people on housing benefit, asylum seekers, short-term lets, properties let to social landlords such as housing associations or local councils or HMOs. Most won't cover properties that are unoccupied for more than three weeks or will limit cover unless the insurer is informed in advance and regular visits to the property are carried out. Others will insist the property is let on an assured shorthold tenancy and that you do proper reference checks on tenants. Where the insurance company perceives that the risk is higher, it may cover it, but charge a higher premium or impose a higher level of excess. Many insurers will not cover theft losses if the building was not properly secured.

Malicious damage by tenants rarely happens but it's some-times not covered, even under some "specialist" landlords' policies. As this can be very expensive, we advise our clients to be covered for this risk.

If you're a nervous first-time landlord with a big mortgage, it might be worth considering a rent guarantee policy which will pay your rent if the tenant defaults. Typically they cost from about 3 per cent of the rent (though some letting agents may include it "free" within their fee for finding a tenant). Typically these policies pay rent for between six and twelve months, although they often don't kick in until two months' rent has been missed. If you buy one, look for one that also covers legal expenses to evict the tenant.

I don't buy rent guarantee cover because I'm confident my vetting procedure will weed out tenants who can't or won't pay. I've also found that, to qualify, the tenant has to score so highly on the insurance company's own credit scoring system, that the chances of his defaulting would be very low anyway! However, I'll admit they do give useful peace of mind (at a cost!).

The level of excess (or deductible) on a specialist landlord policy varies from about £100 to £250 for normal claims though it's normally £1,000 for subsidence claims. Block buildings policies that apply on flats tend to have standard excesses from £250 to £500 (and even higher for claims caused by water damage) and no contents cover at all, so your carpets and curtains will be at risk if you don't have separate cover. Block polices will also generally not have any liability cover protecting you as the flat owner and landlord – and often, there is no loss of rent or malicious damage cover either. If you are worried about this, buy separate additional cover to protect against these risks.

Tell your tenants that you aren't responsible for any accidental damage they do, nor for damage to their own possessions whatever the cause. I always advise my tenants to take out cover for their own possessions, and to ensure that it includes accidental damage cover too.

Most domestic insurance policies do not cover rented property at all so if the property used to be your home, tell your insurers and mortgage company that the property is being let and check if they can provide a suitable specialist landlord policy. But shop around as most ordinary mortgage lenders' policies are poor value, in my opinion.

Good advice for when you make an insurance claim

Most policies won't pay for replacement taps, toilets or boilers, though they usually pay for "trace and access" to find the source of a leak. So tell your plumber or boiler repairer to include "trace and access" on his invoice if he's doing a trace, repair and replacement job. Making too many claims may raise your premiums in future years, so consider this before you make any claim. Keep receipts of all payments made and take photos of damage.

Recent big flood events have pushed up the cost of insurance especially in flood risk areas and there is now a real risk that insurers may withdraw cover completely in areas where flood defences have not been adequately maintained.

As well as not covering very high flood risk areas, the government's back stop "FloodRe" cover will not currently cover any let property nor "commercial" type policies, which includes insurance policies covering blocks of flats. Check whether you are at risk of flood at the Environment Agency website – see Appendix 2. Make sure to tell your tenants to get signed up for flood alerts.

Some portfolio landlords say that they just buy the very basic building and liability cover and this works out cheaper in the long run than covering every eventuality. Whether this is right for you will depend on your attitude to risk and ability to absorb occasional losses.

Keeping everyone informed: Telling people who "need to know"

Being a landlord involves quite a lot of administration. Apart from ensuring that gas, electricity and furnishings are safe and that insurance is in place, you'll need to keep the council tax and utilities people informed too. As soon as you take ownership, take meter readings for electricity, gas and water. If you hope to let quickly, it's probably only necessary to contact them once the property has been let so you can tell them the opening and closing meter readings and the names of the new tenants in one go. If it's likely to be some time until your first let, for example if you are having work done, then give the meter readings straightaway.

Don't forget that even if the property is unfurnished you may have to pay council tax until the property is let, when it becomes the responsibility of the tenant. For short-term lettings it may be simpler to keep utility bills and council tax in your name. It's worth knowing which utility companies are cheapest and, if you aren't likely to be using too much energy, choose a supplier that doesn't make a big daily standing charge.

If you have a flat that will be let out you must tell the freeholder and/or his managing agent. Some blocks don't allow short lets of, say, less than six months so check the terms of your lease first. Also, watch out for local council regulations because some stipulate that all lets should be for more than three months' duration.

If the property used to be your home and you have permission to let it out, tell the mortgage and insurance company. Remember to advise everyone who "needs to know" of your correspondence address and always to keep a record of who you spoke to and when.

To avoid the risk of being a victim of identity fraud, ensure that once the place is let all bills for you are sent to a secure correspondence address by the Royal Mail.

6

How to Get the Tenancy Agreement Correct

Before your first let starts, there are two important bits of documentation you should prepare for your tenant. These are the tenancy agreement and something I call the "House Guide" for the property, which is basically a guide to the property including a list of dos and don'ts and setting out what should be done in an emergency.

In England and Wales, for normal lettings, whilst you don't strictly need a written agreement (unless a selective licensing scheme mandates it), it's best to set down what the tenant can and can't do. It's also harder to evict a tenant if there is no written agreement. For lets in Scotland, new legislation requires tenants to be given a special "tenancy information" pack, so landlords are best advised to issue a tenancy agreement anyway. Also, consultation is currently ongoing in Scotland and Wales on having a new standard form of tenancy. Watch this space.

The different types of tenancy

Assured shorthold tenancies (AST)

The main form of tenancy used today is called the Assured Shorthold Tenancy (AST) or Short Assured Tenancy in Scotland. With an AST, the tenant has the right to occupy the property exclusively and the landlord can charge a market rent. For tenancies starting after 28 February 1997, provided that you don't live there, it is not a holiday let, the rent is under

£100,000 and it is not let to a company, then the tenancy will be an AST unless you stated otherwise. The great attraction of an AST is that you can always recover the property at the end of the fixed term, provided that proper notice of at least two months has been given to the tenant.

The main difference between an Assured Tenancy (AT) and an AST is that with an AST you can always automatically get possession of the property at the end of the six-month term of the tenancy or later provided that you give at least two months' notice, whereas with an AT the only real way to end one would be for the tenant seriously to breach the terms of the tenancy. Also, with an AST, any deposit taken has to be protected in a tenancy deposit scheme.

Rent Act tenancies

Tenancies which started before 15 January 1989 are regulated by the Rent Act 1977 and are often called "Rent Act" tenancies. They aren't as good as ASTs and ATs because with Rent Act tenancies it's very difficult to evict and landlords can only charge a "fair rent". A fair rent is whatever a rent tribunal says is fair and tends to be somewhat below market rents! Also, once a fair rent is set, it usually can't be challenged for two years. And, no, before you ask, you can't convert a Rent Act tenancy to an AST! Evicting a Rent Act tenant requires specialist legal advice. With their disadvantages, these forms of tenancy are declining in number. Properties sold at auction sometimes have sitting Rent Act tenants and this should be reflected in a lower house price.

Company tenancies and rents over £100,000 per year

Where the tenant is a company instead of an individual or the rent is over £100,000, the tenancy agreement may look similar to an AST but there are some key differences. The main difference is that it is not bound by the six-month rule but by common law instead. Again, as with an AT, it doesn't need to be protected in a tenancy deposit scheme. For these sorts of tenancies, whilst the notice procedures in Sections 8 and 21 of the Housing Act 1988 (see Chapter 9) do not apply, a landlord will still need to issue proceedings for possession as the provisions in law for protection from eviction *do* still apply.

The benefits of company lets are that a company can't have security of tenure, payments are often made in advance for a period of three or six months and the company may be more financially secure than an individual. However, be wary if the tenant works for a foreign government because courts can't enforce breaches of contract if the person has diplomatic immunity. Also, if you let to a company you should check their financial position first. If you are worried, get a guarantee against one or more of the company directors so you can claim against them if the company ceases trading.

Many company lets are of less than six months' duration and are popular with companies as they are cheaper than putting an executive in a hotel. Most executives prefer them to hotel living too. Rents should be 10 to 40 per cent above what's achievable on a longer-term let but there may be more voids and frequent changes of tenant mean more work finding new tenants, checking in and out and keeping the property in good repair. If the rent is high and the let short term, the client will reasonably expect higher standards. Relocation agents (acting for companies) are active in this marketplace and many only bill their fees to their client firms, not to the landlord.

Letting rooms in your own home (Licence to occupy)

If you let rooms in your home to lodgers, they have fewer rights and you can end the lodger agreement when you want and without ever needing to get a court order. A written agreement isn't essential but is useful to set out dos and don'ts anyway. A key thing is to specifically make clear you are not giving the lodger exclusive possession (i.e. landlord is excluded) of any part of your property including his own room. This may mean disallowing locks to be put on bedroom doors. It is best if you avoid using the word "tenant" at all in your agreement.

Holiday lets

If the property is let for a few weeks for a holiday, you can evict the occupiers if they refuse to leave without getting a court order. A formal tenancy agreement isn't required but you should keep invoices and correspondence to prove the intention was to be a holiday let.

The assured shorthold tenancy (AST) agreement: What's in it?

Since the most important form of agreement is the AST, it's worth saying some more about it.

Most ASTs are for a fixed term, normally six or twelve months. And many lenders still do not allow initial fixed terms to be more than twelve months. When the term comes to an end, if the landlord agrees, the tenant can simply stay on, with exactly the same terms and conditions as before – this is called a monthly periodic tenancy.

The landlord can get the property back at the end of the fixed term or any time after that, provided that he gives two months' notice.

Where there is more than one tenant on the agreement, each person is "jointly and severally liable" for the full rent. So, if two people sign the same agreement to rent a house at £1,500 per month, if one leaves, the other will have to find the whole £1,500 himself. If he can't, you're entitled to claim against either party for the whole of the rent for any period it remains unpaid. It is important to make this clear to tenants, particularly to groups of friends renting a house together.

In practice, what happens is that the remaining person would get someone new in. However, it's important that anyone new is properly reference-checked and a new agreement issued with both persons' names on it. Again, you should make it clear that they are each jointly and severally liable for the whole rent, not just one half of it. If the old tenant and the new tenant didn't know each other beforehand, this is quite a commitment for them to take on as they need to trust not only you, but each other too!

If you aren't certain that someone can pay his rent, it's worth getting a guarantor who can pay if the tenant defaults. The guarantor will need to be referenced too. (For more on referencing see Chapter 7.) The guarantee can be simply tacked on at the end of the agreement and signed with the signature, dated and witnessed by a independent third party when the letting commences. It needs to confirm he will pay if the tenant defaults or breaches the tenancy agreement in any way resulting in cost to the landlord. Alternatively, the guarantor can sign a separate letter of guarantee. If you later increase the rent or change the tenancy agreement in any way, you must get the guarantor to sign to accept the change – again with his signature witnessed. If you don't the old guarantee will lapse.

The agreement shouldn't contain any clauses that are unfair or which reduce the rights of the tenants as consumers. An example of an unfair term would be one saying that the landlord had the right to come and view the property at any time without giving prior notice. An unfair term wouldn't invalidate the whole agreement – it would just make the unfair clause unenforceable.

The effect of the fixed term is that you can't evict a tenant within that term unless he has breached the terms of the agreement. It also means that if a tenant moves out after, say, three months of a fixed six-month tenancy, you could try to claim rent for a further three months (but only if you hadn't let it to someone else after he'd left). In practice though, you must be flexible. If the tenant had always paid rent on time, and had to leave early due to difficult circumstances, but found a suitable replacement tenant, then you must be accommodating. After all, if the old tenant hasn't got a job, then it's going to be hard for him to pay the rent anyway!

If the old tenant can't find a replacement, I'd let him go with six weeks' notice, during which time I'd be fairly confident I'd find a new tenant. In return, however, I'd make it clear that the property should be left in a pristine condition whenever any prospective tenant came to view. Also, you would be within your rights to charge the early-vacating tenant your reasonable costs in connection with ending the old tenancy and setting up the new one.

The fixed term can be longer than six months. However, I'd avoid making it too long because if, say the tenants kept annoying neighbours or continually paid the rent a little bit late, then you'd want to be rid of them earlier. So, if you've arranged an eighteen-month tenancy, (assuming the mortgage lender allows one over twelve-months duration) you may end up waiting eighteen months to be rid of them. For more on giving notice and getting possession, see Chapters 8 and 9.

A six-month term is also good if you use a letting agent because some agents still take their commission upfront, based on the period of the tenancy. (Too many agents try to get newbie landlords to agree a six or twelve-month tenancy and then a brand new one six or twelve months later for which the agent will naturally charge another set of chunky fees, but this is usually not necessary because you can just let the tenancy "run on" instead, on a monthly periodic basis.)

The agreement will describe the property to be rented, the start date of the agreement and the names of the landlord and tenants. It should make it clear if any part of the property is excluded, such as garages or outbuildings. It will specify the rental amount and should say that it's to be paid in advance and to a specified account. Normally, the rent should be paid monthly. If you opt for weekly payments you should provide a rent book.

Normally utilities (including council tax) will be paid by the tenants but you can pay these if you wish, especially if it's a short-term let or an HMO. The agreement must say who is going to pay these bills.

The amount of the deposit will be stated and mention as to what it will be used for and whether any interest will be paid on it. Most tenants don't expect to receive interest, but it's worth stating so anyway. I normally charge a deposit of about five to six weeks' rent but, if you supply a lot of furnishings, ask for up to seven weeks' rent. Deposits should be less than two months' rent as giving more could give tenants a right to sub-let. The agreement should state how frequently rent reviews will take place – I recommend you do these annually.

Make two original copies of the agreement. You and your tenants (and the guarantor if applicable) sign and date both copies on the day they move in after they have paid the deposit and the first month's rent and before they move in any of their own stuff. Ideally, everyone should initial each page. Each party keeps one copy.

All ASTs where a deposit is taken must have that deposit protected in a tenancy deposit scheme. You should state on the agreement which of the various schemes it is protected in. See Chapter 8 for more on this.

Finally, before a tenancy starts, the tenants must be given the energy performance certificate (EPC) for the property, a copy of the gas safety certificate and, in England and Wales the government produced document called "How to Rent" available online from www.gov.uk. I suggest all three are included with the tenancy agreement and the tenant signs the tenancy agreement to say they have seen these things and that they have also been shown that all the smoke alarms, (and where appropriate, carbon monoxide alarms), work properly. The "How to Rent" document should be sent each time a replacement tenancy is issued to the same tenant.

What tenants need to know: The emergency and maintenance "House Guide"

It's very important to give tenants some guidance to help them look after your property properly. In particular, those who haven't rented before will need to be told what to do in the event of an emergency and how to deal with routine maintenance. Explain to tenants that they are responsible for minor repairs like changing fuses and light bulbs as well as taking prompt action and seeking help if anything more serious happens.

Here's a typical scenario. It's 9 p.m. on Christmas Eve and the phone rings. It's one of your tenants and he's calling to tell you that water is pouring out of a pipe and flooding the hallway, the neighbours in the flat below are going crazy and he doesn't know what to do. This has been going on for three hours, but he's only just managed to find your phone number!

This is the kind of problem many landlords face from time to time and, for some reason, they have a knack of happening at the most awkward times, usually on public holidays, at weekends or late at night. It's a pain because it ruins your weekend; you either have to go and deal with it yourself or pay someone, just when charge-out rates are most expensive. So, how can landlords plan for such events and what should they do when they happen?

The first thing is to make your tenants aware of what to do and who to contact in an emergency. New tenants should be told it's their contractual duty to act promptly to report anything that could damage the property or give rise to a claim. If they fail to do so they could be held liable for the resulting additional avoidable cost!

Give your tenants a written set of instructions (a "House Guide") to follow so they know what action to take to protect themselves, the property (and especially in the case of flats) surrounding properties too. Ideally, the House Guide should cover what to do in the event of a problem with plumbing, drains, gas or electricity and is invaluable because a delay of only half an hour in getting a problem fixed can cost thousands in damage.

Get tenants to look out for problems

Many tenants ignore minor problems until they become serious or affect them directly. A friend of mine had a tenant who ignored the fact that water was flowing from the toilet overflow pipe outside his flat. As the water flowed out from the pipe it cascaded down onto the wall of the flat below where it eventually seeped into the wall and caused damage to the internal decoration. An angry neighbour and a big claim could have been avoided if the tenant had taken action to stop the overflow earlier.

Every time you let your property, talk through the House Guide with your tenants and leave a laminated copy on a notice board, where they can find it quickly when they need to. Show them where the mains fuse board is, how to turn the gas off at the mains, where the water stop valve is and how to work the heating, washing machine, etc, using the operating manuals.

As well as dealing with emergencies, the House Guide should highlight some basics for tenants to look out for. In particular, overflowing pipes, damp smells, mould, flaking wallpaper and short-circuiting fuses are things that indicate the presence of problems that need fixing. Damage caused by water leaks can be very expensive if the problem isn't fixed quickly. The most common causes are boilers, pumps, dripping taps, leaking pipes, leaking drains, toilet overflows and showers. Usually, the cost of things damaged by water is covered under insurance, provided that you (or your tenant) weren't negligent or slow in dealing with the problem. It's worth remembering that, in extreme cases, insurance companies can limit what they'll pay out, or even refuse the claim altogether, if they think you (or your tenants) had been careless or failed to take prompt action to reduce damage.

Extra special care and responsibility is required for flats above another property because in the worst case you could be held liable by a neighbour (or his insurance company) if water escaping from your property causes damage to his furnishings or fittings. This could include the cost of replacing curtains, carpets and furnishings, repairing ceilings, repainting, cost of temporary accommodation, damages for inconvenience and even the cost of a court case. It can all add up, especially if your neighbour happens to be a lawyer!

The House Guide should contain the following instructions:

- In the event of a gas leak, windows and doors should be opened. No one should smoke, use naked flames or touch electrical devices. The gas supply should be turned off by pulling downwards on the gas lever and Transco's twenty-four-hour emergency line (0800 111999) called.
- In the event of a problem with the mains drain, the water company should be called. (Include their number.)
- In the event of a water leak, the water should be turned off at the stop valve. (Say where the valve is.)
- If the property is going to be empty overnight or for more than twelve hours when the weather is cold, leave enough heating on to prevent the freezing of the water system.

- Air rooms, especially bathrooms to stop the build up of condensation – especially where clothes are dried inside the property. (If you have a garden, provide a clothes line outside and get them to use it.)
- Ensure extractor fans are working.
- Regularly check that no water is running from overflows or pipes.
- Look out for damp smells and flaking walls.
- Regularly check that the washing machine remains securely plumbed in.
- Do not allow the washing machine or dishwasher to operate when no one is in.
- Ensure that the shower curtain is pulled across during use.
- Avoid fat, food, tampons, nappies, hair or other obstructions being put down toilets or sinks.

The Guide should contain information on how to relight a gas boiler, where the stop valve (stop cock) is and how to open and close it. A good tip here is that, when opening the valve, it should always be turned back half a turn from the fully open position to avoid the valve sticking.

Relevant telephone numbers for you, your preferred tradesmen (and your insurance company's emergency assistance number, if covered for emergency call-outs) should be put in the House Guide, so tenants can contact them directly in an emergency. It's also worth including the phone number for their water, gas and electricity suppliers.

The House Guide should show the location of the mains fuse box and isolator switch and how to replace mains fuses and smoke detector batteries. Where you have battery-operated smoke detectors, your tenant must be able to get to them easily to replace old batteries.

You could also include in the House Guide useful information like the refuse collection day, details of local doctors and pharmacies, good restaurants and the location of the nearest trains, tubes, trams and buses.

Water damage in blocks of flats is a real headache for flat owners and is one reason why buildings insurance and excess levels in blocks (especially those in which most flats are let out) can be so high. So, if you have a flat which is below another flat, it's worthwhile getting to know the people who live upstairs. Ask them what they would do in the event of, say, a water leak. Do they know how to turn off the gas or water? If the property is let out, I can almost guarantee that their landlord or his agent has left them no instructions at all. In fact, it never ceases to amaze me that some landlords are prepared to spend a lot of money on a flat, only to risk it being badly damaged for the want of a few simple instructions! Do yourself a favour and give them a copy of your House Guide, or even this book! (If their flat is in the same layout as yours, the stop valve and gas shut-off valve will probably be in the same location.)

There is lots more useful information about how to manage damp problems, pests and many other things in Chapter 8.

7

How to Find a Good Tenant

So, you've got the property, it meets all the legal regulations and your tenancy agreement is ready. Now you need to find a tenant. How do you go about finding a good one? There are various options. You could get friends in, use a housing association, a letting agent or find a tenant yourself. This chapter tells you everything you need to know – where to advertise, what to say and how to check potential tenants out. If you use a letting agency, this chapter will tell you how to choose a good one and get them to work effectively for you.

A word of warning! Even if you use a letting agent, you are strongly advised to read the whole of this chapter, especially the parts about referencing tenants because, if your agent gets this wrong and you get a bad tenant, it will cost you (not your agent) a small fortune. This means you *must* make sure that your agent has checked out your potential tenant properly!

This is a long chapter and I make no apologies for that because getting a good tenant is absolutely critical for success as a landlord.

Letting to friends . . . and why you shouldn't!

You may be tempted to let to friends or relations especially if you have some friends who just happen to be looking for a property to rent. Characters on *EastEnders* and *Coronation Street* do this all the time. After all, you won't need to worry about advertising, and, if they can move in right away, there won't be any periods when your property is vacant and bringing in no rental income. And, of course, your friends will move out when you want them to. Well, that's what you hope.

Letting to friends sounds very good but I'd advise against it. They say you should never mix business with pleasure and nowhere is this truer than in the lettings business. Your friends will not like the fact that you have power over them and, despite what they may say, will probably not see the relationship as a commercial one. Even if they did see it as a business relationship to start with they will forget about this a few weeks down the line or as soon as you put the rent up or even when you ask for a deposit. So, if you want to keep your friends as friends don't let to them in the first place. This is real life. You are not on the set of a soap!

Getting your existing tenants to find new tenants

If you are already letting the property to tenants you like, but they have to move on, why not ask them to help find your new tenants? They presumably have friends who may have been to the property and liked it and they will know you are a good landlord.

Letting to a social housing organisation

Letting to a social landlord is becoming increasingly popular at the lower end of the market. Many local authorities and housing associations can take on your property for a long term (typically between two and four years). They will pay you a guaranteed rent which is usually about 10 per cent below market rent and they will frequently look after some of the maintenance for you. They will then sublet to their own tenants, who are usually homeless people in desperate need of accommodation. Your contract is with the local council or housing association not the tenant and rent is guaranteed. Normally, you don't need to supply any furnishings, not even white goods, which can be a big saving! The only real drawback is that you have no control over whom they let it out to, which could be a real issue for you if your neighbours are the type who are active complainers. Keep in view the fact that some homeless people are homeless for reasons of antisocial or odd behaviours.

These types of let are sometimes called Private Sector Leasing Schemes (PSLS) or Housing Association Leasing Schemes (HALS).

In many ways this method is better than letting directly to people who are on housing benefit. With a PSLS, your rent is guaranteed and there is no void nor any chance of tenant default nor of the council clawing back from you money they paid direct to you but which turned out to be based on false information provided by the tenant. Also, you don't have to worry about re-letting the property and finding new tenants for a few years and there is no agency fee to pay. Check with the council or housing association. Some mortgage lenders and some leases do not allow these types of lets and insurance premiums might be higher too.

In recent years some spammy *private* companies have sprung up claiming they can also pay you guaranteed rent by subletting to housing benefit tenants. Some even try to represent they are "working for the councils". But think about it – a company guarantee is worthless if that company goes bust. Many have indeed gone bust and when they do, it will be you who is left with the tenant and a big problem. Don't enter into such an arrangement.

Using a letting agent

Another way to find tenants is to use the services of a letting agent. There are of course many times when you have to use a letting agent. For example, if you don't live close to the

131

property it would be impractical to do it any other way. The other reason is if you simply don't have the time or inclination to do it yourself. After all, why waste time advertising and interviewing tenants if your friendly local agent will do it for you anyway at a fraction of the cost of your own lost work or leisure time?

So, if you live far away, are a high earner in your day job and/ or you are just too busy, then a letting agent may be good for you.

Now, as with anything, there are some agents who are good and some who are poor. In my experience the majority of agents are pretty good but you can often do a better job yourself. I shall discuss how you do it yourself in a moment. But first, a quick look at what a letting agent actually does.

A letting agency can either just be involved in finding a tenant or it can be involved additionally with managing a tenancy. In this chapter, we shall just concern ourselves with their role of finding a tenant. (See Chapter 8 for advice on managing a tenancy.)

Typically the fee a letting agency will charge to *smaller* landlords (i.e. with fewer than, say, three properties) for finding a tenant is between four weeks' and six weeks' rent. For short-term lets, although rents will be higher, the agency's finding and management fees will be in the range from 20 per cent to 40 per cent of the rent.

Look at any letting agency's advertising material and it should be full of the benefits of using them. (If it isn't full of such claims, then you should be very worried – after all, if they can't market their own company, how are they going to market your property?) Some of the ancillary benefits they claim for using their tenant-find services are listed below. However, as you will see from reading about each of these services, their expertise can be acquired easily yourself.

Letting agents prepare a tenancy agreement in accordance with current legislation

Any agent can prepare a tenancy agreement in accordance with current legislation. However, you can easily obtain an up-to-date standard tenancy agreement in any bookshop, online or from a landlords' organisation, such as the National Landlords or Residential Landlords Associations. Once you have your standard agreement, you then need to keep up to date with any changes in legislation and amend it accordingly.

Letting agents can value your property and advise what rent can be achieved

An agent will happily value your property and advise you what rent can be achieved. However, you can get a rough idea of what's achievable by looking in letting agents' windows, on the Internet at sites like Rightmove or in the local paper.

Moreover, if you bought a property with the intention of letting it out, you really should have worked out what the likely rent is before you bought it! For more on estimating achievable rent see Chapters 2 and 3.

The key message is to make sure you do your homework yourself and research what realistic rents are in your area.

Letting agents can advise you about decorating, furnishing and the laws on electrical and gas safety, HMOs and disability

True they can do this. Alternatively, everything you need to know is in Chapter 5 of this book.

Letting agents can do a detailed inventory

An agent can do the check-ins and check-outs, read the meters and arrange an inventory or appoint an independent clerk to do this. There will be an extra charge for handling the inventory. However, if you want to appoint a professional independent inventory clerk to record the condition of the property and the fixtures and fittings, you could appoint one yourself – possibly at less cost. Never skimp on having an *independent* inventory clerk do it for you – essential if you are to win any disputes over damage and retentions against tenancy deposits later. Don't attempt to do an inventory yourself! Making a good inventory is a professional job and best left to professionals.

Letting agents have a shop or an Internet site that will attract tenants

This is where agents really add value because lots of tenants now use Internet portals like Rightmove or Zoopla to find property to rent and any decent agent should be with one or more of these portals. However, whilst an agent will attract people to their shop or Internet site, you can also generate interest through your own advertising and you can get on all the main letting portals via specialist landlord letting sites (so called "online" letting agents) for often less than £100 per property though you'll have to handle all the calls and viewings yourself as well as do the reference checking.

Now, what are the drawbacks to using some letting agents?

Some letting agents have longer void periods

In my experience, properties which are marketed by letting agencies can sometimes suffer longer periods without tenants (the dreaded "void periods").

If you are letting through an agent and there is a long period when your property is between tenants, you can be sure that the agents aren't losing as much sleep as you are. After all it's not their money which is being lost on mortgage loan payments, service charges, etc, whilst no rent comes in!

Some letting agents can be prone to exaggeration

Some of the less reputable agents are prone to exaggeration or even telling downright lies. Here is a typical scenario. You get a phone call from an agent who has seen the property that you are trying to let online. "Hello, Mr L, we saw your ad. We have twenty blue-chip tenants we can send round today for our usual commission."

Now, for some reason these blue-chip tenants never materialise. They either don't exist at all or, if they do, they tend not to be all that blue-chip! Yes, they might work in an investment bank, but they are cleaning it, not talking to clients! If you get such a call from an agent, ask yourself this – if a letting agent was any good would he be wasting time scouring newspapers and cold-calling landlords?

I have experienced agents saying that they have sent people round when they haven't. Try to catch them out – if the property is empty, leave some post right behind the door. If it hasn't moved when you next come round, they are obviously lying about having been to your property. If your existing tenants are still in the property ask them if the agent has really had as many people round to view as he claims.

Most decent agents don't get up to these kinds of tricks, but there are undoubtedly a few odd rogues that do.

Some letting agents are expensive and can hurt your cash flow

Agents can be expensive and hurt your cash flow. They generally charge you upfront, which means that their charges will usually come out of the first month's rent – obviously bad for cash flow. If the tenant leaves early or doesn't pay, you are really stuffed – having paid the agent's fee in full but had no or little rent – so see if you can get the agent's fee paid in stages as the tenancy progresses. (Most will baulk at this suggestion, but you may gain another concession.)

Also, don't forget, some agents may try to charge repeat fees if tenants stay on at the end of the initial six-month term, even if the agent did no work in connection with the re-let or continuation of the existing tenancy. So, unless you terminate the tenancy or have it specially written into the contract with the agent, you could be paying your agent forever. So, read the agent's contract carefully and amend and delete anything you don't like. In particular, strike out any claim for fees where a tenant introduced by them as a tenant later ends up buying your property.

Letting agents have historically charged tenants quite heavy fees for processing applications and other "services", which are often way above the true costs of doing this work. These are now banned in Scotland. England and Wales look set to follow the Scottish lead soon.

Some letting agents aren't as thorough or as quick as you would be

Some agents aren't as thorough or as quick as you could be. Take the job of referencing tenants. I thoroughly vet all my tenants and I can do it in forty-eight hours, because I reverse the whole process by asking *the tenants* to get the references I need to see from their landlord and employer.

Letting agents tend to outsource this job and the firms they use sometimes spend days and weeks sitting and waiting for Personnel or Human Resources Departments and past landlords to respond to reference requests – which means it takes a whole lot longer than it takes me. This is one reason why letting agents' void periods tend to be longer. And I often wonder if those doing the referencing for the agent employ their sixth sense to sniff out a potentially troublesome tenant. If there was a nagging worry about a potential tenant would they reject him?

How to find a good letting agent

Obviously, the best recommendations are personal recommendations.

If you don't know another landlord, ask to speak to two or three of the agency's existing landlords. If they won't let you, go elsewhere. Gauge how much of their business is letting property as opposed to, say, selling houses.

Read their brochures – are they professionally written? I have seen lots which are full of spelling errors. Ask to meet the staff who will be handling your letting. How professional are they? Look at their office – if it's dirty and disorganised, they will be disorganised too and potential tenants will also have a poor impression. What is said about them online?

Is their office in a good location where it will attract lots of potential tenants? Does it open on Saturdays? Do they have an answer phone to take messages for people who call "out of hours"? Do all their properties appear on all the big letting portals like Rightmove? Do they let properties that are like yours or are all their properties more up-market (or down-market) than yours? Pick an agent in *your* market! Do they hold indemnity insurance? Are their photos and property descriptions properly marketing other properties? Is there an EPC available for each property (a legal requirement)? Do they hold client monies in protected client accounts? Do they properly protect tenants' deposits? And if they use the insurance based scheme version of the tenancy deposit schemes then suggest they hand the deposit money over to you. (See Chapter 8 for more.) What is their rent arrears rate? (It should be less than 2 per cent.) Ask to see a typical file – it should include gas safety and electrical checks, EPCs, an inventory, deposit scheme details, etc.

The letting agency should have a contract with you telling you how they will go about marketing your property and the precise detail of what you will pay them for doing this.

Review this carefully and tell them if you want any item amended. Refuse any contract that requires you to give an agent sole agency on advertising your property for a set time period

– you should be free to fire an incompetent agent any time you wish and find tenants yourself without paying commission to the agent.

If an agent wants to take a non-returnable security deposit as part of a "finder's fee", then go somewhere else. Also, if all they are doing is finding a tenant, then they should not hold on to tenants' deposits – these should either be put in one of the tenancy deposit protection schemes, with the money held in a separate client account, or handed over to you for you to protect it in one of the recognised schemes. If the letting agent is protecting it in one of the tenancy deposit schemes, ask to see proof of this as some agents have failed to do this, used the cash as working capital and then gone bust, leaving the landlord liable for the return of the tenants' deposit. Letting agents now have to be members of an approved ombudsman scheme – these offer independent investigation of things like hidden fees or poor service. You should also ask whether the letting agent is a member of ARLA (the Association of Residential Letting Agents), the National Approved Letting Scheme (NALS), the RICS (Royal Institution of Chartered Surveyors), UKALA (UK Association of Letting Agents) or the NAEA (the National Association of Estate Agents). Some of these organisations have a code of conduct and a fidelity bonding scheme (client money protection) which means that if the agent goes out of business the landlord will lose money in suspension but not the tenants' deposit. Check what's available. In Scotland all agents must be registered and in Wales they must be licensed with RentSmart Wales.

Ask the agency what references they ask for and insist on being able to see the tenants' application form and all references obtained. Also insist that you retain the right to accept or reject any tenant they find. (A word of caution here: don't forget to make it clear to the agent – preferably in writing – what sort of tenants you will accept and what sort you will reject. You don't want to waste their time unnecessarily.)

Test the agency. Phone them up anonymously and make an enquiry about exactly the type of property you are trying to let through them. How well did they market your property, if at all? Even better, you could get a friend to do the same thing and, this time, actually get him to go and view your property with the agent. Your friend will be able to tell you how well the agent marketed your property and how knowledgeable he was. Did your agent know his facts about your property? Although most agents are very clued-up, there will be some who are incompetent or in complete ignorance of your property or of the local area. Don't forget to buy your friend a drink or a meal as thanks!

It must be said that some agents can get rents about 10 per cent higher than private landlords can achieve. As this is about the same as the fee that they charge for finding a tenant, it leaves the landlord no worse (or better off). However, very good agents can get higher rents still.

Don't ever ask a friend or relation to act as your "agent" and look for tenants for you. Again, you are not a character on *Corrie*! Letting property is not easy so if you don't want to do it yourself, then employ a professional agent. However, if you use an agent, you need to make sure they are doing the advertising and reference checking of applicants properly. So, even if you use a letting agent, you should still read the next section about doing it yourself. Also, see the section on letting agents in Chapter 8.

Finally, a word of warning. All landlords are bound by their agent's actions, so for example, if an agent fails to carry out an annual gas safety check, the landlord will also be liable for that failure as well. Unless the agent does something that is obviously outside the authority of a normal agent acting for a landlord or acts contrary to the specific instructions of a landlord, the landlord will also be liable.

If you're looking for a tenant yourself

There are three parts to finding a tenant. Firstly, you need to advertise. Secondly, you need to pre-screen and reference check the respondents so that you can separate the wheat from the chaff and find your ideal tenant. Thirdly, you need to make all the final preparations for the tenant to move in. It can be a lot of work.

Advertising your property is simple. It comes down to three things – where to advertise it, when to advertise it and what to say in your advert.

Where to advertise your property

Being on website portals like Rightmove and Zoopla is now essential if you are to access most tenant markets. And to get on the portals you have to go through a letting agent. Just make sure you use one who will upload your property to the main ones.

These days offline publications or sites that don't upload to Rightmove have less clout, though they may still be worth trying in certain niche markets. If the property you have is somewhere posh, then the publication or website you choose should be up-market too.

If you are prepared to let to students, then universities, colleges and hospitals are good places to advertise. Keep in with the Accommodation Officer and time your advertising when students are looking (this varies by college but can be up to nine months before the end of the academic year for returning second- and third-year students). If you are a member of a local or national landlord association, they may have a website where you can advertise for free. You could also advertise on your own work intranet site, if you have one. Specialist commercial websites like AccommodationforStudents are also worth considering for student lets. Sites like Spareroom. co.uk are useful for those letting by the room and are very inexpensive.

Consider also your local supermarket, corner shop, gym and library noticeboards. Contact any large local employer in the area. By all means give it a go but you may find it hard to beat the wide coverage that can be gained from being online on the big portals via professional letting agents.

Today, you can put your own advert on all the main portals by using one of a number of *specialist online letting agents* for £100. It is easy – write some good copy, take some good photos, upload the advert and you're off. Of course, you'll need to handle enquiries, do the viewings, reference checks, prepare agreements and inventories, do the check-ins and all the other work a "full service" high-street agent would do.

When to advertise it

The second decision is when to advertise it. If your property is available for rent, you'll just have to market it, whatever time of year it is. However, it is still useful to know something of the seasonality of the rental market.

In most big urban centres, especially those with student popu-lations, the lettings market goes a bit dead between June and early August and from mid November to Boxing Day. When the students go home, people go on holidays and businesses take breaks, the letting population inevitably falls. There is a pick-up in September and mid January due to returning students looking for accommodation and companies recruiting more staff.

So, if you already have a tenant in place whose tenancy is ending or who calls to give you notice, which would mean advertising for new tenants in the quiet months, do all you can to make him stay that little bit longer. Consider offering a discount on the rent for, say, six weeks if he agrees to stay on for that period. In my experience, you'll get 10 per cent more rent in September than at the end of July so you would soon make up for the discount.

Of course, the holiday rental market has its own peak seasons. In UK seaside and holiday towns the peak will normally be in the summer months or when special local events take place.

In more depressed towns with few employment opportunities and no student or large business population, there will be little seasonality – so one month is probably as busy (or quiet) as any other.

In up-market properties catering to corporate tenants, there will be the same lull in the summer months and the run-up to Christmas when businesses effectively shut up shop.

Another thing to note is that if the weather on the day you advertise is very hot, cold or wet, this will affect the response you get to your advert. Potential tenants don't like trailing round looking at properties if they are going to get sweaty, frozen or soaked.

What to say in your advert

What you say in your advert may depend upon the space available in the publication or website and what that ad space is costing you. Obviously, there are some things that you just *have* to get in and there are some other things that are less essential but, if space and cost allow, are useful to include.

Of course, where the advert is costing you a lot of money, you might be limited to stating just the location and the rent. If you do this, however, you will end up with a lot of enquiries from people for whom the property is unsuitable – e.g. they wanted furnished and your place is unfurnished. You will also get enquiries from people whom *you* may not want – e.g. from people on housing benefit when perhaps you only wanted people in full-time work. Fortunately for most

Internet-based adverts – which is where most people look – text space is usually very generous, if not unlimited, so you can provide full details.

Let's have a look at what you should put in your advert – and why.

State the location

It's important to state the location accurately and not lie about where it is. Don't say it's central Manchester if it's really in Salford. If you do, it will annoy potential tenants because if there is one thing that tenants *are* clued-up about, it's location. If you say it's in central Manchester and it's really in Salford, what will happen is that lots of people just won't turn up for the viewings. Also, use the Google Maps Street View facility to show a video of the road it is in.

Some tenants won't turn up for viewings
Don't expect potential tenants to call you and tell you that they are not coming – in my experience only about 30 per cent of tenants will do this.

Include some other details about the property

If you are renting a flat and it is self-contained with its own entrance, say so. This feature is particularly attractive to those seeking security and people (like me) who can't abide a smelly hallway full of other people's unwanted junk mail and pizza flyers.

State how many bedrooms it has. If it's a modern property or a warehouse style one, then say so. This is useful as some people prefer older buildings and some prefer modern ones. Also, if it is posh enough, put "apartment" instead of "flat" – it sounds better. Avoid using terms like "duplex" or "conversion" though, especially where potential tenants are non-British as they may not understand these terms.

Tenants nearly always ask how big the rooms are – and you need to have measurements in feet (for Brits and Americans) and metres (for everyone else) ready for when they call. If the rooms are large, say so in the advert. I would always say "large bedrooms" rather than "double bedrooms". Suppose you have a two-bed flat and you want to let to a cohabiting couple or two single people. If you put "two double bedrooms" in your ad, you'll attract calls from groups of four single people who want to share the two bedrooms, and this may not be what you would want, unless, of course, you are happy to have twice the wear and tear!

If it's close to shops, buses or transport say so, and, if space allows, say how far it is in distance rather than minutes. If there is a garden it is worth saying so. Also, if there is a shower it might be worth stating this. Some people won't even consider a property that doesn't have one. If it has a parking space and it's in an area where parking space is at a premium, this is a plus point for many tenants.

State whether furnished or unfurnished
People will ask you about furnishings, so it is useful to put something about this in your ad. The problem is that people have very different ideas about what is meant by the term "furnished".

If you are offering a very up-market property catering to corporate tenants, and particularly for short lets, you may have to go the whole hog and completely furnish the property with TVs, videos and high-quality furnishings. For other kinds of property, furnishing to this level isn't expected. Nor is it desirable from your point of view because it will add to your insurance costs, problems managing the inventory including possible disputes about damage, and will mean more things to fix when they break down. (See also Chapter 5 on Furnishings.)

For "furnished" properties in more run-of-the-mill lets, the following would be expected as a minimum: washing machine, fridge-freezer, cooker, beds, wardrobes and chest of drawers, sofa, pots and pans, cutlery and cups.

It is worth stating that, just as with the term "furnished", people tend to vary in their understanding of the term "unfurnished". Some think that they will have to provide their own fridge-freezer and washing machine whilst others think that "unfurnished" means that a cooker, a fridge-freezer and a washing machine are provided as standard.

For this reason, where you intend to provide the basic "white goods", use the term "part furnished" or "kitchen equipment furnishings" in your advert to reduce misunderstanding. Finally, if you can avoid supplying washing machines, then great, as these have a limited life expectancy. If you can't, then always buy upper mid-range, quality machines with a five-year parts and labour guarantee – it's worth the extra cost.

State what sort of tenants you want or don't want

Before you advertise, you must decide what sort of tenants you want. The decision about this will depend entirely upon the type of property and your own preferences.

If you have strong views that you don't want tenants who are dependent on housing benefit to pay their rent, then it's probably worth saying so in your advert. Many landlords just put "No Housing Benefit".

You should be aware that even where you put "No Housing Benefit" and "No students" you will still end up with enquiries from people who are in low-paid work. I never cease to be amazed by the number of people in part-time cleaning jobs who are seeking to rent a £30,000 per annum property. How would they afford the rent? Would they work twenty hours a day and live off rice? Probably they are planning to sublet to ten of their friends or they will be hoping that housing benefit will pay.

An alternative that works well is to put in your advert, "Full-Time Employed Persons Only" and/or "Deposit and References required". You'd be amazed by the number of people who don't think that they would need to provide any form of referencing or deposit. Stating in your ad that deposit and references are required will cut calls from what I call "No-Credit Time-Wasters". In addition, to avoid enquiries from people who may want to turn your home into a doss house, you might want to state the number of persons expected to occupy it by stating in your ad, "Suit Couple" or "Three Sharers".

State the rent

If the custom in the media you are advertising in is to express this in £s per week, then do the same. If the custom is to express it in £s per month then do likewise. However, if you state the rent in £s per week, be aware that you will come across some potential tenants who think that the equivalent monthly rent is exactly four times the weekly rent. If so, politely explain that there are 4.33 weeks (52 weeks divided by 12 months) or 30.42 days (365 days divided by 12 months) in an average month!

Include your contact telephone number

Ideally leave a mobile phone number rather than a landline one. Also, leave an email address. For some reason people are much more likely to leave a message on a mobile phone number than a landline.

Example of a good advert

Headingley, bright attractive 2-bed apartment, wooden floors, furnished, suit couple or 2/3 sharers, allocated parking. Large rooms, all mod cons. Dep. and refs required. No Housing Benefit or agents. £800 pcm.

Tel 0777 777 7777.

Email Joe@InsertEmailAddressHere.com

Give chancers the brush-off

If you are set on doing it yourself, state "Tenant Enquiries Only". This will stop the disreputable (and desperate) type of operator, masquerading as a letting agent, from calling you to claim that he has twenty merchant bankers with glowing references just waiting to rent your property. Just as you should never buy tarmac from the guy who knocks at your door claiming he has "some left over from a council job", so you should never entertain these chancers.

However, if you want to have some entertainment, tell him, "Fine. Send your prospective tenants round tonight." And tell him that your fee for taking these surplus tenants off his hands is 20 per cent of the rent. The 20 per cent must be paid upfront of course! That should put him off. And give you a laugh!

How to screen potential tenants and take references

Once you have got your advert right you should have lots of enquiries coming in. Your next job is therefore to sort the wheat from the chaff or, in other words, to "screen" the respondents.

Just as in selecting candidates for a job, there are three simple stages. Firstly, you do an initial screening when you take phone or email enquiries. Secondly, you screen when you actually meet them. Thirdly, you screen them when you take up their references. Each stage is simple.

Telephone/Email screening

Have a crib sheet with the details about the property on it, which may not have been included already in your advert – room sizes, car parking, distance to transport, level of council tax. You could have this information saved on your computer and offer to send it by email. If you are more flash, you could even have your own website with more pictures of the interior of the property.

When people call, have some paper at the ready to note their details – whether employed, where living now, why they are looking for somewhere new, etc.

Take care with your own security. Take a note of their phone numbers including, if possible, landline phone number, address including postcode, and time of appointment. Check out their landline number by using 1471 and calling them back on it, and leave a note of their details with another person. You could even check that their address matches their postcode through the Royal Mail website (see Appendix 2). Don't be too paranoid though. If it doesn't match up, there could be an innocent explanation. Ask them.

Finally, have an agreed secret coded message with a friend which you can use to let them know you are not comfortable. A good one would be, "I just want to check on the council tax of the property at [state address]."

If you can, arrange appointments at the best time for the property – when it is quiet or when it is brightest!

Tenants love showers (and landlords hate them!)

Most of my flats don't have shower cubicles for the good reason that showers often leak, and I can't be bothered with all the hugely time-consuming business of repairing them, filing insurance claims, dealing with tenants who want you to waive their rent while the thing is being fixed and angry neighbours whose ceiling has been ruined. However, I would not tell a potential tenant that my flat does not have a shower unless he was American or Scandinavian (who all seem to insist on them!).

If there is anything that you know about the property that may make it hard to let, you might want to tell your potential tenants when they call. Whether or not you do this will depend on how many other callers you have still to get back to and how desperate you are. However, you also need to be careful as you don't want to put people off!

If the property is more than half a mile from public transport, I would always say this upfront as some tenants are not at all keen on walking further. (I should add that if a property is more than a mile from transport, then you should not have bought it in the first place!)

You may get calls from people on very low incomes who will obviously have trouble paying the rent unless they get five mates in to share with. So, if you don't want tenants like this, casually ask them where they work and what they do.

If you have someone who is probably not really suitable, then tell him, gently.

Make brief notes on the tenants as you speak to them on the phone and take these with you to the appointment.

I try to avoid doing a viewing with just one tenant, as the sad fact is that, even if you make an appointment in the morning for that evening, about 30 per cent of people won't turn up (or will let you know so late that you have already journeyed to the property).

If I have only one or two potential tenants coming to a viewing, I would call them just ahead of the viewing to confirm that they are still coming. I *always* reconfirm if the appointment was made the previous day because, for some reason, these ones have a much higher chance of not turning up. Perhaps people don't own diaries! Perhaps they think that it is less rude just not to turn up than to call you and tell you that they have found another property after all.

Some people call when they are minutes away and still fail to turn up. Perhaps they met a friend and went down the pub, perhaps they were hit by a bus, or maybe they were abducted by aliens! Who knows!

I mentioned that it is often a good thing if your property is easy to find. It also helps if the street has a simple, familiar name and if it is listed in the street atlas. If they drive to the viewing, check out the cleanliness of the car. If it has a filthy untidy dashboard full of old crisp wrappers, that's an indication of how they will probably treat your property.

If you are letting a property that is in a street that has been built at any time in the last twenty years, check if people who are coming to view it have an up-to-date street map downloaded from the Internet (but bear in mind new streets may not yet be listed).

Even if the road is easy to find you'll get people who will telephone you six times while en route and ask for directions because they haven't got a street map, don't possess a street-map app or couldn't be bothered to download one. I would reject these people out of hand as potential tenants – if they haven't got the intelligence to bring along a map with which to find the property, what will they be like as tenants? Chances are that they will call you every time a fuse for a plug needs changing. Save yourself the trouble and avoid them.

Also, avoid people who turn up more than twenty minutes late for a viewing, and can't be bothered to think of a good excuse or let you know of the delay in advance.

Interviewing potential tenants

When arranging viewings, get to the property at least fifteen minutes early to turn on lights and heating and generally make the place look as nice as possible.

Stagger viewings about twenty minutes apart. This gives you enough time to meet the individuals and make some notes about them – what they do for a living, where they are living now, how long they have been there, what they are like generally and whether you like them and think you can trust them. If the viewings overlap and the next viewer is having to wait outside, don't worry, as this will tend to also create its own demand.

Your aim should be to seek the following information (ideally for each tenant):

- Name and date of birth. Occupation.
- Where living now – full address with postcode. Whether living with parents/renting/friends.
- If renting – is this with a letting agency or private landlord?
- For how long have they been living at their current residence?
- Addresses with postcodes over last three years.
- Do they have a good relationship with their current landlord?
- What is their contact telephone number or email address?

When meeting tenants it is important to have all the information available that they are likely to need to know about the property. This is where you can make a significant impact compared with most "jobbing landlords" and some letting agencies who can be woefully unprepared to answer tenants' basic questions. Also, if you make no charges to tenants for inventory checks or referencing enquiries, it is worth pointing this out to the tenant. (Some letting agencies in England and Wales still charge sums of over £300 for "registering" tenants, doing reference enquiries and inventory checks.)

You should know the following:

1. If your advert states the rent as a weekly amount, what this translates to in £s per month.
2. How much the deposit is – this should be a minimum of five weeks' rent, but less than two months' rent.
3. The form of the contract – e.g. "Six-Month Fixed-Term Assured Shorthold Tenancy becoming a Periodic Tenancy at Landlord's Discretion at the End of the Six-Month Term".
4. The current rate of council tax (available from the local council).

5. The estimated cost of electricity, gas and water and whether the water is metered.
6. Where the nearest public transport is, the frequency of service and journey time to major centres.
7. Where the nearest good shops, pubs, restaurants, schools and gyms are.
8. What parking facilities are available and whether any local parking restrictions apply.
9. Any restriction that your tenant should know about – e.g. no pets.
10. What will be included in the way of furnishings.

The last point is very important. Make clear what items will be included in the inventory – i.e. what furnishings will be in the property when the tenant moves in. This is particularly important if you are showing a property where the existing tenant is still in residence and the tenant's furnishings are still in place. Don't allow the prospective tenant to make any assumptions about the inventory. Don't let the tenant think that you will be providing beds or cutlery if you are not.

I have found the best thing is to give tenants a list covering all these points, including details (phone numbers and locations) on all the local services and culture. They can then take this away and study it at their leisure. This makes you look prepared and professional and ensures that there are no doubts and uncertainties to plague the start of your relationship.

When you go into a room, allow the prospective tenant to go in first. You take up space and you want to maximise the impression of space!

Even if you think you have found a good tenant, I would continue to show other candidates because people sometimes change their minds. For me (but not for agents!) it normally takes only about two days to complete the take-up of references as I ask *the tenants* to get the references and documents I need. If, in this time, the tenant you had lined up changes his mind, then you have to start again. And if your property is already vacant then you will be into a void period with no rental income. If you have got someone else lined up, then hopefully he can step into the breach.

How a listing magazine helped me!

I once had a flat in an area of south London that was up-and-coming but was still perceived by those not in the know to be a haven of criminals and graffiti. For this place I always gave prospective tenants a copy of an article plucked from one of the issues of *Time Out* (a London leisure guide) which extolled the virtues of this part of London. This worked well and won over many younger people, who were keen to live somewhere that was up-and-coming but still cheap. It's also worth preparing a guide about the property and the area – anything that will help rent it.

Taking up references

The third stage is to take up references. What references you check and how thoroughly you go about this is one of the most important things you will do as a landlord. If you don't believe this just ask landlords who have suffered with bad tenants – they will all agree that, if they had taken more care in checking their tenants out, they would probably not have had problems.

The purpose of references is to confirm that the person is who he says he is, that he can afford the rent and that he doesn't have a history of not honouring his commitments in the past.

If you don't bother referencing a tenant properly, you will eventually end up losing a lot of money. Just in case you think that referencing is not important because you could kick out a bad tenant the next day, I would urge you to read the box overleaf on the cost of a bad tenant.

What references you should ask for will depend on the type of tenant you are seeking. However, the following are essential for an employed tenant and should be obtained for each person.

1. An employer's reference.
2. A reference from a previous (and preferably last-but-one) landlord.
3. Proof of identity.
4. Proof of current address.
5. A satisfactory credit reference report and sight of at least three months bank statements (six months for the self-employed).
6. Proof of permit or visa entitling the tenant to work in the United Kingdom (non-EU nationals only).

A prospective tenant should be able to get all these references within two working days. If he is unable to get them within this time frame, tell him that he risks the property being let to someone else.

There are some exceptions to this list. If you are letting to tenants who are depending on housing benefit to pay their rent, then they may not be in full-time employment and therefore you will not need to ask for an employer's reference, though you may want a guarantor. In such circumstances, the other checks are even more important. I shall discuss each of the references in turn.

Employer references

The employer's reference should state how long the person has been employed, the nature of the employment contract – e.g. permanent/temporary – the salary and a statement that the person is not under notice to leave.

The cost of a bad tenant

If you have a tenant who doesn't pay the rent, the only way to get him out is to apply to a county court to start possession proceedings and have him evicted. You cannot "send the boys round" or in any way harass the tenant by calling at 4 a.m. or cutting off his water, etc. If you do this, it is a criminal offence and you'll be the one in trouble.

You can only start court action for eviction after a period of two months of unpaid rent. In addition to this, you will have to pay a court fee to start the action. If your paperwork is OK, the court will grant an order telling the tenant to leave. (A Notice to Quit.) If the tenant doesn't leave by the date in the Notice, then you'll have to pay another fee for bailiffs to come in and remove him. If it goes this far, you'll probably already have lost about four months' rent as well as court fees too. (If the tenant persuades the court he has a valid excuse not to attend a hearing or has a counterclaim, the whole thing can drag on longer.)

During this time you will, of course, have to pay the mortgage and all the usual running costs of the property. Additionally, you'll almost certainly find that the tenant has not been paying any of his other bills too and you'll have to deal with a small mountain of post from his debt collectors. He may also have damaged electricity and gas meters to obtain a free supply. Some tenants even deliberately damage the property or at least leave it in a dirty condition. Bad tenants never make great neighbours, so you may also have to deal with angry neighbours too.

If you want to recover the money you are owed, this is yet another separate court action with additional costs, and your chances of recovery are not high unless your tenant is in the UK, is traceable and has a job.

As well as the cost of evicting a bad tenant, there is also the time and stress. So pick your tenant with care. (For more on bad tenants and eviction, see Chapter 9.)

To save time you should ask your tenant to get this reference from his employer himself rather than you writing to the employer and then waiting ages for the response to come back. When you get the reference back, read it carefully. Does it give you all the information you asked for? Ideally it should be from the Personnel or Human Resources Department but a reference provided by a senior manager is usually just as good.

You should *always* telephone to verify the reference. Rather than telephone the referee's direct line, go through the main switchboard of the company, check the referee's job title and only then ask to be put through to the referee. Then identify yourself and check that he provided the reference and validate what it says. All employers should be happy to do this for you. In phoning the employer and checking the referee's job title, you are just confirming that the reference is not written by a mate of your prospective tenant.

Many people nowadays work on a contract basis or are self employed. If so, they should be able to provide you with evidence of their current contracts. Where someone works on a freelance basis for many clients, you should ask for evidence of regular income from his bank statements over a period of at least six months. His agent or accountant may be able to provide proof of past and/or future income too. Clients may be prepared to provide proof of future work in the pipeline. These references should be followed up.

If he has his own company, ask to see its last two years' reports and accounts. If it hasn't been trading for that long, you will need to look for other evidence that he can pay the rent, so the other references listed here will need to be very good.

It is important to check if what the tenant said to you when you met him ties in with what his employment references say.

That's why it's useful to make notes of even those casual "getting to know you" conversations on the phone or when he first came to view your property. If there is a discrepancy, gently probe further. If you have real doubts, walk away!

How much should they earn?

At the first phone call, we generally tell applicants that their combined income should be at least 2.25 times the rental amount. However, this is a starting off point. Some people may earn four times the rent amount but also have hideous outgoings and already be overdrawn. In the absence of other information, we would reject such candidates. To establish this we ask to see at least three months' worth of bank statements. Conversely, some people may only have income of say just two times the rent, but that income is set and reliable and they may also have very low outgoings, especially if they have no kids. Pensioners often fall into this category. We can be flexible in a way most letting agents often cannot be.

Previous landlord reference

A previous landlord reference, especially one from a *good* respectable letting agent, can be very reassuring. Ideally the landlord reference should be from the landlord before his current one as his current one may be prepared to say anything just to get rid of him.

The reference should state the start and end dates of the tenancy, the rent amount, whether this rent was always paid on time, his conduct as a tenant and whether the referee would recommend the tenant as being reliable, honest and trustworthy. Again, always phone to validate it. If it's from a large letting agency, always call the main switchboard number first and validate the referee. If the agency is local, go and see them. You might find that when you speak to the landlord he is not as glowing about the tenant as he was in writing.

Of course, not all people can provide a previous landlord reference for various good reasons. For example, they may have never rented before or their landlord may be hard to get hold of or uncooperative.

Therefore, one of the things I always try to find out when I first meet tenants is where they are living now and whether they are currently renting. If they say they are renting, I always ask them what their landlord is like. I have met quite a few sets of tenants who have said that the reason that they are moving out is that their landlord is awful – he doesn't fix things, they have had a hole in their wall for six weeks and damp in their living room for months. They can never get hold of him and have had enough.

The chances are that these people will be unable to get a reference from their landlord. Of course, if they are genuine and their landlord is the idiot that they say he is, then they will probably appreciate a good landlord like you!

Naturally, you have to be alert to the fact that the reason that they cannot get a previous landlord reference is because it was they who were awful and so their last landlord will not give them a reference. Some tenants might be so awful that a previous landlord will say anything in a reference if it helps to get rid of the problem onto someone else. Unfortunately, there is not much that you can do about this. After all, it's very unlikely that you could ever prove that a landlord gave a misleading reference and, even if you could, then so what? Giving a misleading or untrue reference is hardly something the police will be interested in. That is why a reference from the landlord *before the last one* is usually the best of all.

If the reference is from a landlord in another country who doesn't speak English, you will have to find someone who speaks the same language to validate the reference. Make the effort. It only takes a call and will give you extra peace of mind. Finally, you can check whether the previous landlord really owns the property he says he let to the tenant by running a check on the Land Registry website for £4. This is a very useful "background check" that few landlords or agents do.

Proof of identity

Obtaining proof of identity is a must and may soon be a legal requirement. Ask for sight of an official original document proving the person's identity – usually this will be the person's passport or new-style driving licence. Keep a copy of the photo and a record of the passport or identity number.

Checking addresses and the credit reference

The reason for checking the tenant's current and previous addresses is linked to the running of a credit reference check. I normally ask to see the last three utility bills, mobile phone bills (or even better bank statements) in that person's name to check his most recent address. A bank statement for that person's *current* account can be particularly useful as this will give you an idea of whether he is in credit and whether sufficient income from a job is being regularly paid into the account and rent is being paid out. Used in this way it acts as an additional check on the employer's and landlord's references.

You can do a basic credit reference check on a tenant for less than £15 and there are a number of suppliers who provide this service. Normally, the credit referencing company will issue a form on which you fill in the full name of the prospective tenant, his date of birth and his addresses over the last three years. Some companies will also ask you to state the amount of the rent.

You simply complete the form and get the tenant to sign it or get an email from them giving their consent to the credit check. The credit referencing company can normally send you a report immediately and you can use it to assess whether the tenant is a good risk. More importantly, the report should tell you whether this tenant has something negative in his credit history like a County Court Judgment – i.e. a debt that he hasn't paid.

You need to use common sense to interpret a credit report, but it also helps to know how credit scoring works. I'll try to explain.

A person's credit score is basically a reflection of how he runs his finances. If you own your own home and have lots of accounts on which you honour your commitments then you will have a very good score. You could, of course, have lots of overdrawn accounts but, as long as you are meeting repayments, then your score will still be good. Conversely, a young student, who has been renting for a few years, hasn't bothered to register on the electoral roll, has moved addresses a few times, doesn't pay the utility bills where he is living and has a short credit history, will have a low score. (See also the section on credit scores in Chapter 4.)

Therefore be careful when using credit scores. If you are letting property to young recent graduates, the chances are that they will have low credit scores. The key thing to look out for here is that they don't have a negative credit history – i.e. outstanding County Court Judgments. However, if their score is particularly low, you might want to seek a guarantor such as a parent.

If someone has a County Court Judgment against him, he should tell you before you do the credit reference enquiry. In some cases it may be that the debt is due to a past business failure that is about to be cleared. Ultimately, you will have to weigh up what your prospective tenant tells you about previous debts with the other information and the other references and come to a decision. The key thing is, if in doubt, don't let to him.

If you are letting to foreign nationals who have recently moved to the UK, credit referencing is of more limited use because most credit referencing companies still don't have

160

lots of data from foreign countries. (If you are deciding which referencing service to use, it is worth asking them which countries they cover.) This is particularly relevant in the big cities and at the lower end of the market where the majority of potential tenants may be from overseas.

It is possible for anyone to obtain their credit report online and give this to you instead. That's fine, but if they do this, check the report is a current one.

Non-EU nationals – work permits

For a national of a country outside the European Union, you are now legally obliged to check his entitlement to live and work in the UK at the start of tenancy and ongoing. (Yes, landlords are now amateur immigration officers too!) And if he can't work, he probably won't be able to pay rent! Fines can be imposed on landlords who fail to do this. A government online checking facility has been developed to help landlords do these checks more easily.

The facility is called the "Right to Rent" checks and you can see the latest requirement via the government website, www.gov.uk. Go there and search for "Right to Rent". You should keep copies of passports and other relevant documents in case you need to prove you did the appropriate checks at a later date (though it is also good practice in case you later need to trace a tenant). Of course, you need to check and keep copies of passports of *all applicants* not just those who "look British". This is good practice and doing otherwise is clearly discriminatory.

Other checks

Some landlords ask for bank status enquiries in which they write to the tenant's bank and ask for a report on their creditworthiness. I wouldn't bother for the reason that the banks take far too long to respond and the wording of their responses is usually confusing and vague. Of course, the far better alternative is to ask your prospective tenant for sight of his last three months' of bank statements. Most tenants are happy to comply.

Some referencing companies offer a service where they do a credit reference enquiry and also check the employer's and previous landlord's reference – basically doing the whole thing for you. However, I can't see the point of paying a third party to check employer's and landlord's references when that is something that you can do much quicker yourself and at the cost of a couple of phone calls.

If you are letting to students, their parents should sign the tenancy agreement as guarantors. This means that the parents will be jointly and severally responsible to pay the whole rent if the student doesn't. All the usual checks should be done on the parent as you would do for any other potential tenant. Guarantors should be used for any person who, for whatever reason, can't provide all the references or pay the rent out of their own resources. This would include any self-employed person whose real income may be greater than can be proven in a bank statement and some housing-benefit recipients. Guarantors must be UK home owners – and you can check if they are through the Land Registry online. (See Appendix 2.)

Finally, it's also useful to have a record of the tenant's National Insurance number.

Gut feel

When making a decision about whether to let to someone use each of the references and exercise common sense. In addition, don't be afraid to see if the applicant has an online business or social media presence, including Google images – and assess what these say about them and if it confirms other information they have given you. However, the most important thing is probably gut feel as you'll rarely find the tenant whose references are immaculate in every way. If the references are in any way deficient or you have only slight doubts, you could ask for three to six months' rent in advance. This could be in addition to the provision of a guarantor. Make sure you make it absolutely clear in writing that this money is rent and not a deposit.

Don't lose sight of the fact that the vast majority of prospective tenants are basically honest and only about 2 per cent will be cheats and con artists. However, be particularly wary of well-dressed and plausible-looking people who just *have to* move in today. They'll always promise that they will have the money tomorrow. If you let these people into your property, you'll probably get no rent and you will have a very difficult job of getting your property back, as they know every trick in the book and will use the system to their advantage. You have been warned! If you have a nagging doubt about someone, you *must* walk away even if your property is proving hard to let and *never* let someone in to your property until you have obtained cleared funds for both the deposit and rent. Never be tempted by someone who offers to pay six or twelve months' cash in advance with no reference checks unless you are also happy to have your house turned into a cannabis farm. Always do thorough checks!

The good news is that if you or your letting agent use a referencing system such as the one I've described, you will almost certainly avoid the bad tenants. Bad tenants know that they can't provide the documentation required by a proper reference check and, when faced with one, will go away and seek a more gullible landlord or duff letting agent elsewhere.

Letting to companies

What about letting to companies? First check whether it is a limited company and assess its financial worth by obtaining a copy of its report and accounts from Companies House.

If there is any doubt about the company's stability then put the tenancy in the tenant's name rather than the company's, especially if he has assets like a house elsewhere. Then, check the individual's references as you would any other person. Insist on a homeowning guarantor if you are worried.

Many of the more up-market fully furnished properties are let on short-term contracts to companies or relocation agents direct. Avoid letting to a foreign-based company as it would be expensive to pursue a claim abroad – again it would be better to let to the individual rather than the company; and be wary of letting to workers for foreign governments who may have diplomatic immunity.

Don't accept a "letter of guarantee" from a company; insist on a deposit and cleared funds before anyone moves in. See also the section in Chapter 6 on company lets.

Letting to individuals in a house share

You may be letting to individuals in a shared house. This entails more work than where you let out a whole property, as people will be coming and going more frequently. Each person may have his own agreement to let a room.

All the tenants should be checked and referenced in the same way as before and, to save your time, you should put the responsibility on them to find replacement tenants when they move out (still subject to all your reference checks and agreement of course). Also, be aware that the property could be counted as an HMO – with possibly more regulations to comply with. For more on this see Chapter 5.

What if they are on housing benefit/local housing allowance/universal credit?

If a tenant is on housing benefit (HB), it may be possible under certain special circumstances to have some or all of the housing benefit paid direct to you, the landlord, by the State. And the local council may run a "bond" scheme in lieu of a deposit to protect the property from damage – though these can be limited in cover and hard to claim against. HB tenants can be profitable, stay a long time and be problem-free but extreme care is needed these days as a result of well meaning but flawed government "initiatives" in recent years, which have made this an ever more difficult part of the market to operate in. The main problems are lower (i.e. sub-market rent) benefit levels, the risk of tenants spending the benefit money on something else other than rent and delays in processing applications.

The tenant should apply to the housing benefit officer well before the planned move-in date. Tenants should sign a letter of authority allowing the HB staff to talk to the landlord regarding the progress of the application and ongoing for the direction of the tenancy. Keep in mind that the amount paid by the authority will be limited by the size of the property required for the tenant's needs – i.e. a single person aged over thirty-five with no kids will only get HB payment for a one-bed not a three-bed flat! Single people under 35 will only get enough for a room in a shared house. Different areas have different rates.

It's worth keeping on good terms with the HB Office at all times. (Please also see Chapters 8 and 9 for more on managing HB tenants.)

Housing Benefit is being gradually replaced with Universal Credit and the rules for this keep changing as the new system starts to be rolled out.

Final steps and what happens on move-in day

Assuming you are happy with the potential tenants you should ask them to pay a cash reservation fee of three weeks' rent as proof of their commitment to proceed. You should emphasise on your email correspondence and receipt that this fee is *not a tenancy deposit* and is non-refundable if they change their minds for any reason and decide not to move in or fail to show up on the agreed move-in date.

At this stage you should give them a *draft* copy of the tenancy agreement and ask them to read it through carefully. I have emphasised the word draft, because you should not sign the formal tenancy agreement until after they have paid you the deposit and the first month's rent. (Once they have done this, the reservation fee can be repaid.) Endorse that it's a draft or specimen tenancy agreement by writing *draft* or *specimen* across each page of the agreement.

You can then make the final arrangements prior to the tenants' moving in. This will involve the tenants contacting the electricity, gas, water, phone and council-tax people. I also ask tenants to ensure that their own contents insurance has accidental damage cover included – so they can "make good" if they, say, spill red wine on the carpet.

I always ask tenants to ensure that they have set up their standing order and to make sure the rent payments are in my account on time. With some banks it can still take three working days for money to go from one person's account to another. Therefore, to allow for this and the additional effect of week-ends and bank holidays, I ask tenants to ensure that the money leaves their account six calendar days before it is due in mine.

On move-in date, tell tenants in advance that the formalities will take about an hour. Agree and sign a detailed inventory check, preferably one done by an independent inventory clerk which should include date-stamped photos and even videos these days – and note any marks, chips or damages to every item in the inventory or any carpets or walls and describe every item of furnishing in detail. The inventory should also note the meter readings in case of disputes later. Show them how everything works using the House Guide as explained in Chapter 6.

Oh no! I can't find a tenant! What do I do?

What you must avoid is the dreaded void period, where you don't have a tenant but of course you still have to pay the mortgage and all the other bills. Firstly, do not panic. Secondly, examine the possible causes of why you aren't managing to let your property.

If you are advertising it yourself and getting few calls, ask yourself the following questions:

Is it advertised in the right websites/publication(s)? Look at other properties advertised in the same places. If these properties are much smarter than yours or vice versa, perhaps you are in the wrong publication. Would a better quality, wider-angled set of photos help? Remember too, your rent should be less than similar advertised properties. Other properties that have been advertised for weeks on end are, by definition, at too high a rent.

Are there too many properties of the same type on the market? If so, can you differentiate yours in some way? If not, then you are going to have to cut the rent.

Is it the time of year? Over the summer and at Christmas it goes very quiet in most big towns, especially college towns. Hang on until mid August or January.

Is the weather too hot, cold or wet? When the weather is very horrible (or very nice), tenants don't go looking for accommodation.

Are you excluding groups of people unnecessarily? For example, if your ads exclude students, you might like to consider them. If you are worried about students causing more damage to your property you could always ask for a higher deposit, do reference checks on students' parents, make them guarantors for the rent, or restrict the let to more mature (and hopefully more responsible) postgrad students. (I know one experienced student landlord who accepts all students with the exception of first year ones who he says are too irresponsible, too likely to party and too likely to fall out with each other).

Also find out if the college has a "head lease" scheme that could see the college guaranteeing the rent and/or managing the tenancy for you. Perhaps you could allow pets – if so, make sure the pet is described on the tenancy agreement and you may want to consider requesting special end of tenancy cleaning and asking for a higher deposit as risk of damage will be higher. Request a reference for the pet from the previous landlord.

If you are getting enquiries and/or viewings but no conversion, perhaps your advert is "overselling". Maybe there is something else wrong with the property. Perhaps it needs to be decorated better? Contact people who have rejected it and ask them for their honest opinions.

If you are using a letting agent and not getting the property let, get a friend to pose as a potential tenant and see how your agent performs. If he performs poorly, get a new agent.

Finally, the tenant should pay the deposit and the first month's rent in cash or cleared bank transfer. (At this point you should also return the reservation fee.) I would advise against accepting a banker's or building society draft as there is always a small risk it could be stolen or fraudulent. You should both sign the tenancy agreement of which there should be two original copies – one for the landlord and one for the tenant. It's worth also taking next of kin details in case anything should happen to the tenant.

8

How to Manage the Tenancy

How to manage the tenants

After a couple of months, go and visit your tenants and take a look at the property. You can use this opportunity to run through the House Guide again (see Chapter 6) to see that they know what to do in an emergency. After that, if everything is OK, I tend to leave my tenants alone apart from annual check-ups. My view is if they're paying the rent, they're probably also looking after the property too and will know to let me know if anything is wrong. The only exception is if a letting agent is managing it, where I'd insist on visits and reports being done each quarter.

Only go to the property after arranging an appointment, except if there is an emergency that needs fixing immediately and you can't wait for the tenant to be on-site.

Check your bank account on the date the tenants' money is due. If it isn't there contact them straightaway. It may be just an error at their bank. If this is the excuse, to avoid further delays get the tenants to pay cash, either direct to you or by direct same-day transfer. If they are late paying, don't accept a cheque or a re-sent standing order as it takes too long to clear.

If a tenant says it's his bank's fault, then his bank should resend it.

If a tenant still hasn't paid after a week, then telephone or visit. Be firm and polite. If the tenant makes a formal complaint to anyone about you, stop calling round and make future rent demands in writing. I'll explain more about what to do with problem tenants in Chapter 9.

More up-market properties, especially those that are fully furnished, let on short-term contacts or to companies, will command higher rents, but will require more management because tenants' expectations will be that much higher and the more frequent changeover of tenants will mean more checking in and out. Your challenge will be to meet tenants' higher expectations whilst keeping voids to a minimum.

How to manage housing-benefit/local-housing-allowance (LHA) tenants

Tenants on housing benefit (or Local Housing Allowance) need to be managed slightly differently. Most lettings to housing-benefit tenants work well once they've been set up and the tenants tend to stay longer too, thus reducing void periods and re-letting costs. But getting the forms filled in right and understanding how the process works can be hard work for the novice.

In some areas housing-benefit officers take ages to process new claims. In other areas they are much more efficient. If things are moving too slowly, formally ask the housing-benefit people for an interim payment. They will then either have to pay in full or make an interim payment fourteen days after having all the information necessary. You should always ask the tenant to keep you informed at all times.

The Government is now rolling out the new Universal Credit system – so it is all change once again. The key difference under the new system is that tenants (not the landlord) will usually get money paid direct to them. Of course, this change clearly increased the risk that the tenant spends the money on something other than rent and, unsurprisingly, landlords don't think it was a great idea. However, if the tenant is in two months' rent arrears or they are deemed to be highly "vulnerable", the landlord can apply to be paid direct. As processing can be slow, don't wait for two months' arrears to build before applying for direct payment – notify the housing benefit officer there is a problem as early as you can!

Where the benefit is being paid direct to you and the tenant is later found to be ineligible, the council may try to recover the money from you. In order to safeguard your position, visit the property regularly during the tenancy to ensure that the tenant hasn't vacated and that there aren't any other circumstances that could affect their benefit. Examples may be someone else moving into the property or the tenant getting a different job. Again, any such visits must be arranged with the tenants in advance.

Provided that you have done all you can reasonably do to check that no fraud is going on, it will be hard for the housing benefit office to claim back overpayments from you, though don't be surprised if they initially adopt a very heavy legalistic attitude. Most overpayment claims can be resisted successfully. I always advise any landlord involved with "benefit-dependent tenants" to get familiar with the detailed but very mind-numbing Local Housing Allowance Guidance Manual. Mistakes by staff are all too common, unfortunately, so if you are in this end of the market, you *must* get clued-up and understand the rules they should be working to.

How much local housing allowance a tenant gets will depend on rents in the local area (each area of the country is divided into Broad Market Rental Areas) and the size of the property he is deemed to need. Use the government's look-up tables to find out the maximum levels paid in your area.

Bear in mind that the now massive bill for housing benefit is a political football and the coalition government has already cut the cost by reducing rates, cutting entitlements and breaking the link with local market rent levels.

These big changes are progressively rolling out. But as landlords are increasingly voting with their feet and leaving this end of the market where they can, we predict the government will have to backtrack or else face the cost of having to put more people up in B&B accommodation.

Despite the risks and challenges and the constant tinkering by government, if you are in the right location, if your lender and insurer allow these lets and you are happy dealing with extra paperwork and potentially more difficult tenants, it can be very lucrative, socially satisfying and worth the effort. And this type of tenant tends to stay longer too, so less voids.

How to manage a letting agent

In Chapter 7, I explained what sort of things to look for in a letting agent who will just *find* a tenant for you. Of course, such agents can also be used to *manage* your property too, which may be useful if you live a long way away and don't know any local plumbers or other tradespeople. If you're going to use an agency for management, you must be clear about what level of service it is going to provide. You can get an idea by asking the agency the following questions:

1. How quickly after they receive the tenant's money will it be in your account?
2. How frequently will they pay visits to inspect the property?
3. What will they look for when they do inspection visits?
4. If maintenance work is required, whom will they call? Do they have their own maintenance people or will they just get someone out of the phone book?
5. Are their maintenance people members of the appropriate bodies, e.g. NICEIC for electricians, IPHE, etc, for plumbers, Gas Safe Registered for gas? Do they check their membership?
6. Will they arrange the annual gas safety check?
7. Do they have a special telephone number for tenants to call for maintenance out of normal office hours?
8. How quickly will someone be on site if there is an emergency such as a burst pipe?

9. Do they request an estimate for routine works first?

10. Will they clear the cost of work with you or just go ahead? Above what amount will they request your authorisation?

11. Can they advise what the average cost of a sample of typical maintenance jobs is? (Are the costs reasonable?) Do they take commissions from tradespeople for being on their list of approved contractors and do they mark-up contractors' invoices?

12. What money float do they require you to provide to cover maintenance?

13. How will you be invoiced for maintenance work?

14. How frequently will they send statements?

15. Are they members of a property ombudsman scheme? Are they members of one or more of RICS, NAEA, NALS, ARLA or UKALA schemes for agents? (These umbrella organisations may operate a bonding scheme protecting your money in the event the agent goes bust.) In Wales, are they registered with RentSmart Wales?

16. How do they protect tenants' deposit money? What are their procedures at the end of the tenancy, including for the hand-over of the deposit?

17. How will they prove they have protected tenants' deposits in one of the schemes? You are responsible for this so make sure they have done it!

18. If it is an HMO, do they have experience of managing this kind of letting? (It is essential that they do as fines for non-compliance can be stiff.)

19. If a landlords' licensing scheme applies locally, how do they deal with this?

As well as this list, see also Chapter 7 on how to use a letting agent for finding a tenant and the questions you should ask them about this aspect of their work. From their responses, you'll be able to assess their degree of professionalism and whether your property is safe in their hands. If they haven't got a clue, go to another agent.

A letting agency should earn its management fee by doing regular inspections and should be prepared to talk through your House Guide with your tenants, demonstrating how things work and what to do in the event of an emergency. They should be able to show you a list of things they look for on inspection visits. Ideally, this should be a pre-prepared list that can be given to anyone doing inspections. It should include a list of things to look for which might indicate damp, overflowing pipes, etc. A really good agent would complete a report after each inspection visit and send it to you. Many agents will have people who can competently carry out emergency repair works at a reasonable cost.

You must make sure that you are getting value for money from this aspect of their work and ensure that you are getting what you are paying for, especially if the emergency work is not covered by your home insurance or other maintenance contract that you have set up. Don't forget to tell a letting agent if, say, you have the white goods covered under an existing agreement. You don't want to pay for fixes unnecessarily.

Most letting agents sell property as well as let it, which is fine. Where this is the case, try to ensure that the letting agent devotes as much time and interest to the letting side of their business as they do to selling properties. Since margins are tight and the work dull and admin heavy, some letting agents will be tempted to cut corners by sending the office junior to do an inspection or "forget" to do it at all.

If you ask all the questions above and get sensible answers, you'll have a good agent who will treat your account with respect but you'll still need to keep on top of them. Letting agency staff move often, so don't leave new staff in any doubt about the standard of service you expect!

How to manage maintenance

Too many landlords fail to manage their properties properly and when faced with emergencies they often do the wrong thing and end up paying out far more than they need to.

As a landlord you have a legal duty to keep your property in good repair, so this means spending some time managing people who come to fix things when they go wrong. If you live close to your property, are good with your hands and have the time, you can of course do it yourself. However, there are some exceptions. If you aren't a Gas Safe registered gas engineer you can't try to fix gas appliances. If you do, you are breaking the law. Also, most significant electrical work now requires a qualified electrician.

For other things too, it's important to know what you're doing, so, if you don't, get the job done by a professional who does! They'll also get it done in half the time.

If you find a good tradesman, pay his bill on time and cultivate a good relationship. Then, when the big freeze comes you should be near the front of the queue. If you've got a number of properties, try getting your tradesmen to agree a service-level agreement and a fixed price list for emergency and other call-outs.

Get things fixed as soon as possible. If there is going to be an unavoidable delay, tell your tenants as soon as possible. Also, let them know in advance when you or your tradesmen will be on site and never go in without making a prior arrangement unless it's an emergency. If you don't fix things quickly you'll lose tenants. If you don't fix them at all, you could get a court order compelling you to carry out repairs and you'll have to pay court costs too. Also, if the local authority upholds a complaint about disrepair, you won't be able to issue a Section 21 Notice for six months or until the matter is resolved.

If the property (or part of it) is uninhabitable, for example following a leak, give your tenants a rent reduction or waiver.

You'll generate good will and the lost rent and cost of alternative accommodation should be covered by insurance anyway!

Self-managing landlords should have a local "always available" key holder who can be available to give keys to tradesmen and hand out replacement keys for tenants who find themselves locked out. If tenants frequently lock themselves out you should charge for letting them in (and if this persists, maybe you'd be better off with new tenants).

Always keep records of monies paid out that can be recoverable in the event of an insurance claim.

Dealing with leaks and heating problems

Water damage in a property can be very expensive. The most common problems are to do with showers, boilers, pumps, dripping taps, leaking pipes and toilet overflows. Things like dripping taps should take no more than forty-five minutes to fix. Your tenants are, of course, your front line for dealing with emergencies like a burst main or boiler leak and they should know what to do to minimise damage. See Chapter 6 for what should be in a tenant's emergency "House Guide".

Let's assume your tenants have followed the instructions in their House Guide and have stopped the flow of running water. The next step is to get the thing permanently fixed. There are a number of options here.

If there is a management contract with a letting agent, call him. For landlords doing their own management, the initial response of many of them is to get an emergency plumber from the Internet, but this may be expensive and there is no guarantee of competency. However, if you *must* do this, don't use people who charge "by the hour". Insist on getting them to agree a fixed quote (not an estimate!) for the repair. (You will, of course, have to pay the first call-out fee which should also be agreed in advance.)

It's possible to take out a separate "Home Emergencies" contract to cover household emergencies. Schemes on offer from some utility companies cover a number of contingencies from plumbing and gas central heating to electrical appliances though I have found call-out times are rarely guaranteed. Also, the schemes usually don't cover replacement of appliances, kitchen and bathroom fixtures, tap washers, showers, the mains electricity supply or rewiring. Even worse, I have heard of stories where the firm's engineers are all too ready to condemn a boiler so they can get commission on installing a new one.

If your insurance policy offers emergency cover free of charge then it's definitely not worth bothering with a separate Home Emergencies contract.

Landlords with two or more properties should have a reliable plumber and qualified gas engineer on their books. For water and heating, there is the Institute of Plumbing and Heating Engineering (IPHE) and the Association of Plumbing and Heating Contractors (APHC). See Appendix 2.

Don't forget that being on the Gas Safe Register is a requirement for anyone working with gas but it gives no guarantees at all when it comes to plumbing.

If you have a flat, you'll probably have to contact the freeholder's managing agent, even if it's just to register the insurance claim or get into another property to stop a leak. Many landlords say that their managing agents are good at just one thing – collecting the ground rent/service charges – and are pretty useless when things go wrong. If this sounds like your freeholder's agent, think about buying your freehold, applying for commonhold or getting the freeholder to get a new managing agent, preferably one who is a member of the Association of Residential Managing Agents. (See Appendix 2.)

Most leases require the freeholder's consent to major works, so if you have suffered from a leak from an upstairs flat that was caused by works, check that the freeholder's consent was given. If not, the freeholder should take action against the upstairs flat owner.

Problems with water leaks in flats are worse where a flat has just bare floorboards because water will pass straight through, causing more damage. If your tenants are continually flooded by careless occupiers of flats above them, check if the flooring in the offending flat complies with the lease as many leases have a requirement that flats be kept carpeted. Also, keep a diary record of all flood damage, with photos as supporting evidence. If problems continue, try to get the managing agent to instruct a solicitor to enforce the lease provisions.

Often leases have penalties for persistent careless behaviour, and freeholders can ultimately forfeit the flat owner's lease. However, getting a managing agent/freeholder actually to do anything is often a challenge in itself! Finally, don't forget, within the terms of most leases, that managing agents/ freeholders and residents in neighbouring flats have the right to enter another flat to do emergency repairs, if the problem is affecting them.

Get some heaters

It's worth investing in some electric heaters which can be made available for tenants, if their heating breaks down in the middle of winter and there is a delay of a day or so in getting it fixed.

Getting a new boiler

As central-heating boilers get old the cost of maintaining and repairing increases and most boilers have a life of no more than fifteen years. Normally, it's best to replace with the same energy source as before. In rural areas, there may be no mains gas anyway so oil or electricity will be the only sources of heating.

Where the property is small, a "combi" boiler which in summer heats the water only when taps are on will be best. Combis also don't require a hot-water tank, thus saving on space but an under-powered one can take longer to run a bath as the water is heated through the burners.

Look for a boiler carrying the Energy Efficiency Recommended logo which guarantees that the boiler has met strict efficiency criteria.

The new condensing boilers are cheaper to run because they extract the remaining heat from the water cycle when it returns to the boiler for reuse. They are roughly about 90 to 95 per cent efficient at converting fuel into heat where as a ten- to fifteen-year-old boiler may be only 65 per cent efficient. It's worth checking if any help is available from the government at the Energy Saving Trust website, www.est.org.uk . Look out for manufacturers who offer seven-, and even ten-year, guarantees on their machines, though these long guarantees are often only available when the machine is installed by certain gas fitters. Otherwise you may only get a standard two-year guarantee.

Non combi boilers are best where the boiler is likely to be used a lot, for example in properties with more than one bathroom. If space is limited, a combi might be the best option. If you have a new efficient boiler, tell any prospective tenants as it will be they who'll enjoy savings on their fuel bills. If they are deciding between renting your property and another, this could just tilt the balance in your favour!

When installing a new boiler, put in a timer and thermostats to make them even more efficient. If it's a solid fuel or gas boiler you must have carbon monoxide sensors fitted.

Finally, for all AST agreements landlords have by law to provide their tenants with an Energy Performance Certificate (EPC) showing the energy efficiency of the property. The certificates are valid for ten years. Search for "Domestic Energy Assessors" on the Internet to find an assessor.

Dealing with drainage problems

The drains in your property including the pipe connecting to the sewer are your responsibility and your plumber should be able to look after your drainage, whereas the water company is responsible for mains drainage. If the problem is somewhere between property and road, but it's unclear exactly where, I've found the water company will usually do the job if you complain hard enough and to a high enough level (letters to the Chairman of the company usually do the trick). For flats, the pipes serving your flat are your responsibility and not that of the block. However, where the pipe serves more than one flat, the maintenance responsibility belongs to the freeholder and their managing agent.

Things to check as part of your maintenance programme

- Check that the water stop valve can be opened and closed easily. If it sticks, spray on some WD40.
- Clear drains, down pipes and gutters of leaves and moss.
- Lift manhole covers to check if drains are flowing freely.
- Lag any boiler pipes that are exposed.

Dealing with damp problems

People often worry about damp and mould unnecessarily as often the cause is just condensation resulting from poor ventilation and is common in house-to-flat conversions. A simple solution is to install a quiet extractor fan in the bathroom and get tenants to air the property regularly and dry clothes outside whenever possible. If necessary, put in some air bricks. Other causes are plumbing leaks, localised failure of the damp proof course and water penetration from blocked gutters or from outside pavements that have been built too high. Sort out the possible causes first and if there is still a problem get a quote from a specialist buildings surveyor.

Tips for Preventing Condensation and Damp

Extractor fans should be quiet running. If not tenants may disconnect them. And they should be powerful enough to hold up a bank note.

Tumble driers should be vented outside.

A small amount of cold water put in a bath first will reduce condensation from this source.

Avoid putting large items of furniture against cold outside walls.

Dealing with electrical problems

Get a properly qualified electrician to check thoroughly any property you buy and to deal with any problems that come up. Put hard-wired (i.e. fitted into the mains) smoke detectors on each floor, including near to the kitchen, in hallways, landings and the main living room. Lightly vacuum detector elements once a year. Install a hard wired heat detector in the kitchen. This overcomes the problem of tenants neglecting to replace old batteries. Ensure doors are fire-resistant. Stand-alone appliance cover is available for things like washing machines, though many are poor value for money as nowadays quality equipment rarely fails in the first five years. Only buy new machines that come with five-year guarantees.

Dealing with pest problems

First, ensure tenants are not leaving food out. If the problem persists, call the local council. They may deal with the problem free of charge or for a small fee depending on what the infestation is.

How to manage a problem neighbour

Just because it's a rented property, don't think that the fact that the neighbours are awful won't matter to you. It will matter to your tenants, so it will end up mattering to you if they are made so unhappy they end up moving out.

Nobody should have to put up with neighbours from hell and the Government now seems to be taking the problem seriously by issuing criminal behaviour orders. However, they are only applied when things are really very bad. In most cases, you'll still have to try to work out the problem yourself.

The first thing is try to talk reasonably to the neighbour to see if he can stop doing whatever is causing the problem. Only if the problem persists should you take the matter further. If it's noise, contact the Environmental Health section at your local council. If the offending property is rented and the occupier is breaching the lease, tell his landlord. If it's a flat in the same building as yours and with the same freeholder, try to get the managing agent to take action. Keep a diary log of all events and correspondence, including phone calls.

Complaints about neighbours must be declared when you come to sell the property, even if that complaint has been resolved. You're also supposed to declare any complaint made about you and any you've made about the freeholder or their agents. If the complaint has been resolved, this will probably satisfy most potential purchasers. If the complaint is ongoing, it may make it harder to sell and could affect the price you get too. Lots of people don't declare complaints or disputes in the hope their buyer won't find out. This is risky because it may come to light when the buyer moves in and meets the neighbours. In the worst case you could even end up being sued. So, if you're thinking of selling the property soon anyway, consider whether it's really worth making a formal complaint at all.

If it's your tenant who is causing a nuisance, talk to the neighbours and deal with their concerns as soon as possible. I once made the mistake of not doing this and it ended up costing me money. It was on my very first letting and I had a tenant from hell. (I'm glad to say it was the last time I had a tenant like this and my experience with him later inspired this book!)

When it's not worth complaining

I used to own a top-floor flat in a converted house where the front garden was a mess. It put off potential tenants and would do the same for any potential buyer of my flat. The garden belonged to the basement flat whose owner didn't seem to be interested.

I considered sending a formal letter to the managing agent asking him to write to the owner to get her to tidy it up. However, I knew I'd have to declare this when I came to sell the property. So, instead, I decided that whenever I wanted to re-let my flat, I'd just go round and tidy the garden myself. It took about two hours each time. One day, the owner of the basement flat popped out and gave me money to cover my time and trouble. I hadn't expected it, and, although it wasn't much, it made me feel better about the hassle!

My problem tenant left eventually. Later, when I re-let it, there was a small leak in my flat. Unfortunately, it wasn't detected quickly and it caused some damage to the flat below me which prompted the neighbour who lived there and his brother to turn up at my own home one day, demanding all sorts of compensation. They looked pretty hard cases and it wasn't a pleasant experience. I had to pay all their vastly inflated damage claims which luckily were mostly picked up by my insurance company. I reflected that if I had offered the neighbour more tea and sympathy when the problem tenant had been around, he may have been more accommodating when the leak happened.

How to end your tenancy

How to give them notice

An assured shorthold tenancy will end at the end of the fixed term (unless both parties accept an extension). However, even where a fixed term of, say, six months exists, you *still* need to give the tenant at least two months' notice. Let me explain. Suppose on 1 January you set up a fixed six-month tenancy – ending on 30 June. You can't just walk into the property on 30 June. You would *still* need by 30 April to issue notice to leave. I know it sounds stupid, but that's the law!

If both parties agree to extend after the fixed term ends, you don't need to do anything special apart from getting your tenant to confirm in writing that he wishes to stay on. Later, if you want him to leave, it is best to give at least two months' notice and this notice must be dated to expire "after the last day of the tenancy". So, in the example above, the period of the tenancy is from the first to the last day of each month. Therefore, if you give notice on 10 August, the period of notice wouldn't actually start until 1 September and would end "after 31 October".

If there was no fixed term in the first place, then the period of notice must still be two months but again it must state that it ends *after the last day of a "period" of a tenancy*. If, after the end of the fixed term, it's the tenant who wants to leave, he should give you at least a month's notice. Make sure you write the period of notice you require him to give you in the tenancy agreement.

In England, the form of notice given to assured shorthold tenants requesting they leave is called a "Section 21 notice".

Giving notice is important because, if you don't, you won't normally get a possession order in the unlikely event they don't leave and you end up needing to evict through the courts. (For more on evicting see Chapter 9.)

There is no need to pay a solicitor a fortune to draft a formal Section 21 notice for you. You can obtain a blank one from Oyez Stationers (see Appendix 2), your landlords' association and lots of places online.

If you compile your own letter, you need to make clear that you require the property back "after the appropriate date", giving the correct period of notice and stating that you require it back under Section 21 of the 1988 Housing Act. You need to include your name and address, the tenant's name and address and to refer to the property in question specifically. The letter must be dated and it's important to keep a record of the date and time of giving the notice and the method used – e.g. posting it or putting it through the letter box. You could email a copy of the notice too. Keep copies of all correspondence.

The formal Section 21 notice has a lot of legalese, including a bit which basically tells the tenants that if they don't go, you have to apply to the court for a possession order. It's best to include this too.

Problems can arise when it's not certain if a tenant has left because you could end up being charged with unlawful eviction. Normally, you'll be on safe ground if the fixed term has ended and the tenant's possessions have gone, especially if the keys have been left at the property.

In the unlikely event that rent is in arrears, the tenant isn't contactable but his belongings are still at the property, it's best to get a possession order through the courts. For more on doing this, see Chapter 9. Meanwhile, try and make every effort to contact the tenant. If you have a telephone number or email address for friends, parents or work, try these.

It's worth pointing out that you cannot issue a Section 21 notice if you have not protected the tenancy deposit within 30 days of receiving it, if you did not provide the tenant with an energy performance certificate, if you did not provide them with a gas safety certificate, if you did not give them the government's "How to Rent" guide or if a complaint from a tenant about you has been upheld by the local authority. You also cannot serve one during the first four months of a tenancy.

Section 21 notices have been removed in Scotland and look likely to be dropped in Wales too. This is a huge change for private renting, which effectively means landlords will no longer have the automatic right to get their property back unless the tenant has breached the lawful terms of the tenancy.

A letting agent can issue a Section 21 notice on your behalf but they cannot issue claim forms for possession proceedings.

How to deliver a notice letter

Don't use recorded delivery to issue a notice, because if the tenant isn't in or refuses to sign, the letter won't be delivered. Use normal post and get a proof-of-posting certificate or hand deliver with an independent witness to verify it was delivered. Add extra days if the notice is sent by post as the two months' notice starts from the day the notice letter arrives. As an alternative, you could use a "Process Server" to do it all for you.

Other things to do to make sure the end of tenancy goes smoothly

Lots of landlords and tenants who have otherwise had a perfectly good relationship end up falling out at the end of the tenancy over the return of the deposit. This is a shame because, with a bit of planning and hand-holding, you and your tenants can remain on good terms.

The problem is that at the end of the tenancy most tenants don't know what they've got to do to get their deposit back. If they bothered to read the tenancy agreement and returned the property in the same state as when they let it, they would (or should) get all their deposit back. Unfortunately, many just file the agreement and inventory report away and forget the state and condition of the property when they first moved in. I'm pleased to say I've never fallen out with a tenant over deposit money because I have a good system in place. Here's what I do.

When a tenant gives notice to leave, I first ask him to confirm it in writing. Once I have his confirmation letter, I then send him a letter setting out what he needs to do and what happens next. Often, there will be something that the tenant hasn't told you about before because it was too minor. Now is the time to find out and fix it ready for the new viewings.

Sample letter prior to leaving

Dear **NAME OF TENANT**

I acknowledge receipt of your letter and I'm sorry you are leaving. Leaving date is INSERT DATE/TIME. You must continue to pay rent up to the leaving date and under no circumstances use the deposit in lieu of the last month's rent. If you should wish to move before this date, please call me as I sometimes have people who like the property and may want to move in earlier. If this should be the case, it might be possible to close the tenancy earlier.

Please note the following approximate times when I propose doing viewings with prospective new tenants: INSERT TIMES AND DATES. I'd be grateful if you can keep the house as tidy as possible at the set times. Occasionally I may have someone who wishes to view at another time. If so, I will call you first to let you know and see if that time is convenient for you. I will accompany all viewings.

187

Please let me know if you are aware of anything in the property that needs repairing.

Finally, please read the "Important Notes" carefully. These notes simply highlight items in the Tenancy Agreement or relate to things that you need to do before you leave the property. If you have any questions or are unsure about anything explained here, please contact me as soon as possible.

If all is well, I'll be happy to provide a good reference. I will send further communication prior to the leaving date so watch out for this.

Yours sincerely

David Lawrenson

Important Notes
Please ensure that you have done the following:

1. That all the keys are returned.
2. That the property, including the garden, is returned in the same state at the end of the tenancy as it was at the start and after all your personal items have been removed. A deduction will be made from the deposit to repair and/or replace any damaged items or make good any damaged property, fixtures, fittings, furniture and effects. (Fair wear and tear excepted.) Please take care not to damage walls when removing your own furniture! It is recommended that you use a properly qualified removal firm.
3. That all items in the inventory list are left in the same positions as they were at the start of the letting. The position of each item is listed in the Agreement under the section headed "Inventory". Any items that have been stored off-site must be returned.

In addition, I kindly request that you:

4. Provide all gas, electric, telephone, council tax and/or any

other utility suppliers with a final meter reading and your forwarding address.

5. Provide me with a forwarding address and contact phone number.
6. Forward your post via the Royal Mail redirection service.
7. Arrange with the council for any bulky rubbish you no longer require to be collected before you move out.
8. Remove vehicles from the allocated parking bay.
9. Replace dead light bulbs.
10. Arrange to have the carpets professionally cleaned.

Note on cleaning

For cleaning, you should pay attention to the following:

- Cleaning outside and inside all cupboards, including kitchen cupboards.
- Removal of all stains and fat marks in the kitchen area (including on top of the kitchen units).
- Cleaning kitchen floor.
- Cleaning oven and grill including trays and racks.
- Cleaning bathroom area including removal of scale from taps and bath/shower fittings, inside and outside pan in WC/toilet and around rim of toilet.
- Cleaning and dusting including windows, windowsills (inside and out), around and inside all light fittings, skirting boards, dado and picture rails. All surfaces.
- Defrosting and cleaning of fridge-freezer.
- Wiping down doors, door frames including street door and all woodwork.

Please note this is a guide, not an exhaustive list. If property is not cleaned to the state as was recorded and agreed in the inventory at the start of your tenancy agreement, additional cleaning that is required to be performed/arranged by the landlord will be charged and deducted from the deposit.

During the last few weeks of the old tenancy, I do a formal visit to see that everything works as it should. I check the oven, the shower, the central heating and whether the windows open properly. I test and check every item on the inventory including the beds, sofas and wardrobes. If things have been damaged (beyond fair wear and tear) I obtain two quotes and send these to the tenant with an explanation that this amount will be deducted from the deposit, less any fair wear-and-tear deduction.

I may also go to the property a few days before the leaving date to check if the cleaning has started and to deal with any final questions the departing tenant has. On the leaving day, I meet with the tenant and check the inventory with him together with the inventory clerk. In case of dispute, I take along the "start inventory" and any photos or a video showing the condition of the property when he moved in and check and agree meter readings for electricity, gas and water. If you can use the same *independent* inventory clerk who did the inventory and schedule of condition on move in, so much the better. It will seriously reduce the chances of a dispute.

Check everything thoroughly

After one tenant had left at the end of his tenancy, I made a cup of tea and sat down on one of the beds. It promptly collapsed! I checked the other bed – the same thing happened. Ditto the wardrobes! The tenant had obviously dismantled all the furniture to replace it with his own, and found it wouldn't go back together easily. Unfortunately I hadn't checked the furniture before he had left with his deposit. I had to pay a carpenter to put everything back together with extra supports. So, I now check all furniture when a tenant leaves and have inserted a clause in my agreement saying tenants must not dismantle any furniture.

If all is well, I return deposits (less any costs) on the leaving date itself when the tenant hands over the keys. Some tenants ask for it in cash, which I'd avoid, but if you must do this, make sure you get them to sign for it and have their signature witnessed.

If you hold the deposit, you should not hold onto it for more than ten days after the end of the tenancy. The only possible time I might hold onto the deposit for a couple of days is if the rent is paid directly to me by the housing-benefit office. If so, I check with the housing-benefit people that it's all up-to-date and they have made no overpayment. (The rules on payment of housing benefit are constantly changing, but you may be justified in holding onto some deposit money for a few days in case the housing-benefit authorities later try to claw it back from you.)

It's worth noting that once final utility meter readings and a forwarding address have been taken by you in good faith, the council-tax authority and utility suppliers can't come after you for money owed to them by your tenants. So, again, you've no reason to hold any of their deposit pending final bills.

I usually allow a few days between the old tenants leaving and the new ones moving in, in case anything needs fixing or if the previous tenants have not cleaned up properly.

If you do all this, or check that your agent is doing it, you'll never have an argument with your tenant about the return of his deposit. If you part on good company, ask your old tenants if they would be happy to provide references on you, the landlord, for other prospective tenants! Many will be delighted to do this and only too pleased to tell people what a good landlord you have been.

Respecting your tenants' privacy

When planning viewings with prospective tenants, I always fix a few specific times during the week and stick to them. Only if I have someone who sounds really good, and who can't make one of these times, will I call my existing tenant to make an appointment for another time. That way, I respect my existing tenants' privacy. It's worth including a clause in your agreement allowing you to do viewings with prospective tenants in the last month of the tenancy.

When the property is vacant between tenants I always ensure it's properly locked and secured. I leave a few lights and a radio on a timer switch to give the impression someone is in. It's best to visit regularly and pick up the post, especially if it is left in a public area like a communal hallway. Don't allow a "To Let" board as it's a dead giveaway the place is empty.

Squatters look for empty properties where an agent's board is outside, post is piling up and there aren't any lights on. There are websites out there telling squatters to look for just these kinds of unsecured houses. You've been warned! If you leave a window open and they get in without using force, you'll have a lot of hassle getting rid of them.

Finally, if from your visits to the property, it is clear that your tenants live in filth, that they have never cleaned in their lives and would not even know the difference between a duster and vacuum cleaner, it will be a waste of time giving them a cleaning list. Your best route is to point them to a good professional cleaning firm to do an "end of tenancy clean". Of course, the tenants will have to pay for this, but it is remarkably inexpensive.

Tenants who leave stuff

If the tenancy agreement has ended and tenants' belongings have been abandoned, write a formal letter giving them ample time to come and retrieve them. Inform them that if they don't, the items will be disposed of or sold off – with sale proceeds less your reasonable costs returned to them.

Tenancy deposit schemes

Things have changed in the way landlords have to handle deposits. All landlords who take deposits on assured shorthold tenancies have to join government-approved tenancy deposit schemes (TDS) which have the aim of protecting tenants' deposits. The schemes (run for the government by private approved organisations) have dispute-resolution procedures in place for landlords and tenants who can't agree about the deposit at the end of the tenancy.

The new rules were brought in to try to make it easier for tenants to reclaim their deposits at the end of the tenancy since it was felt that many landlords were unfairly holding onto them.

There are two types of TDS: a "custodial" scheme where a third party holds the deposit; and, in England, Wales and Northern Ireland (but not Scotland), an "insurance" scheme where the landlord holds it. Landlords have to tell tenants which scheme they are in and provide full details of how the scheme works, including sending tenants a signed copy of the protection certificate, the scheme rules and other prescribed information within thirty days of receiving the deposit. (The schemes come with downloadable documents and certificates of deposit protection.) If landlords don't do this, penalties include having to pay the tenant an amount up to three times the deposit and the landlord becoming ineligible to regain possession under the so-called Section 21 and "accelerated possession procedure" (unless the deposit has been returned in full or with the tenant agreeing to deductions from it).

The insurance scheme seems to be the better option as it is relatively cheap and allows landlords to hold onto their deposits rather than paying them over to the scheme – much better for cash flow. The only downside of the insurance schemes is that landlords have to pay a small fee to join and for each deposit taken. With the insurance-based schemes, only if at the end of the tenancy is there a dispute must the landlord lodge the disputed amount with the scheme until the dispute is resolved – with the rest being returned to the tenant. If, for any reason, the landlord does not pay the disputed amount into the scheme, the administrators will return the disputed amount to the tenant (if they are entitled to it) and chase the landlord for recovery of the money. The landlord and tenant can opt out of the schemes' free dispute-resolution service, if they wish, and go to court instead.

There is just one custodial scheme, at www.depositprotection. com. It is free but uses the interest on landlords' deposits to pay for the administration.

There are two insurance-based schemes. One is run by Tenancy Deposit Solutions (www.mydeposits.co.uk) and the other is run by the Dispute Service Ltd (www.thedisputeservice. co.uk).

The schemes do add extra work and cost for landlords – and the administrative requirements are a bit of a pain – but once you have done it a few times it gets easier.

Landlords should note that the very existence of the schemes makes it all the more important to appoint an independent inventory clerk to do a thorough inventory with time-dated photos, thus evidencing the state and condition of the property at the start and end of each tenancy. (Bear in mind that successful damage claims under the various TDS schemes are not awarded on a new-for-old basis – wear and tear and age of the item is taken into account. The expected lifespan, location and amount of use of an item counts too. So, a carpet in a bedroom may be expected to last ten to twelve years, whereas in a hallway it might be expected to last for eight years, or even only for five years in a large shared house.)

You can avoid TDS completely by issuing an assured tenancy instead of an assured shorthold one, but if you do this you will not be able to regain possession unless the tenant seriously breached the tenancy agreement or left voluntarily. I would advise against doing this.

If you use a letting agent to handle the deposit, you *must* check that they have protected the deposit and complied with all the scheme's rules or you could end up out of pocket if the agent goes bust. If you don't trust them to do this right, protect it yourself, especially if the agent is using the insurance-based scheme. After all, why let the agent have the benefit of the deposit cash, when you could be earning interest on it instead.

How to manage utilities and council tax

In between lettings you'll have to pay the utilities and, depending on the local authority, possibly also the council tax too. For utilities, keep a note of start and end readings and supply the tenant's forwarding address for bills. It's worth keeping a record of all conversations because I once had the council-tax people incorrectly sending bills to me at my rented property instead of my correspondence address. The tenant forgot to send me the bill and I nearly ended up in court for non-payment! Luckily I had a record of the phone call where I gave the council my correspondence address.

I now put in my tenancy agreements that tenants must forward any post addressed to me personally or to "the owner" as soon as possible. Post addressed to "the occupier" must be opened by them and passed on to me if it's relevant for me to see it – for example, if it is related to construction work or a planning application nearby.

In the agreement I also advise tenants that I'll pass on the names and forwarding addresses of *each* tenant to utility companies and the council-tax people when they move in and leave. Council taxpayers living on their own are entitled to a discount so if you have more than one person renting your property, it's best they don't try to cheat the council by pretending they're living alone when they aren't.

Tenants are free to change their utility supplier as they see fit.

How to manage paperwork

One thing that soon becomes apparent to new landlords is that there is a lot of paperwork and online admin to deal with. As well as the usual bills to pay for each property, there are also tenancy agreements, inventory/condition lists, invoices and mortgage statements to file.

It's also useful to keep your own record of where the stop valves/fuse boxes are, how the heating system works, room sizes, the location of the meters, parking space, communal bins and any other useful information on the property. Keep a diary log for each property to record notes of any conversation or phone calls with tenants, agents, even the meter readings given to the water company! I keep leftovers and samples of the types of carpet and paint used in each room for when I need to replace it.

If you have a flat you'll be a leaseholder or you may own the freehold on your own or with others. The lease contract sets out who should do what in relation to the property and the various rights and obligations on each side. Keep a record in your diary log of all events, phone calls and copies of all correspondence with other leaseholders, the freeholder and managing agent. See the section in Chapter 3 on Freehold or Leasehold.

You need an up-to-date filing system for all this and to keep invoices and statements for up to six years to satisfy the Revenue for income-tax purposes and for as long as you own the property should you want to claim a cost against capital gains when you come to sell it. I file my records by property and my rents and invoices in date order. These can then be re-sorted by property, supplier or type of bill. Sorting by bill type makes it easier to complete your tax return because HMRC requires that costs be grouped into different categories. For more on reporting for tax purposes, see Chapter 11.

You can buy software, where if you enter information in, say, an invoice file, it will automatically fill in another form which can be sent to the Revenue or update a management report. It's worth looking into these especially if you have a lot of properties.

How to keep up to date

The law on letting property and the requirements made of you as a landlord change from time to time so you need to keep up to date. The property pages of the national newspapers are a good source for finding out about the basic changes and, if you use a good letting agency, they should be able to keep you up to date too. Make sure to ask them though because keeping you informed won't be their top priority!

Better still, join a landlords' association. They offer a way to meet other landlords, receive information and updates and use free helplines. Of course, there is also my own site, www.LettingFocus.com which also has a useful and regularly updated blog. Finally, there is the occasional property show you can attend. These have lots of useful seminars you can go to for a small fee. Be careful, though, estate agents and property syndicates occupy about 80 per cent of the stands at these shows. They are all hungry for your money, so leave your chequebook at home!

One last thing, if you are a member of a landlords' association (or are accredited with your local authority or university) you may get a discount on the cost of your licence application (if you have a licensable HMO) and on the cost of things like Energy Performance Certificates and tenancy deposit schemes. To find out if your local authority runs an accreditation scheme for private landlords ask your council's housing department or check their website.

Preventing Fraud

The Land Registry has a useful anti-fraud feature where you can register up to ten addresses. The Land Registry will notify you if there is any attempt to sell one of your properties.

9

Difficult Tenants and How to Deal with Them

The vast majority of tenants are good and there are only a few bad ones who could cost you a fortune. The good news is that provided you or your agent reference, ID and credit check your tenant properly (see Chapter 7) then it's very unlikely you'll end up with a bad one. However, I can't stress enough that it's essential to ask for and check references thoroughly and never let a tenant in until all checks have been done and both deposit and rent have been paid – in cash or by a cleared bank transfer. Even if you use a letting agent make sure you always double check the references yourself.

The sorts of things that can go wrong . . . and how to deal with them

Things that can go wrong with tenants boil down to one or more of the following:
- They don't look after the property properly.
- They annoy the neighbours.
- They don't pay the rent.
- They don't move out when they're supposed to.

If they don't look after the property or they annoy the neighbours but are paying the rent, then you just need to change their behaviour. In these cases, it's often that they are young people away from home for the first time. They simply need to be put on the right track!

For example, if they've painted a bedroom black, you need to explain that they must put it back to the original colour before the end of the tenancy. If they allowed an obvious water leak to continue without telling you about it, tell them they may be liable for the cost of repairing the additional and avoidable resultant damage. If they annoy neighbours with loud music, explain that other people have to get up for work in the morning! If they've broken something, tell them they'll be liable for the cost of repair.

If they are students with parent guarantors tell the guarantor about the problem. Parents usually come down heavily on wayward offspring if they're behaving unreasonably. Go through the tenancy agreement and House Guide again and remind your tenants of their responsibilities to look after the property.

Ask if there is anything you can do to help. If the garden is a mess, do they have tools to keep it in good order? If not, get some. If damp has built up, did you impress on them the importance of opening windows regularly? Could they do with another clothes line to dry things outside? If they just live in a mess then that's not your business, though you should make it clear that the property must be left clean and tidy at the end of the tenancy. If the rent doesn't show up in your account, it might be that they have just genuinely forgotten, in which case a polite phone call and written reminder will do the trick.

Sometimes you need to be flexible. Suppose you have someone who has rented from you for a year and he contacts you to say he has lost his job so the rent will be two weeks late. In this case, I'd agree to the delay but I'd get him to commit to the exact date the rent would be in my account and make it clear that I would not allow any further delays.

Where a person loses his job, he may be entitled to housing benefit/universal credit. However, it's usually paid a month in arrears and is always less than market rent. If you accept payment through the housing benefit/universal credit system, you are advised to do all you can to help the tenant with the claim. Offer to take the tenant to the housing-benefit office and help with his application, request to be kept informed by the housing-benefit office, monitor the claim progress carefully and if there are arrears apply to get the benefit paid to you directly. If you can't wait for the housing benefit to come through, you may need to give notice to leave. Whilst you can be sympathetic, you must remember this is a business. You don't have a duty to house people who can't afford to pay and the failings of the benefit system aren't your problem! Your tenants can always move somewhere smaller and cheaper.

If it's mid way through a fixed term contract, you're better off letting the tenants leave early as there is no point insisting they pay until the end. Point them towards a good source of other lettings and say that, if they go early and you don't incur actual losses, you'll still give them a good reference.

If a tenant's rent is late, he makes no effort to contact you and avoids you when you call, then you may have a bigger problem. He may have no intention of paying – either because he can't or he would rather spend the rent on other things. Again, you should give him an option to leave early but you may have to take legal action to evict him through the courts. What if a tenant doesn't move out when he is supposed to? If a tenant pays the rent on time but doesn't move out when he should, this will usually be due to a misunderstanding. Sometimes it happens that the property that he was moving to has fallen through and he needs to stay just a few more weeks. Try to be as flexible as circumstances allow!

An agreed surrender of the property can happen at any time in the course of a tenancy, even in a fixed term. This might happen if a tenant found he could no longer pay the rent and you were happy for him to leave, to avoid you suffering losses. It is prudent to get an agreed surrender in writing from the tenant, preferably witnessed by an independent person.

How to evict a tenant

In this section, unless stated otherwise, I shall cover the situation as far as Assured Shorthold Tenancies are concerned in England. For a guide to the different kinds of tenancy see Chapter 6.

When evicting tenants, you need to have a "ground" for eviction and to have served a proper notice on the tenant before legal proceedings are started.

There are seventeen different grounds for eviction and these can be either "mandatory" or "discretionary". Where the ground is mandatory, provided that your paperwork is OK, the judge must grant an order for possession. With discretionary grounds it's up to the judge. Most landlords therefore use a mandatory ground. (If only discretionary grounds are claimed, the tenant may be able to get legal aid to help his defence, and you could have a big legal bill to pay if you lose. Public funding may also be available for mandatory grounds if the tenant's lawyers can identify a defence e.g. the initial notice was invalid, etc.)

The main mandatory grounds are:

- Where the fixed term has come to an end (called the short-hold ground).
- Where there are serious rent arrears (sometimes called ground 8).
- Where the landlord previously occupied the property (sometimes called ground 1).

Let's look at each a bit further.

Where the fixed term has come to an end

Where the fixed term has come to an end and you have given at least two months' notice to quit in the form called a Section 21 notice, you will automatically get a possession order should it come to court. You cannot obtain possession under this ground during the first six months of the original tenancy.

A Section 21 notice can also be served if the tenancy is periodic, i.e. running from month to month. Where the tenancy is periodic or the notice is served after the expiry of the fixed-term tenancy then the notice must expire on the last day of the period of the tenant's tenancy – the problem of accurately identifying the date can be avoided by giving the tenant notice that possession is required "at the end of the period of your tenancy which will end next after the expiration of two months from the service upon you of this notice". For more detailed advice on how to issue a Section 21 notice at the end of the tenancy see Chapter 8.

There is a strong possibility that the Welsh Assembly will follow Scotland and remove from landlords the facility to use the no fault possession (Section 21 notice) – a very significant change to the private renting landscape.

Where there are serious rent arrears

Where there are rent arrears of at least two months' rent (in the case of a monthly paid tenancy) when you serve notice (a Section 8 notice), you will always be granted possession at the date of any subsequent court hearing. If the rent is payable weekly, quarterly or yearly this ground requires rent arrears of eight weeks, three months and six months respectively. (Note that as rents should be paid at the start of the "rental month", two months' arrears will actually exist as soon as the second months' rent payment is missed, i.e., effectively after just a month and a day.)

The Section 8 and Section 21 notices are easy to complete and can be obtained from legal stationers like Oyez (see Appendix 2), online or from landlords' associations. If you serve a Section 8 notice for serious rent arrears, you must give the tenant two weeks' notice that you want possession. If he doesn't leave, you then have to go to court to seek a judgment in your favour – so more delay!

If you use this ground, claim at the same time under the discretionary grounds for general rent arrears (ground 10) and persistent late payment (ground 11) so you can get a judgment for rent arrears owed too.

If the property was previously occupied by you

If you occupied the property before the tenancy started and wish to occupy it again (or if it was previously a holiday let), you need to give written notice to the tenant before the tenancy starts that possession may be granted on this ground. Then, when you need the property again, give the tenant a Section 8 notice at least two months before you want possession. If he doesn't go, you would then go to court and be automatically granted possession. Again, it's worth claiming under grounds 10 and 11 (if appropriate) too.

Severe Anti-Social Behaviour

A new mandatory ground came in in 2015 called Ground 7A and it can be used in cases of extreme anti-social behaviour in the locality of the property being rented.

How to serve a notice

The service of the correct form of notice in writing must be done before you can get a possession order. If you can't prove that you have done this, you will not usually obtain your possession order. The correct notice to be served will depend upon the ground you are using and whether or not the fixed term has expired.

Keep a record of the date and time and method of how the notice was served. Ideally it's best to deliver it through the tenant's letter box yourself, witnessed by an independent person (i.e. not related to you), so the tenant cannot say it got lost in the post. Alternatively, get a proof-of-posting certificate from the post office or use a Process Server. Don't use recorded delivery as the tenant can simply refuse to accept it.

Section 8 notices remain valid for one year so you can start court action to evict at any time until twelve months after the date the notice expires. If, for some reason, you don't start court action within this time you'd have to send a new notice. For Section 21 notices, the validity period is six months from the date of service, so if a landlord doesn't issue possession proceedings in that time, he will need to serve a fresh notice.

Possession proceedings

The court procedure for evicting a tenant who won't go or who owes you rent is relatively simple and you follow a straight-forward county court process. You'll need to fill in a few forms, which you can do yourself without a lawyer but it's imperative the forms are completed correctly. The staff at the court can help and will check your documents for you, though they can't offer legal advice.

Two types of court proceedings are available: "normal" and so called "accelerated" possession proceedings.

Accelerated possession

Accelerated possession can only be used if you're claiming on the shorthold ground – i.e. because the tenant hasn't moved out after the end of the fixed term and a valid Section 21 notice has been served and expired. You can't use accelerated possession to claim arrears of rent.

Evidence is presented in writing so you don't have to go to a court hearing. Once the court has issued papers to the tenant, he has fourteen days to reply after which an order for possession will be made and the tenant told to leave within fourteen days. Although you'll have to pay the fairly modest court fee upfront, the order will be made for the loser, in this case the tenant, to pay this cost.

The court judgment will be against anyone in your property at the time. So, if your tenant has decided to sublet your property to another unsuspecting third party (as my problem tenant once did) then that third party also has to go on that date. If the third party has been a victim of fraud by your tenant, that's tough; he still has to leave. The possession order gives a date for possession. If on that date the tenants or anyone else is still there, you'll have to fill in another form and send another fee to the court for them to appoint a bailiff. This will add on another three to five weeks depending on the local court. Are you beginning to see the importance of checking references carefully at the outset to reduce the chance of having to deal with all this nonsense?

Please note, even when you have a possession order, you can't make the tenants leave yourself. You need a court bailiff to do this. When the bailiff goes in, you need to be there to take possession formally. You'll also need a locksmith in attendance to change the locks.

Normal possession

"Normal proceedings" is the name for the court process used for all types of possession other than accelerated possession. Normal proceedings will involve a court hearing which you'll have to attend. You will normally get a money judgment for arrears due and an order that the tenant pays you until he leaves. If the tenant doesn't pay up, which he normally won't, you'll have to fill in some more papers at court and another small fee to "enforce the judgment".

However, before you embark on trying to get money out of a tenant through the courts, you need to decide if you're ever going to get it back anyway. If not, and if it's near to the end of the fixed term, you might be best waiting and going down the accelerated possession route to get him out.

There is much useful guidance to help with pursuing possession procedures in material published by the Court Service (see Appendix 2). You'll also get excellent advice if you join a landlords' association; their helplines are staffed by fellow landlords who have been there before and can give good free advice as well as offer sympathy.

Using a solicitor

If you feel you really must use a solicitor, use one experienced in landlord and tenant work and get a firm quotation upfront. Get him to agree to a fixed price for the eviction and not just working unspecified hours at an hourly rate.

How to make a claim for money owed

Occasionally, you might want to make a claim for money you are owed but without the need to claim possession. It might be that the tenant has already left the property owing money or that the condition of the vacated property will cost more to put right than the amount of deposit.

Where money claims are for small amounts, currently under £10,000 for most types of claims in England and Wales, they are dealt with by what is called the "small claims procedure" in the county court. Again, you simply get the forms from the court and complete them yourself following the easy-to-read leaflets. If you are claiming damages, obtain a couple of estimates for the cost of the work and submit any documentary proof (e.g. photographs) to back up your claim. You also need to provide a copy of the tenancy agreement and any rent books. Only if the claim is defended will you have to go to a hearing. There is a small court fee to pay.

Occasionally, landlords have to defend claims where the tenant is seeking return of his deposit, which perhaps was withheld due to damage. If so, you'll need evidence to back up why the deposit is being withheld. Such claims are normally handled through the tenancy deposit schemes dispute resolution procedures, but they can go to court too.

Most money claims aren't defended by tenants. If you win, the tenant will be told to pay you and the court fee too. You'll then have to hope the tenant actually pays up. Many don't, which means that you'll have to go to court again to get them to enforce the judgment. However, if the tenant has left you'll have to find him to get payment due to you and this may involve employing a tracing service/debt collector.

If the tenant has no money, it may be a long time before you are repaid (if at all). Sometimes the tenant will counterclaim, in which case it will probably be decided at a court hearing.

Despite the problem of actually getting your money back through the courts, I would urge all landlords who are owed money at least to sue in the small claims court and get a judgment against the tenant, even if you can't be bothered actually to enforce the judgment to try and collect the money owed. The court fee is small and it will at least make it more difficult for the tenant to get credit or to rip off another landlord, as it will show up under his name at that address as a County Court Judgment (CCJ). You can see it as your duty to other landlords and will be at least some form of retribution!

Some useful tips

If you're taking someone to court for non-payment, don't discuss the matter with him. Provided that you did all you could to get in contact with him beforehand, there is nothing

---

left to say. Don't listen to sob stories; remember it's not personal it's just business. Your only reason to stop a court order would be if he pays up all that is owed immediately, which means in cash or cleared bank transfer today. You should accept nothing less because once you stop a court order, that's it – you'd have to start the whole thing off again from the beginning.

Ensure that there are no grounds that the tenant can counter-claim on, such as repairs not being done. For some claims you can use the courts' online claims service.

In fact, the possibility that a tenant may have a CCJ is the main reason why it's important to perform a credit reference check against each tenant's name at his previous addresses. (See Chapter 7.) If he is reluctant to give you evidence of previous addresses and/or a reference from his last landlord, it might be that he is hiding a County Court Judgment. In these cases, you should be very wary of letting to him. You have been warned!

Many tenants will pay up at the threat of court action. They know the problems they'll have with a CCJ against their name. Some, unfortunately, are too far gone to care or are moving back abroad where the judgement may not affect them.

When you have a judgement in your favour you can ask the bailiff to sell any goods in the property to satisfy the judgement. Most will have little value though.

There is also a procedure that allows a landlord to serve notice on the tenant's last known and any alternative addresses, requesting they collect any goods or belongings left and advising they will be sold or disposed of if not collected. Recorded delivery letters must be used and a fair notice period would be 28 days. You are entitled to deduct storage and disposal costs.

Finally, you can apply to the court which granted possession for permission to transfer the matter to the High Court to use a High Court Enforcement Officer. Serious rent arrears and anti-social behaviour may qualify for this. Permission is not always granted and the cost is about four times the County Court Bailiff fee, but orders can usually be enforced in weeks not months, so this is often a sensible course of action to consider, especially where rents are high.

Evicting squatters and Rent Act tenants

In law there is no legal definition of a squatter, just a trespasser. If a trespasser is in occupation you can rely on self-help measures (i.e. not involving the court) to get the property back. Clearly, what you will have to do is somehow get into the property and change the locks and secure it. But although you can do it yourself – and you would be wise to have the police there when the squatters come back – what you cannot do is use violent entry if one of the squatters is actually in the property at the time and opposes you. Of course, clued-up squatters know this, so they change the locks and always make sure that someone is in the property – not hard for them as most won't have jobs anyway. They will no doubt quote the relevant law – which is Section 6 of the Criminal Law Act 1977 – and call the police and friendly lawyers to stop you from trying to evict them.

So to counter this you will need to use the special court process for trespassers. Usually these can be issued quickly – often in less than four weeks. For most people this will be the most attractive option and is usually easier than waiting in vain for them to go out before you can go in and change the locks. It is also much better from the point of view of your own physical safety.

The good thing about going to court is that the squatters will almost certainly go just before the bailiffs arrive, taking their stuff (or at least the stuff they want to take!) with them. If the property was your former home, or was somewhere that you were about to move into, then you have a right to get back in as a Protected Intending Occupier (PIO) under Section 7 of the 1977 Act. You will need to prove that it was your former home or that you have recently bought it and intended to move into it – which you can do by getting a written statement and having it witnessed by a solicitor. You then go to the police and request their assistance with gaining re-entry and effecting the removal of the squatters.

You can also use this approach if the squatters had got in while the property was empty between tenants and you have already got a tenancy agreement with new tenants.

A new law criminalising squatters under the criminal law was passed with much fanfare in 2012 but many lawyers are sceptical that it will continue to be effective in practice. I am too, as I am convinced any savvy squatter will find it easy to get around it. And I cannot see the police prioritising these offences either.

If your tenant lets the squatters in (and assuming you did not allow your tenant to sublet to them), it gets a bit more complicated. In this case it's probably best to be safe and pursue the normal track possession route through the courts to get possession. (In other words, you would still in effect have to assume that your tenant was in possession!) In this case, your possession order is in effect made "against the world" – meaning against anyone who happens to be in your property, irrespective of whether they are mentioned in court papers or not!

To avoid people just letting themselves into your property and becoming squatters, keep your property secured at all times, especially between tenancies and before the completion of the conveyancing.

Windows should not be left open because with no evidence of forced entry, squatters cannot be treated as burglars.

Dealing with squatters and also taking action against "Rent Act" tenants is complex so I would strongly advise you to seek legal advice from a solicitor experienced in dealing with these issues.

Whatever you do, don't harass!

By now you're probably thinking the law is a bit of an ass to allow a former tenant to stay in your property rent-free for three to five months while the legal process drags to its slow conclusion and you finally get your property back. Well, if it's any consolation, thousands of other landlords agree with you. That's why it's so important to be very careful with reference checks. Tight checks (and a deposit of at least five weeks) will put off bad tenants. They'll seek an easier sucker landlord or duff letting agent elsewhere.

Landlords who suffer from bad tenants experience a feeling of anger, rage and impotence that someone can effectively steal from them in this way. Not only is there the lost rent, but you'll incur about £800 court costs if it has to go all the way to a bailiff eviction, much more if you employ a solicitor. And a bad tenant is bad through and through. As well as spending time filling in court forms, you'll have to change locks, clean up after the tenant, deal with sending back all his other unpaid bills (get some "Gone Away" stickers made up!) and possibly angry neighbours too.

The anger is all the more acute when the tenant clearly has money but chooses to spend it on other things. In some cases, tenants even insist you do repairs, despite having not paid rent! They may also run illegal activities from the property. Faced with this kind of professional tenant conman, many landlords are tempted to get heavy, use threatening behaviour, try to evict the tenant themselves, enter the property without consent, change the locks or cut off the tenant's electricity.

However bad the tenants are, you must always follow the correct legal procedures, even though it takes time. If you resort to "self-help" measures as practised on *Corrie*, you have a very good chance of facing criminal or civil action. Naturally, any civil action from the tenant will probably be financed by legal aid so, if you lose, you'll have to pay not only damages but legal costs too. Landlords who don't know the law are sitting ducks for rapacious no-win no-fee solicitors. So, be careful.

What to do if a tenant dies

It's rare but it can happen that a tenant can die whilst renting your property. If you've referenced the tenant, you should be able to get in touch with his employer or his next of kin fairly quickly. If it's a joint tenancy, the other tenant(s) would remain responsible for the rent.

You can hold the tenant's estate liable to pay the rent until the end of any fixed term, although in my opinion this is a bit unethical. However, it would be reasonable to expect to recover any expenses you incur out of the rent that was due. This would include any costs incurred for storage and cleaning.

What to do if a tenant abandons the property

Sometimes a tenant can stop paying the rent and apparently abandon the property and this can be a real headache for a landlord, especially if the tenant has left some belongings there. If there is any real doubt about whether the tenant has gone or not, it might be best to go for an order through the courts, (Section 8 or 21 Notice followed by possession proceedings). If say a TV or computer has been left, there is a small chance they may not have abandoned the property. In this case the best route is to put a notice through the front door saying that unless the tenant contacts the landlord within 14 days, the landlord will take action to repossess. Get the delivery of the letter independently witnessed. Landlords should also enquire at other addresses – email and postal (including work addresses) in their records.

Then, if nothing has been heard after 14 days, affix an Abandonment Notice to the front door and change the locks. This notice should give the landlords' contact details, so the tenant can contact the landlord to recover anything they want but also state that unless the tenant makes contact, the landlord will assume the tenant has abandoned the property. If there are serious rent arrears and a Section 21 notice has not already been served, it will be better to go down the Section 8 route as it will be faster because if the tenant has gone, the claim will be undefended anyway. And also, you can make a money claim at the same time for any rent that is owing. Storage and disposal costs of abandoned goods can form part of that claim.

How to solve housing benefit/local housing allowance problems

If your tenant is on housing benefit, and if the rent is also paid direct to you, the council may ask you to repay it if, for example, the tenant was caught working and wasn't entitled to the benefit. If this happens, write to the council asking for the exact reason for the overpayment. Then ask for a review of the decision, putting all the blame on the tenant's failure to notify a change of circumstances. (Remind the authorities that it is not your job to keep badgering the tenant to tell you every time his circumstances alter!) If this fails to satisfy them, you are entitled to have an independent appeal tribunal decide the matter.

As a pre-emptive step, make regular quarterly or twice yearly visits to the property to ensure that any such tenant's circumstances haven't obviously changed, e.g. he has got a job or moved someone in. If they have changed, tell the housing-benefit officer. For advice on how to speed up payment of housing benefit see Chapter 7 and for more on fighting overpayment claims see Chapter 8.

Questions and answers

Q. My AST tenant is behind on his rent? What do I do?

A. It depends how long the arrears are. You have to wait until he is two months in arrears as the judge is then obliged to make a possession order. Then, send the tenant a Section 8 notice citing grounds 8, 10 and 11 and stating you require possession in fourteen days' time. If he doesn't go, go to the county court and ask for the appropriate forms to complete. A hearing will take place about four to eight weeks later which you must attend. Alternatively, if the fixed term has ended, use the Section 21/Accelerated Possession route, as it is usually faster.

Q. I have had complaints that my tenant is running a brothel from the house he rents from me.

A. Send the tenant a special Section 8 notice quoting ground 14 with just one day's notice. Proceedings can be commenced immediately the notice has been served. Ask at the county court for the appropriate forms to complete.

Q. I issued a Section 21 notice and the tenants have not left. Can I kick the tenants out?

A. No, the tenants don't have to leave until evicted by the bailiffs. Your next course of action would be to ask at the county court for the forms for Accelerated Possession. Then, if they don't go, use a court bailiff.

Q. My tenants owed me over two months' rent so I went to court and got a possession order giving the tenants fourteen days to leave. However, they are still there. What can be done?

A. Obtain from the court the appropriate form to instruct the bailiffs.

Q. I bought a house with some "Assured Tenants" in it. They don't have a written tenancy agreement. Will this be a problem?

A. If the tenants were there before 28 February 1997, they will be "assured" tenants unless you specified otherwise. You don't strictly need a written tenancy agreement to have a tenancy. However, if they are not assured shorthold tenants and there is a problem, you won't be able to use the Accelerated Possession procedure. In order to evict, you would need to prove a serious breach of the tenancy and attend a hearing.

Q. The annual gas inspection is due, but the tenant won't let my gas engineer in. What can I do?

A. Write to the tenant and explain that it's a legal requirement (under Section 11(6) of the Landlord and Tenant Act 1985) for the landlord to obtain access to the property at reasonable times of the day on twenty-four hours' written notice for the purpose of viewing the condition and state of repair. Keep copies of all correspondence and a diary log to record visits and phone calls, in case of dispute later.

Q. My tenant has left owing me money and I don't know where he has gone. I know he has money so I could make a claim against him. But how do I find him?

A. Consider employing the services of a tracing agent. Contact the Credit Services Association or the Association of British Investigators.

Q. Can I make a possession claim online?

A. Yes you can, using the Court Service online facility, and it can be faster.

Q. Are attachment of earnings orders to reclaim money owed of any use?

A. Yes, especially if some time has passed. A tracing agent can find out where a former tenant lives and works and with an attachment order a court can order an employer to make deductions from salary each month.

Q. Can a letting agent sign claim forms for possession proceedings?

A. No, only you as the litigant or your solicitor can do this. If your letting agent does it, it will be rejected. They can, however, issue notices to quit.

10

When it's Time to Sell

Professional landlords are always evaluating their property investments against other properties (and other investments) elsewhere. So should you. If the property has gone up in price but the rent has stayed the same, then it might be worth thinking about selling and investing instead in another area or type of property with better yields or better growth prospects.

When thinking about selling it's important not to forget to include all the legal costs as well as the cost of any agent involved in the sale. Also budget for any costs needed to smarten up the property for sale as well as any period when the property is empty and no rent is coming in. Include transaction costs for any new property in your evaluation. Finally don't forget about possible capital gains tax implications too. See Chapter 11 for more on this.

When it's time to sell, you'll want to get the best price as quickly as you can. Of course, a property that appeals to first-time buyers will always sell faster as there will not be a "chain" to delay things. This short chapter provides some help and advice about selling a property, whether it will appeal to first-time buyers or another sort of buyer.

What's the best time of year to sell?

If you can pick the ideal time of year to sell, the best time to get property on the market is late February. The market starts to hot up with lots of buyers through late February and into March, April and early summer. It tends to die off in high summer, picks up a bit in September and October and dies the death by November and December.

How to sell successfully through an estate agent

Selling through an agent is a tried and tested way of getting a sale. Estate agency fees for selling vary depending on the state of the market, the type of property and how hard they think it will be to sell it. Typically they vary from 0.5 to 2 per cent. Negotiate as hard as you can and get valuations from at least three agents. Also, consider using an "online" estate agent – however, you will have to do most of the work yourself, though this will not be a problem for most people.

Look for the following:

- The agent should have a good website and advertise on the major portals such as Rightmove and Zoopla.
- The agent should try to advertise in local papers as there are still some buyers who will only look at local press property ads.
- They should be able to provide evidence that they have sold lots of properties like yours. It's worth checking what kind of properties they sell, because some agents will be too up-market or down-market for your type of property. If they have an office, it should be in a busy, prominent and accessible location. If they have more than one office or franchise, they should actively sell your property from their other offices too. Test them out.
- Their "For Sale" boards should be attractive and eye-catching, the pictures they put online should show the property in the best light and the written copy should sell the benefits.
- They should be prepared to explain how their valuation was arrived at.
- They should have good staff. Not just the manager but all staff, including Saturday ones, should be professional, efficient and easy to get on with.

- They should be prepared to negotiate on their fee and should consider performance-related fees linked to the sale price achieved or speed of sale. There should be no additional fees for any special marketing they do for you. They should take care in producing accurate property details that present your property in the best light for potential buyers. (Floor plans and colour photos are plus points here!) They should open on Saturdays.
- They should give you feedback following viewings. They should properly "qualify" potential buyers. (If you are concerned that a buyer is "flaky", ask the agent for sight of the mortgage offer. If there is no sign of a surveyor/mortgage offer or legal progress within two weeks, insist that the property be remarketed. If it's a cash buyer, ask his bank to prove that he really has the funds.) The estate agent should keep you updated as the sale progresses.
- Ask who the buyer's proposed mortgage company is. Some lenders are known to be slow at processing transactions. Your mortgage broker will know which lenders are slow coaches.
- They should allow you to suggest improvements to their advertisement for the property.
- They should work quickly and efficiently.

Check your contract with the agent carefully. In particular:
- Don't sign a long contract with an agency, but give them at least three weeks so that they have a real chance of selling it. Sole agency is usually best unless you have a good reason to go for multiple agencies. If you must go multiple, avoid a cluster of For Sale boards outside as it looks desperate (and very untidy). If you change agents, make sure the old board is removed from the property.
- Don't accept "sole selling rights" as this would mean you would have to pay them, even if you eventually sold it privately to a friend.

- Don't accept a clause whereby you still pay them fees if you withdraw after they've found you a buyer.
- Keep the external photos up to date. (If the photos were taken in high summer and it's now midwinter, it may be obvious from the shots that it has been on the market a long time.)

Don't give the buyer or an agent too much information about your personal circumstances. If he knows that your tenants have gone and you are no longer getting income on it, he'll think you're more desperate to sell and will accept lower offers. Do listen to feedback from viewers and the agent. If it's not selling because something basic needs fixing, then fix it. If it's a mess, tidy up! If the furnishing/presentation/paint colour is awful, get it sorted. Read the section in Chapter 5 about decorating for tenants as the tips explained there apply equally well if you are selling a property too. If all else fails, consider reducing the price.

Selling at auction

Alternatives are selling at auction and selling it yourself. If you sell at auction, you will, at least, have serious buyers with the necessary deposit who can complete within a month. Auctions may be a particularly good idea if your property is run down or in any way unusual. Fees are roughly equivalent to sales through estate agents. However, you will probably get less than if you had sold through an agent. Try to have your property come up around a quarter of the way through the lots listed, when more bidders will be actively bidding.

Selling it yourself

Selling it yourself can work too, though it can be time-consuming. You may be able to advertise in the local press, on your company website or on public notice boards in supermarkets and libraries for free. Online estate agents such as Purple Bricks are also worth considering. Other landlords might be interested in buying it as a going concern with your tenants in place and this will save you from having a void period before you sell it. Advertising to sell with tenants in place will of course work best where the tenants keep the property clean and tidy.

Home Information Pack (HIP)

In Scotland, the whole conveyancing process is much easier and faster than in England and Wales. Here, the contract becomes legally binding much earlier. This stops people making multiple offers on different properties and minimises the risk of being gazumped. Also, since a formal moving date is set, it is much easier to co-ordinate sale and purchase, thereby removing some of the problems of being in a chain.

Think about the time of day that best shows off your property and do your viewings then. Allow potential buyers to walk into the room before you because, if you go first, you'll take up space and the property will seem smaller. If you market it yourself, keep an eye on your personal security: see Chapter 7 for more on this.

Never say that the property is empty at any time or leave it unsecured. If it's empty, give the impression it's occupied by setting internal lights on timer switches and think carefully before putting up a For Sale sign, especially if it's in a crime-ridden area – you could attract squatters or burglars.

Why it pays to be prepared

Don't give away too much information if you are desperate to sell. If an agent or potential buyer asks how long it's been on the market, answer vaguely; it's not on the list of questions that you must legally answer!

Negotiate coolly and be unemotional about it. Have all necessary information ready to answer positively any possible question – e.g. whether it's south-facing, when the windows were put in, the level of council tax, parks, transport, improvement plans for the area, good local school results, lack of crime, etc.

Speed up the sale process by having additional documents like insurance policies, warranties, guarantees, manuals and instructions available for the buyer. Use a good conveyancing firm to speed up the sale process – see also Chapter 4 for more on this.

11

Tax

Ah, you are probably thinking, here is a nasty, boring subject. Also, you might be worried it's a bit hard to understand. Well, the good news is that taxes on property are not too harsh. In fact, Her Majesty's Revenue and Customs (HMRC), or "The Revenue" as I will usually refer to them here, is reasonably kind to property investors. However, property tax is a teeny bit complicated, mainly because there are so many nooks and crannies within it, but understanding it means you can significantly reduce your tax bill.

I'll do my best to make it as simple and interesting as I can. However, you may need to read this chapter a bit more carefully and slowly than the other chapters in this book. So, relax, get a cup of coffee and take your time and you'll be well on the way to becoming an expert! Before we start I'll make it clear that for convenience I have used the term "couple" or "married couples" to refer to "legally married couples" and to same sex partners in civil partnerships – who have the same rights, of course.

First, two quick words of warning! The Revenue change their rules often so check their website for the latest position (see Appendix 2). Don't bother phoning them unless you want to waste a few hours waiting for them to answer.

Also, to find what is best for your own circumstances seek advice from an accountant, tax adviser or specialist. Check that whoever you employ is good at advising on property and get a fixed quote for what you want him to do.

Unfortunately, there are many different taxes that affect

landlords (and this chapter is focused mostly on advice for people who are primarily *landlords who are UK residents* rather than property developers or traders or investors from overseas).

Let's look at the various taxes.

When you buy a property, like anyone else you'll probably have to pay stamp duty land tax. When it's rented out, you may have to pay income tax. If you set up a company and use this as a vehicle to buy your properties, your company may have to pay corporation tax. When you sell, you may have to pay capital gains tax (CGT). Whenever you buy goods and services, you'll have to pay VAT. And when you die, your estate may have to pay inheritance tax (though at least when you die, CGT is not chargeable; a small blessing, I guess!).

Finally, if you have lots of properties and have to employ other people to manage them, then you'll have to pay employer's national insurance contributions.

However, the main taxes that matter significantly are capital gains tax and income tax so I'll focus mainly on these and touch on some of the others where relevant.

If you live abroad

If you are a non-UK resident, the situation may differ slightly from that explained here and you may also be taxed in your country of residence subject to any double taxation agreement the UK government has set up with the country where you live. Check with the Revenue and your local tax authority. For a brief analysis of the tax position on investment properties abroad, see Chapter 12.

Completing the tax return

Landlords should not register as self-employed but they should register for self-assessment within three months of starting letting their first property.

When you do your tax return, you have to write down your income and costs from property letting on the special supplementary pages for property. You can get these by downloading them from the Revenue's website. The Revenue should then send you the pages every year automatically.

Completing the supplementary pages is easy. Simply follow the help sheets and list separately the income and costs from normal property lettings and furnished holiday accommodation. You will need to tick the "rent a room" box if applicable. Overseas lettings go on the foreign pages and capital gains go on the capital gains pages. You need to keep all records, invoices, receipts and statements for at least six years.

All about income tax

For most landlords, costs and income have to be accounted for in the tax year when the bill is incurred or arose rather than when it's paid or received. For example, suppose you've got a bill for repairing some windows. If the work is done in February 2017, you can deduct costs for the tax year ending 5 April 2017 even if you don't actually get the invoice until May 2017. So, if you made a big profit from renting, but have big repairs, it's worth getting them done before the end of the tax year.

Where costs and income are ongoing and spread over different tax years, like rent or insurance, then they should be split over the different tax years. So, if your rent runs from the 25th to the 24th of each month and the old tax year ends on 5 April, only twelve days of the rent would go into the old tax year, the rest should be accounted for in the new tax year.

If your annual total rent is under £15,000, the Revenue may allow income and expenditure to be recognised when it is received or paid rather than when incurred, so there will be no need to split it in this way.

What costs can be deducted from rental income?

Costs that can be deducted are the following:
- Financing costs.
- Repairs and maintenance (but not property improvements).
- Replacement furnishings and fittings
- Heating and lighting (where paid by the landlord).
- Insurance.
- Letting agency fees. Advertising for tenants. Accountancy fees.
- Professional and legal fees in connection with the tenancies (but not legal costs related to the purchase or sale of property or planning applications).
- Ground rents and service charges. Cleaning and gardening costs.
- Bad debts.
- Capital allowances on office or other equipment used in the course of running a property business.
- Administrative expenses including wages (if you run as a company) and also the cost of phone calls, stationery, subsistence, travel and an appropriate proportion of household expenses if you run your property business from a room in your home. (HMRC has detailed rules on what household expenses are allowed and how the proportion is calculated.)

Financing costs can be deducted for income tax purposes, include the cost of interest on any loan taken out to purchase the let property, loan application/arrangement fees, valuation fees and broker fees. It all adds up! Make it all count as the financing costs are usually the biggest costs a landlord faces. If you remortgage a property (which can include your own home) and use the funds for another let property or to let the first property, you can deduct the interest cost of this loan as well. The key principle is that the money must be borrowed for and used for the *purposes of the property business,* (which could also include loans for repairs and improvements), with the amount borrowed being no more than the value of the property when it was first let plus any capital expenditure made on buying it, improving it and making it ready for letting.

And you can also deduct redemption fees and early exit fees on relevant mortgages and loans too!

The borrowed money doesn't have to be in the form of a mortgage. Interest on a personal loan to improve a property which is then let out can be deducted.

Keep records of all borrowings made and a record of what purpose they were used for too, in case of challenge by the Revenue.

Where you are paying off interest and capital on loans, you are only allowed to deduct the interest, not the capital. Mortgage and loan providers should give you an annual statement showing the breakdown of interest and capital repayments.

Unfortunately, and to the chagrin of landlords, over the coming years the tax relief for interest and finance costs will gradually be reduced to the basic rate of tax only. See the next section for more on this.

Take care only to book costs that are wholly to do with running the lettings business and where you actually pay the costs yourself. If you are in the habit of getting tenants to pay for small repairs and then reimbursing them, you would be on safer ground paying the supplier yourself. That way, you can more easily show that the cost is a legitimate expense.

Where a cost is split (say, half was for your own use and half for your rented property), you can apportion the cost and deduct the appropriate half as an expense.

Professional and legal fees can include membership fees of landlords' organisations, in addition to any money you pay to help with recovery of debts or any advice to do with renting such as the purchase of books like this one which keep you up to date with landlord issues.

When you buy a property with a mortgage or remortgage it, get the solicitor to split out their fee to show the cost of dealing with the lender and mortgage, as this is a deductible cost too. However, you can't deduct legal fees or your own surveyors' fees on the initial purchase or the sale of a property (unless you are trading as a property developer or trader) though you can claim them to reduce any capital gains tax liability when you later sell the property. So keep the relevant receipts safe for as long as you own the property!

When you replace furnishings or fittings for a let property the costs for this can be deducted as a valid expense for income tax purposes and it doesn't matter to what extent the property was furnished. The replacement of things like baths, wash basins, fitted kitchens and boilers which are non-moveable (or "integral") to the property should be classified as repairs and claimed too. (Note: The old "wear and tear allowance" of 10 per cent of net rents no longer applies any more.)

Bad debts can be deducted but a general provision for bad debts, e.g. 5 per cent of rents each year, isn't allowed. Administrative costs must be reasonable and capable of being supported by phone/mileage records or other receipts. However, there can't be what's called a "duality of purpose", so you can't claim for buying a newspaper because you could clearly read the rest of the newspaper not just the property section! Also, you can't charge your time as an expense.

If it's cheaper to replace something with a more modern alternative such as replacing single glazing with equivalent double gazing, rather than just repairing it, the fact that this is an improvement can be disregarded and the cost *still booked as a repair* and hence deducted from rental income. The same would apply if you replaced an old kitchen with a new one which had a broadly similar set and number of work tops and units of an equivalent quality.

Even where you make a loss, you *must* declare it, not least because it's the law but also because you can carry it forward and set it off against rental profits in the next or subsequent tax years. Indeed, UK rental losses can be carried forward as long as you have a rental business, but they disappear when your UK rental business ceases or when you die. However, you can't normally set it off against income from, say, your day job.

However, where your property business is primarily that of a property developer or where you are dealing and trading in property, trading losses can be set off against all other income and capital gains for the same tax year or the previous one.

Unmarried joint owners can share rental income in different proportions from their legal ownership. If you do this, make a written record of the arrangement to avoid challenge.

Property income counts as an "other" or "non-savings" part of a taxpayer's income. Interestingly, and annoyingly, people with total income over £100,000 lose £1 of personal allowance for every £2 by which their income is above £100,000 – which creates an "effective" income tax rate of 60 per cent on any income falling between £100,000 and £121,200. Ouch!

Individuals who face higher rates of tax could consider making pension or gift aid contributions to extend the basic rate band, especially for those years where income from property is likely to temporarily push them into a higher rate band.

Special and separate rates of income tax may apply in Scotland and Wales in future years. Watch out for this. They are bound to be higher!

All change for tax relief on interest

The Summer Budget of 2015, in defiance of all business accounting principles, introduced measures to restrict tax relief for interest and finance costs paid by residential landlords to basic rate only. This is being phased in over a four year period starting in 2017/18. So in the year 2017/18, 75 per cent will be deducted as normal and 25 per cent relieved at the basic rate. The percentage relieved at the basic rate will then rise to 50 per cent in 2018/19, then 75 per cent in 2019/20. From 2020/21 all interest and finance costs will be relieved at the basic rate.

For many people, this will turn pre-tax profit into post-tax losses and put many more into the higher tax rate bracket.

Holiday lets and people running their business under a property investment company structure are not affected, (at least for now!). Unsurprisingly, investing via a property company looks more attractive now than it did pre-2015. Add the other main attractions of running a property company – the fact that corporation tax is generally lower than the higher rate of income tax and indexation relief is available for capital gains – and suddenly there is real interest in company structures.

But people thinking of setting up a company should bear in mind that a company doesn't get Principle Private Residence or Private Letting relief or an annual exemption from capital gains. Also, there may be tax to pay when taking profits out of the company and you'll have the cost of setting up the company and making annual returns each year too.

In a company structure, salaries can be taken for real work by family members though if this takes them over the personal allowance it may be better to arrange to make them a shareholder and pay them a dividend.

Flexible commercial finance is available to companies, but deposits, interest rates and fees are all usually much higher than on buy-to-let mortgages.

For new landlords, whether it's worth setting up a property company will depend on your own circumstances. Unfortunately, for established landlords, moving from an individual basis of ownership to a company one would mean a SDLT and CGT bill for most, so transferring won't be a smart move for many people, (though some think that rolling over incorporation relief may get round the CGT problem).

It's complex! Landlords will now, more than ever, need to use all the tips and advice contained in this chapter to make sure they are legitimately cutting tax in other ways. Going further, the advice of an accountant with a very good understanding of investment property and company and personal taxation is recommended!

All about capital gains tax (CGT)

Most people know that they don't have to pay capital gains tax (CGT) on their main residence. However, every time you sell a property that has been rented out, you may have some capital gains tax to pay. The good news is that with a bit of planning and understanding you can significantly reduce, and often eliminate, any CGT liability. So, it's worth knowing how to do it! The bad news is that recent governments have removed all indexation reliefs and taper reliefs, creating a crazy system that allows them to tax gains that may be purely due to general inflation and to take no account of that inflationary effect or for the time period the asset has been held. The other bad news is that CGT can be complicated (though ironically a lot less so than it used to be when we had indexation and taper relief) and a little boring. I'll try to keep it simple!

All about capital allowances

Certain equipment used mainly for your letting business, such as office equipment, furniture and garden tools, etc., qualifies for a capital allowance though, if there is private use, the cost must be apportioned. You cannot get allowances for furniture and fittings in residential property but you could claim allowances for the office chair you used yourself. A writing

---

down allowance is available each year, calculated on a reducing balance basis.

Property developers generally have much greater scope to claim capital allowances than private landlords.

The Government is currently reviewing capital allowances and changes look likely for future tax years. Check with HMRC for the latest position.

What is a capital gain and how do you calculate it? Obviously, you need to calculate the amount of capital gain. This is the "net proceeds" from selling the property less the total costs of buying it.

The first thing is to work out the net proceeds. This is simply the price the property sold for, less all the costs associated with selling it, including advertising costs, estate agents' fees and legal costs. (If you sold the property to a relative other than your spouse or to anyone else at below market value, the Revenue will insist that the figure used is the *market* value of the property.)

The second thing is to work out the cost of the property. This is the basic cost when it was bought plus all the costs associated with buying it (this would include stamp duty land tax, legal fees, surveys you initiated, etc.) plus the cost of any enhancements made during the time it was owned (building a conservatory, adding a loft, making it habitable and fit for letting or the cost of extending or renewing a lease). If you inherited the property from a relation or friend the basic cost is the market value used for probate purposes at the time you acquired it.

You then simply deduct the total buying costs from the net proceeds at sale and you have the capital gain. So, if your costs of buying the property plus enhancements were £100,000 and your net proceeds after selling costs were £220,000, the gain is £120,000.

Principal private residence (PPR) and private letting relief (PLR) exemptions

If you ever lived in the property you get a whole raft of exemptions. Every unmarried person and each married couple/civil partnership is entitled to what is known as "Principal Private Residence" (PPR) relief on their only or main residence. What's less well-known is that this exemption can be extended to cover any period where the let property was your main residence *plus in each property, your last eighteen months of ownership.*

So, suppose you bought a property in year 0 and sold it after 5 years and 6 months and you lived in it from year 0 to year 4 as your main residence but rented it out thereafter. The first four years wouldn't count as it was your main residence but the last eighteen months wouldn't count either – i.e. there would be no CGT to pay.

Tip 1

If you've bought a property that requires substantial construction work before it can be occupied as your main residence, the PPR exemption can be extended for up to a year. You can also extend it if you're unable to occupy it due to a delay in selling your old property. In this situation, it's possible to have both properties covered by the PPR exemption.

Tip 2

If you have more than one main residence you should tell the Revenue which is your main one within two years of acquiring the second. Obviously, this must be your own private residence where you habitually live, not a property that you rent out. If you are lucky enough to have two homes that you can live in (neither of which is rented) and fail to nominate one, the Revenue may make a nomination for you based on the facts,

---

as they see them. If you live in both, choose the one that will have the biggest capital gain or perhaps the one you wish to sell first as your PPR. Once you have elected a property as a PPR, you can change it at any time by writing to the Revenue. However, it will only be effective for a period beginning less than two years before the date of your election to change.

Tip 3
If you take in one lodger in your own home, your PPR exemption will usually not be affected but if any part of your property is used exclusively for business purposes, the PPR exemption is not available for that part of the property for the period in question. However, if you have an office at home and sometimes use it for other home uses, then the PPR exemption may still be usable in full.

Now, suppose you rented out the property for longer – say, up to year seven. In this case, there may still be no CGT to pay. The reason is that another very useful and significant relief called "Private Letting Relief " (PLR), comes into play! This Private Letting relief is the lowest of:
1.   The amount of gain already exempted under PPR.
2.   The gain as a consequence of the letting period.
3.   £40,000.

Private Letting Relief applies to any property which qualifies for exemption under PPR and which has been let *at any time* during the ownership of the taxpayer. In our example we already know that the first four years that you lived in the property as your main residence are exempt plus another eighteen months out of the seven – i.e. 5.5 years / 7 years (78.6 per cent) of the gain is exempt. This leaves only 1.5 years / 7 years (21.4 per cent) chargeable.

If the gain was £90,000, the amount that is chargeable would be 0.214 x £90,000 = £19,260

The amount exempted under PPR would be 0.786 x £90,000 = £70,740.

As the lowest figure of £19,260, £70,740 and £40,000, is £19,260, this amount is also automatically exempted as a result of PLR.

The chargeable gain before PLR of £19,260 less PLR of £19,260 leaves zero gain! As you can see, the Revenue is exceedingly generous to landlords who let out their *former* homes.

It's also good to know that the £40,000 Private Letting Relief applies to every property which has ever been your only or main residence at any time during your ownership – so even if you sell two previous homes during one tax year, you could still get up to £40,000 of PLR on each property! And joint owners each get £40,000 of PLR.

Those familiar with UK politics will know that some of our MPs were effectively "flipping" between properties on a grand scale. Following the outcry over this, it is thought by some that some of the PLR exemptions and the PPR extension of eighteen months (it used to be three years!) could be cut in a future budget.

However, for now, the combination of PPR and PLR still remains a very powerful way to cut tax bills for people with a former home they now wish to dispose of and for anyone planning a future of tax-free capital growth.

Because PPR works by giving you exemption for the period you lived in the property *plus, in each property, your last eighteen months of ownership,* this exemption works best if you move into the property as your main residence straight after purchase.

To be a main residence and to get PPR, you must *genuinely* live in the property and in borderline cases HMRC will look at the address on your tax return and where your utility bills and bank statements go among a number of other factors to establish the "true quality" of your occupation.

Annual exemption

Each taxpayer gets an annual exemption from CGT. In the year 2016–2017 it was £11,100 and the amount usually goes up each year. So, if you had a potential capital gain of £13,000, you'll have to pay tax on £1,900.

You can offset any capital losses, including losses from previous years, against any chargeable gains. So, if you make a good gain on a property but lost a load on shares you sold, then you can offset the losses of one against the other.

With a bit of luck, and if you've used all the relief and exemptions available to you, you may have found you have no capital gains tax liability at all! Give yourself a pat on the back! If you do have some, you'll need to work out how much tax you actually have to pay. This is easy.

Tip 4

If you own a property with your spouse, any income or capital gain will be split between both of you in whatever proportion you own it and each person can apply his own CGT annual exemption to his part of the gain. Where husband and wife pay tax at different rates, it's worth planning to share ownership of the property in a way that minimises total tax liability. For jointly held properties, each person will also have a £40,000 limit for Private Letting Relief. Even if you already own it, it's possible to follow a simple legal process to have it transferred into joint or multi ownership but it's best to do this before the property is put on the market for sale. There are no CGT consequences in transferring ownership between husband and wife but there may be CGT to pay if you transfer ownership to other family members or non-relatives. Non-married people who own as tenants in common can split the property profits for tax purposes in whatever way they choose.

Tip 5

If you buy a new residence whilst keeping the old one for letting, you could nominate the new one as the PPR within two years of buying it, but gain the PPR exemption on the old one too for the last eighteen months before you sell it (provided that you had lived in it). In this way you can gain exemptions on two residences at once for up to eighteen months. However, if you nominate a property as your PPR, you must have genuinely lived there for at least part of the time. You should be able to prove this from your financial statements and from all the information held on you by local government and the Revenue.

Tip 6

As part of the PPR exemption, the Revenue provides concessions when you can't live in your house because of work requirements and if your job takes you overseas.

The CGT rate payable by landlords is either 18 per cent for basic rate taxpayers or 28 per cent for higher rate taxpayers, though an entrepreneurs' rate of 10 per cent may be available for landlords with furnished holiday letting properties.

The higher rate of 28 per cent applies to capital gains made by people whose taxable income for the year (after deducting their personal allowance and any other available deductions) was above the income tax higher rate threshold for that year.

Basic rate taxpayers will pay CGT at 18 per cent on the first part of any gains until their basic rate band is exhausted. After that point they will be taxed at 28 per cent.

The total amount of CGT must be paid by 31 January following the end of the tax year in question along with the rest of your tax.

Tax on UK and European Economic Area (EEA) Holiday Lets

To qualify as a "holiday" let, the property must be furnished to a degree necessary for normal occupation, be in the European Economic Area (EEA), available to let to the public for at least 210 days a year, actually be let for at least 105 days a year and not in the same occupation for more than 31 consecutive days any time in at least seven months out of the same 12 month period. Lettings must be at market rents, not peppercorn rents to friends as the letting must be commercial, i.e. with a view to making profits. The property does not need to be in a "holiday" area but must be let to tourists or holidaymakers.

Landlords with furnished holiday lets enjoy some special tax advantages including being able to claim rollover relief on replacement of business assets and capital allowances on the costs of fixtures and fittings.

Losses from furnished holiday letting businesses can be carried forward and set off against future profits from the *same* business (but be aware that a UK holiday let business must be kept separate from a holiday let business elsewhere in the EEA). UK holiday lets require separate accounts to be kept. The lower entrepreneurs' rate should also be available for these lets if the whole business is sold.

How lets in the EEA will be taxed in the future will, of course, depend on the precise nature of any deal done as part of the UK's exit from the European Union.

Tip 7
CGT liability can be deferred or your income tax liability reduced if you reinvest your capital gain in an Enterprise Investment Scheme or a Seed Enterprise Investment Scheme.

However, be wary as these are at the risky end of company investment and you could lose the lot! Check the trust or scheme out carefully.

Tip 8

Be honest with the Revenue. Fraud is illegal and there are high penalties for evaders. The Revenue has a powerful database of who owns what and they do a large number of investigations each year. Some will be random and some will be triggered by information they hold directly, obtained from other sources or from information that you yourself have given.

Tip 9

Keep all your receipts, bank records, statements as well as contracts for sale and purchase for at least six years and for as long as you own the property if they count as a deductible cost against capital gains. You'll need these if you are subject to a Revenue investigation.

Tax on other foreign holiday lets outside the EEA

Where a property is let abroad and outside the EEA, none of the additional relief allowed on UK or EEA holiday lets is allowed. However, travelling expenses are allowed if incurred wholly and exclusively for the purposes of the overseas let. Some UK investors have bought abroad using offshore companies to avoid local land taxes but this may have complex implications. If you are thinking of doing this, it's worth discussing your plans with an accountant who is an expert in this area.

The rent a room scheme

If you rent out a room in your home, you won't have to pay any income tax if the rent is below a certain amount. At present this is £7,500 per annum.

Canny investors know that if they buy a property for their son to live in whilst at university and the property is put in his name, he can then later rent out a room and get the rent a room relief as well as benefit from the principal private residence exemption and from his own personal income tax and capital gains tax allowances. Of course, the property must be his and not all parents feel happy with being quite so generous.

All about stamp duty land tax

Stamp duty on home purchases in England and Wales applies as follows: no tax up to £125,000. Between £125,000 and £250,000 the rate is 2 per cent. Between £250,000 and £925,000 the rate is 5 per cent. Between £925,000 and £1.5 million it is 10 per cent. Above £1.5m it is 12 per cent. These "progressive" rates removed the old "slab system" that prevailed before December 2014.

In Scotland, the equivalent Land and Building Transaction tax have the following rates: no tax up to £145,000. Between £145,000 and £250,000 it is 2 per cent. Between £250,000 and £325,000 it is 5 per cent. Between £325,000 and £750,000 it is 10 per cent. Over £750,000 it is 12 per cent.

If you buy a single property consisting of a number of self-contained flats, the Revenue should count each flat as a separate dwelling, allowing you to claim the average relief and potentially a lower stamp duty rate.

Buyers of "additional rental properties" which, of course, includes most landlords, have to pay an additional three percentage points above the current rates of Stamp Duty Land Tax for all properties where the value is over £40,000.

Tip 10

If you move abroad and become non-resident in the UK and non UK ordinarily resident, and then sell your investment properties, all the gain should be CGT free if you remain non-resident for five full tax years. If you've been letting your own home while working temporarily abroad, your PPR relief is still available for the time you are away.

Tip 11

If you are purely buying and developing property as a business no CGT applies at all, but there will be income tax to pay on any profits you make in selling your property. You will also be liable for National Insurance.

Tip 12

Moveable fittings escape stamp duty land tax but HMRC will carefully scrutinise transactions where the cost of moveable fittings bought with the property appears excessive, especially those purchases close to the SDLT tax bands.

Tip 13

It can be a really smart move from a tax point of view to let out your existing home to fund the purchase of a new property for you to live in because (1) both properties will attract PPR (because of the eighteen month rule) thus meriting a saving on potential capital gains and (2) equity in the former home can be released via a mortgage loan and used for any purpose whilst the interest on the loan (up to the value of the property when first rented out) can be deducted from rental income thus saving income tax. You may even be able to avoid the need to take out any mortgage at all on your new home.

Tip 14

If you expect to be in a higher tax bracket next tax year and there is a profit on your property letting business, consider delaying maintenance expenditure until the next tax year if it helps reduce income tax liability. Conversely, reduce CGT liability by selling in a tax year when taxable income will put you in the lower CGT band. Unused CGT allowances for any tax year are lost if not used.

Tip 15
Keep your tax liability under regular review and remember that just because most loans used for the purposes of letting property are tax deductible, this is not a good reason to over borrow and risk bankruptcy. Also, don't remortgage constantly and end up giving yourself a huge future capital gains tax liability when you come to sell that you cannot afford to pay.

Tip 16
Landlords who are only letting property should not register as self-employed. Self employment attracts National Insurance but rental income doesn't.

Tip 17
This chapter is only a rough guide to a very complex subject and focussed mostly on landlords rather than property developers. HMRC publishes detailed guidance and notes on what is allowed and what isn't but there are still grey areas. Check their guides and if in doubt seek the advice of an experienced advisor in this area.

Tip 18
The tax treatment for property developers and traders is very different from "property investment" (which is what most buy to let investors approximate too) and it is usually, though not always, less kind. HMRC may look closely at what your starting and later intentions were (i.e. whether to be a landlord

or a developer) in deciding how you should be treated for tax. So, for this reason, it can be a good idea to keep documents for as long as possible to help prove what your intentions were. Things that are likely to make the Revenue think you are a developer/ trader rather than a landlord are a high frequency of transactions in a short time period, short term financing arrangements, short ownership periods, not letting properties out for long and not living in them for reasonable periods.

"SIPPS", Syndicates and "REITS"

If you venture to property shows, you may hear about investing in property syndicates. These special purpose vehicles can come in a variety of guises including unit trusts, both onshore and offshore and joint venture agreements. Some can be structured to benefit from the tax treatment within Enterprise Investment Schemes. Then there are Self Invested Personal Pension Schemes (or SIPPS) which can invest in Real Estate Investment Trusts (REITS), property unit trusts, hotel rooms, student halls of residence and residential property syndicates of eleven or more people.

If you put your money in a SIPP you can qualify for tax breaks within the pension fund rules. The syndicate must be worth at least one million pounds and it has to have at least eleven investors because you are not allowed to have over 10 per cent of the holding. This spreads the risk over a number of properties. All eleven investors must be "unconnected" and you have to think carefully about what happens when any individual wants to sell.

Where hotel rooms or other holiday accommodation is bought by the syndicate, any personal use of the property by a member of the scheme is not allowed – and the Revenue has heavy penalties if you break this rule. Annual management fees are not cheap and often multi layered, so if you are thinking of investing in one of these types of schemes, you are strongly advised to take qualified independent legal and tax advice. Proceed with extreme caution.

Finally, there are Real Estate Investment Trusts (REITS). These can invest in residential property and aim to produce a more "liquid market" with investors able to buy and sell shares in the REITS rather than buying or selling properties themselves. However, investors are taxed on the income they receive from the REIT and on gains made when selling their investment in the REIT.

12

Jet to Let: Diversifying Your Property Portfolio

There are many ways to diversify in property. Many people start off with a basic longer-term let property. However, there are of course other opportunities; in holiday and short term "Airbnb" type lets both in the UK and abroad as well as in lets to longer-term tenants in overseas markets. As getting round the world has become quicker and the world more integrated, buying overseas where property is often cheaper is becoming increasingly attractive to UK investors, a phenomenon which is now wittily called "jet to let".

By investing in different types of letting markets you can spread your risk too. However, these alternatives usually involve more work and higher costs and always come with added risks. This chapter looks at these alternatives in detail.

UK and EEA holiday lets

Buying a holiday let has become increasingly attractive in recent years. You don't usually need to worry about people not leaving when they should and you don't need a formal tenancy agreement either (though it's sensible to keep documentation to prove that it was your intention that the let was just for a holiday).

Also attractive is the fact that property prices in the more desirable UK coastal resorts have tended to do very well in recent years, helped in part by people buying second homes for their own use as well as for holiday lets and by generally warmer weather. I expect these trends to continue.

However, running costs and marketing expenses are higher than in longer-term lets. You'll have more periods when the property is empty but you will still have to pay insurance (which will be higher because the property is empty), utilities and council tax. You'll also need to have good security in place to deter would-be squatters and burglars and there will be marketing costs and the cost of cleaning between lets to consider too. There may be restrictions on short term lets imposed by a local authority or within the terms and conditions of a lease or your mortgage. Finally, if you don't use an agency, you will need a local person who can be relied upon to maintain things promptly and deal with emergencies. And don't forget, older cottages, often favoured by holidaymakers, tend to have high upkeep costs.

Getting finance may be harder too. Few lenders offer or allow mortgages on holiday lets so you may have to fall back on a commercial loan. The deposit may be higher too. However, if you can get it right you can do very well on holiday lets. The key is to buy in an area where you can let it out for most of the year, preferably for periods of a few weeks at a time. As with any other letting proposition, look for areas where demand is high and supply of other properties is low and where changes are coming to make the area more attractive. For example, if a new leisure complex is planned or the roads are being improved this should bring more holidaymakers into the area, so demand can be expected to rise.

Investing in property abroad

In the last few years there has been a massive increase in interest in buying property abroad. Right now it seems you can hardly turn on your television without another programme showing happy people jumping on planes to buy overseas. The trend is driven in part by rising British property prices. Property abroad is usually cheaper, often considerably so. The opening up of new destinations by budget airlines and cheaper air fares has also helped things along.

Buying abroad can work really well but there are things you need to be aware of. For a start, the legal systems in other countries will be very different. In most places you will be committed at an earlier stage than would be the case at home. It can be difficult just establishing a good legal title to the property and even confirming that the person you are buying from really does own it in the first place! Checking rights of way over land can be more complex and there may be differences in the way that planning permission operates too. Of course, properties can run the full gamut from ready to move into up to major restoration projects. If you are doing up a property, it will be more difficult if language is a barrier and if you are not on site to control things. In some areas, properties must be renovated or built using local materials and techniques, thereby raising costs. Some countries have imposed outright bans on short-term holiday lets in some areas especially in cities popular with tourists. Even with brand-new properties there may be unusual residents' regulations to comply with. Also, local property taxes, legal fees, land registry and mortgage costs all tend to be higher outside the UK.

The advice contained in all the earlier chapters of this book applies equally well to buying abroad. Just as in the UK, you need to do your own research and keep an open but slightly sceptical mind. Read all you can about an area and speak to as many people as possible, especially people who can be relied upon to give you impartial advice. Even more than in the UK you need to employ good lawyers, architects, surveyors and builders, so you must spend some time checking their credentials to ensure you've got the best people working with you. Also, talk to people who have done it before and find out what problems they found and how they overcame them.

There are many reasons for buying abroad. You can buy to live in it permanently as your main home, as a holiday home for your own occasional use or with the intention to let it out either as holiday accommodation or for longer-term lettings. In fact, people often buy for a mix of all these reasons. For example, someone may buy a second home that they will ultimately retire to but will in the meantime use as a means of generating income from holiday or longer-term lets as well as for the odd holiday for themselves.

It's OK to have a mix of reasons for buying, but, if you do, it's important to set out what your objectives are, how much you wish to spend, how much you think the property will bring in rent (if that's your intention) and what the costs will be. If you are thinking of ultimately retiring there at a later date, think about how suitable the property will be when you're that much older. Also, check with the Department for Work and Pensions if you will be able to access your British pension overseas. The state of local healthcare and whether you qualify for free or reduced cost care is also worth looking into. The Department of Health may be able to advise on what you are entitled to.

Of course, if you are buying purely as an investment then your own personal preferences won't count at all. In many ways this is easier than trying to balance investment with buying for your own use because you can focus on things like demand, occupancy, advertising, agent fees and rent, unencumbered by any other personal objectives.

Holiday homes

A good holiday home must be easily marketable and accessible to prospective holidaymakers. Outside the main tourist areas there may be a more authentic feel, but if it's too far from the nearest airport, up a long bumpy road and miles from the nearest shop, people will be put off. The main seaside tourist areas will invariably be more expensive and will get good rents but may be difficult to let outside the summer season. Properties in major cities may be attractive for year-round holiday lettings and for the longer-term tenant market. It all depends on local demand and supply so you need to do your research on each specific location following the guidelines set out in Chapter 3.

If your property is served by a single local airport and a single budget airline there is a risk that they could stop flying to that destination. If your lettings market is wider and people can reach your accommodation by other means your risk will be less.

Someone reliable must be on hand to deal with changeovers, cleaning, maintenance and any on-the-spot problems.

Don't forget to check out local holiday letting rules and regulations. Some places will require you to register to carry out a tourist rental, require you to collect a tourist tax or give passport details of visitors to the police. Do occasional checks to ensure the local agency is not "skimming" by letting out and not telling you or failing to pass on the money.

Co-Ownership, Time-Shares and Leaseback

There are many variations on holiday-home ownership. You could buy with other owners so that each of you has a share of the property or you could sell time-shares to others on a commercial basis. This would, of course, involve a special form of legal contract and consideration of what would happen if someone wanted to pull out or sell his share. Another alternative, popular in France, is the "leaseback" scheme in which you buy the property then lease it back to a developer or manager who guarantees a fixed income and/or an agreed number of weeks for your own use. Again, have the small print carefully checked.

Longer-term tenants

In the longer-term tenant market you'll need to check out the local tenancy laws and regulations carefully. These will differ hugely from the UK and you need to find out the procedure in whatever country you invest in.

You may find that longer-term tenants will have more protection than they do at home so it may well prove much harder to evict a bad tenant. Also, rent controls may exist which may set a limit on what you can charge and tenant demand and overall rent may be much lower.

Things you need to know – some other considerations

Whether investing for the holiday market or for longer-term tenants the logistics of the arrangement will be more difficult if you are not based locally. You therefore need to budget for the costs of marketing the property, maintaining and insuring it, paying agency and service charges, cleaning it and dealing with any local issues as they come up. Obviously it's worth checking even before you buy that you'll be allowed to let it out in the first place, what safety measures you have to comply with and how to account for your income locally.

For property buying, selling and renting you need a good local lawyer. You can find lists of British solicitors with offices outside the UK from the Law Society. In many European countries you'll also have to deal with a public notary. In Europe, the notary is usually a civil servant (not a lawyer) whose job it is to check the title deeds, draw up contracts and make a record of the sale. However, it is not part of a notary's job to advise you, so you'll still need to appoint a lawyer. For lawyers and notaries, make sure you take time to check their credentials with their local body.

Although you'll probably want to employ a local architect and surveyor, the Royal Institute of British Architects and the Royal Institution of Chartered Surveyors are worth talking to first. Both have databases of practitioners abroad. If you can, get a local person so as not to offend local sensibilities.

Getting finance

Some UK banks are lending on foreign properties, sometimes in foreign currency, and banks in Central and Eastern Europe too are increasingly waking up to buy-to-let. Also, mortgage brokers can usually be relied upon to source finance. Borrowing locally from a foreign bank may involve paying higher fees and the lenders in more remote markets may only look at your net income to assess whether you can afford it rather than taking any note of rent-to-income multiples. Loan to Value levels will generally be much lower than in the UK.

Fixing the exchange rate

When you buy abroad and borrow in the local currency or a third-party currency you'll always be at the mercy of exchange rates. Adverse exchange rates movements can massively increase the sterling cost of mortgages taken in a foreign currency, as British buyers of Cypriot property (who often financed in Swiss Francs) found out the hard way. If you are buying a property off-plan or which must be paid for in stages, you could fix the rate by buying the currency now. If you don't have the money, you could buy a forward contract with a bank. Of course, the whole time you own the property, changes in relative exchange rates will affect the value of your investment when you come to sell.

Getting insurance

Some British insurance brokers offer good insurance policies from well-known insurers for places like Spain, Portugal and France. This avoids the complications of a policy written in a foreign language. Check that you are covered for the period between exchange and completion, for unoccupied periods and for the cost of emergency travel and temporary accommodation following a big claim.

Unfortunately, for many countries, cover for a foreign property is only considered if your UK home is insured with the same insurance company. For more out-of-the-way countries, you may have to seek out an insurer in the country concerned. Policies may be quite different though. For example, subsidence and flooding cover are not covered at all in some countries and public liability cover may not extend to holidaymakers or tenants!

Watch out for "community insurance" and residents' schemes too, as these are often limited in what they cover. Finally, if you end up in dispute with a local insurer you'll have the expense and hassle of having to fight it out in a foreign court.

Investigate the risk of hurricanes, tornadoes, earthquakes, floods, landslides and even tsunamis in the locality and try to get cover for these risks. Local insurers may be more prepared than UK ones to consider these risks as they'll have more data. If the property is out of action for a long time following, say, a hurricane, it will not be generating revenue. Can you finance this yourself or can you insure against this risk? If the property is unoccupied for a long time, you may be able to reduce the extra premiums by paying someone locally to look after it on a regular basis.

Where to buy and what to buy abroad

The most popular countries for Brits to invest in have long been Spain, France and Portugal. These countries are also close to the UK and relatively easy to get to. Prices have been moving down for a few years in most areas and some observers think the massive oversupply of new buildings in some parts will continue to drive down rents and house prices in the medium term. But even these established markets are not without other risks. For example, in recent years many British buyers were running scared of Valencia's so called "land grab" law in which local developers could compulsorily purchase land from existing owners because cowboy developers had reclassified land without first asking the landowner's permission.

Other places that seem to be attracting the interest of British investors are Eastern Europe and Cyprus as well as more far-flung places like the USA, South Africa and Dubai. Whether these areas can produce a decent return to investors will depend, as ever, upon the type of property, the area it's in, the market for tenants and/or tourists, exchange rates and whether the local market becomes oversupplied.

Other countries that are attracting speculative investments are Croatia, Turkey, Northern Cyprus, Morocco, Brazil and Cape Verde. All these new markets are at risk from oversupply because the temptation for local governments and landowners to sell huge tracts of land to build holiday homes to wealthy people from Western Europe and North America is very great indeed.

If you read the previous chapters, you'll know there are good places and less good places to buy within any country or city. Do your research and look out for areas that are changing for the better. Look out for regeneration initiatives and change that will drive an area forward.

Check what will happen near to your preferred location. If you bought for that sea view, check that the land in front of you can't be built on and find out about planning restrictions generally. Some councils have tight planning laws meaning that the area will not be swamped with hundreds of me-too or high-rise developments while others have an anything goes approach.

If a big new airport or connecting road is being built, that's good news if you are in the holiday letting business, provided that you aren't under the flight path or too close to the motorway!

All about taxes on foreign property

Wherever you invest there is one constant: tax! As long as you are a UK resident, you are liable to UK income taxes on rental profits from properties abroad as well as capital gains tax on the money you make when you sell. The only exceptions are for people who come from another country (called "non-domiciled").

It's beyond the scope of this book to look at domicile as it's quite a complex area (more permanent than residence but different from nationality!). However, it's worth saying that a non-domiciled taxpayer is only taxed on profits or capital gains from foreign investments if and when they bring money back to the UK. This means that if you are a married couple where one of you is non-domiciled, you could make foreign investments in the name of the non-domiciled person and free from UK tax as long as no funds are remitted to the UK.

"Non-doms" in the UK have to pay tax on all income and gains wherever they arose or instead pay a charge. Check with a tax expert first for the latest position.

If you are UK-domiciled but have emigrated you'll be exempt from UK tax on foreign property (though you will still be taxed on income from any UK property you own). So if you want to invest abroad for the long term and also emigrate at some point, you may be better off investing overseas. Once you have emigrated you will be exempt from UK capital gains tax wherever the properties are abroad. However, you must stay away for at least five whole UK tax years.

Many people set up companies as a vehicle to invest in property abroad especially if they are going to invest for the long term. In some countries too, investing through a local company may be the only way that you, as a foreigner, can actually buy property. If you don't intend to emigrate, it may be a good thing to use a UK company as a vehicle to invest, but it will depend on your own circumstances and how long you want to invest for, so speak to tax advisers in both countries.

If you intend to emigrate (or you are non-UK domiciled) you'll want to avoid using a UK company for foreign investments. Indeed many British investors have bought abroad using companies which are based offshore to avoid local land taxes. However, this may have complex implications. If you are thinking of doing this, it's worth discussing your plans with an accountant who is an expert in this area. If you do set up an off-shore company it must be set up and run properly. It's not cheap either, and income and gains while the controlling shareholder is still a UK resident will be taxable in the UK.

As well as UK taxes you'll also need to consider local taxes which are often higher than in the UK. Most countries will tax foreign property owners on their income and capital gains. Our Government does allow some relief through something called "double tax relief" agreements with some countries which is intended to ensure you are not taxed twice, but you are still usually taxed at the higher of the two countries' rates of tax! So, if the foreign tax exceeds your UK liability, your double tax relief is limited to the amount of your UK tax bill, thus reducing it to nil. In other words, our Government won't compensate you for the higher tax burdens you face in a foreign land!

When investing abroad think beyond income, capital gains and stamp duty land tax types of taxes. Other countries often have many other weird and strange forms of tax that we don't have. Double tax relief will not apply for these taxes because there is no UK equivalent and even foreign land taxes, the equivalent of stamp duty land tax, cannot be set off against any UK tax. There are extra complications when you die because inheritance rights and inheritance tax overseas is applied very differently and getting probate can be tortuous. So, find out about every other type of tax or fee that can be applied to your type of investment *before* you invest.

Finally, it's worth noting that schemes to avoid tax could be based on loopholes that are already closed by the local government or are about to be. If you cheat the local government of their tax, you could face consequences. For example, in some countries, it's common for people to pay local land taxes on the basis of the price declared in the deed of sale and not what was actually paid. If you are found out there could be heavy penalties including compulsory state purchase of the property plus big fines. As in life, there's really no such thing as a free lunch!

Other opportunities

If you are an active investor, lots of other opportunities may come your way. Some of these may give you an element of diversification. For example, people may ask you to look after their properties for them – in effect, acting as a managing letting agent. Other people may come to you with schemes to invest in. Two new ones doing the rounds in the last few years have been units in large managed student halls of residence and apartments in hotels – both having the attraction of potentially being "SIPPable". For more on this see Chapter 11. Look at every opportunity as just that, an opportunity! Appraise each one dispassionately and plan for the future. Good luck and successful investing!

Appendix 1

A Sample Assured Shorthold Tenancy Agreement

Where necessary, and by way of explanation, I have included in *italics* in square brackets my own comments.

Assured Shorthold Tenancy Agreement

This agreement is made **INSERT DATE** between **INSERT LANDLORD'S NAME**, who is referred to here as "the landlord", and **INSERT TENANT'S NAME(S)**, who is referred to here as "the tenant", who, if more than one, are each jointly, individually and severally liable under this agreement.

("Jointly and severally" means that if the tenant shares the cost of the tenancy with another tenant, then if one does not pay his share, the landlord will seek the balance of the rent owing in full from either tenant.)

By this agreement the landlord lets and the tenant takes all of those rooms of the property known as **INSERT NAME AND FULL ADDRESS OF PROPERTY** hereafter referred to as "the property" together with the fixtures, fittings, furniture and effects therein (as set out in the Inventory) for a term of XXX months, starting at **INSERT START DATE** and ending at Noon on **INSERT END DATE**.

[Initial tenancy fixed terms should be less than twelve months – see Chapter 6. If it exceeds three years, it would need to be witnessed as a deed. And it should never, under any circumstances, exceed seven years.]

The tenant agrees that if the property is permanently vacated by the tenant at the tenant's own request before the

---

last day of the term, the tenant shall remain liable to pay to the landlord the full unpaid balance of the rent receivable by the landlord had this agreement run the full term.

If the tenant is unable to pay rent until the end of the fixed term but finds another tenant prepared to take on the property, then, provided that the new tenant is acceptable to the landlord, the landlord will be prepared to accept the tenant's request to close the tenancy early, though the tenant will be liable for the landlord's reasonable costs associated with the re-letting.

The rent amount is **INSERT AMOUNT** pounds per calendar month payable in advance. The tenant agrees to pay the rent in advance by a single bank standing order by the **INSERT DATE OF RENT PAYMENT** day of each month without deduction or set-off. *[The rent money should leave the tenant's account six days before the due date, as this will allow time for inter-bank transfers and long weekends. If more than one tenant, get them to set up just one standing order.]*

The payment of the first month's rent is due on signature of this agreement. If any rent or other money payable by the tenant is not paid within seven days of the day on which it is due, it shall be payable with interest at the rate of 4 per cent per annum above the base minimum lending rate of **INSERT ANY UK BANK NAME**. This will be calculated on a day-to-day basis, from the day upon which it became due. If payment of rent is not received on the date it is due and the landlord needs to write to or visit the tenant, an additional administration fee may be charged to the tenant.

The tenant also agrees to pay the landlord on the signature of this agreement a deposit of **INSERT AMOUNT OF DEPOSIT** as security against the failure by the tenant to make good any reasonable demand by the landlord, and at the tenant's expense any damage by the tenant to the property or to any fixtures and fittings, furnishing and effects and as security against any expense or other nuisance caused to the landlord by the failure of the tenant to behave in a tenant-like manner or to return the property to the condition in which it was let (fair wear and tear excepted).

This deposit will be held by the landlord as stakeholder and lodged with a tenancy deposit protection scheme through the term of the tenancy without any deduction being made. The tenant will be advised by the landlord within thirty days of the start of the tenancy which scheme is protecting the deposit. No interest will be paid on the deposit. *[Landlords have to tell tenants which scheme they are in and provide full details of how the scheme works, including sending tenants a signed copy of the protection certificate, the scheme rules and other prescribed information within thirty days of receiving the deposit.]*

If, at the end of the term of the tenancy agreement, the tenant wants to continue the tenancy and has not received from the landlord two months' notice to end the tenancy, it will carry on from month to month as a monthly periodic tenancy. The arrangements in Section 21 of the Housing Act 1988 for the landlord to repossess the property apply to this agreement. This means the tenant cannot claim any legal rights to stay on once the tenancy has ended and a court order says the tenant must leave.

The landlord may seek to start action to repossess the property if the tenant fails to pay rent fourteen days after it is due, if the tenant becomes bankrupt, if any of the grounds listed in Schedule 2 of the Housing Act 1988 as amended by the Housing Act 1996 apply (these include not paying the rent, breaking the tenancy terms and causing a nuisance or annoyance) or if the arrangements for the landlord to repossess in Section 21 of the Housing Act 1988 apply. The landlord will obtain a court order to repossess.

Should the property be the landlord's main or principal home before the start of the tenancy agreement, the provisions for recovery of possession by the landlord in Schedule 2 of the Housing Act 1988 will apply.

[If applicable you should also include this clause: The property is subject to a mortgage granted before the start date of this tenancy agreement which gives the mortgagee the power of sale and that possession of the property may be recovered by the mortgagee under the provisions of Schedule 2 Ground 2 of the Housing Act 1988.]

Deposit

Provided that the tenant has vacated the property and has returned all keys to the property to the landlord, the deposit shall be returned to the tenant following the end of the tenancy. It will be returned after deducting any rent and other sums referred to that may be owed by the tenant – the reasons for these deductions will be notified to the tenant in writing.

The contents of the property at the start of the tenancy shall be assumed to be in immaculate order unless noted otherwise on the inventory.

Occupation only by the tenant

The tenant agrees not to sub-let or part with all or a share of possession or occupation of the property without the consent of the landlord (whose consent shall not unreasonably be withheld).

Utilities

In addition to the rent, the tenant is responsible for payment of all utilities including council tax, refuse collection charges, water rates and/or charges, electricity, gas, telephone, broadband and TV licence during the term of the tenancy, for making arrangements for meter readings at the start and end of the tenancy and advising the landlord of the readings. *[You need to check meter readings too but having the tenant do it will save some time on move-in/out days!]*

General

The tenant **must not**:

1. Make any alteration or addition to the property.
2. Damage the property or the fixtures, fittings or furnishings or remove them from the property. No screws, nails or bolts are to be attached to any wall or part of the property and no "blu-tack" or similar substance may be attached to walls. *[Put in a few picture hooks and tell the tenant he must only hang pictures on these.]*
3. Dismantle any item of furniture. *[Some tenants may dismantle and store your furniture if they plan to put in their own. If you've ever tried putting self-assembled furniture together after it's been disassembled, you'll know why this clause is here!]*
4. Bring in any item of furniture that doesn't comply with the Furnishings Fire Safety Regulations.
5. Interfere with the internal or external decorations of the property though reasonable requests will be considered.
6. Change or alter any locks on any door or window. (If any keys have been lost, the tenant must notify the landlord and pay the landlord the cost of fitting new locks and obtaining replacement keys.)
7. Have any additional keys made without permission of the landlord or allow any key to be in the possession of any other person except those who are party to this agreement.
8. Permit any illegal or immoral act to take place at the property.
9. Allow anything which is or may become an annoyance or nuisance to neighbouring premises or to the landlord.
10. Carry out any trade or business in the property or use it as other than a private residence. *[A tenant working on a computer from home is fine. Holding items of stock is not as it may invalidate the insurance policy and annoy neighbours too.]*

11. Allow anything on the property that may render void any policy of insurance maintained on the property. *[If you have this clause in the agreement, you must give the tenant a copy of the insurance policy so he will know what he can and can't do!]*

12. Keep any flammable items such as gas cylinders, paraffin or oil on the property.

13. Insert any rubbish, refuse material, food, corrosive substance, cooking fat, wet wipes or sanitary towels in any sink, toilet or pipe.

14. Keep any bird, reptile, dog, cat or other living creature in the property without seeking the landlord's permission (such permission shall not be unreasonably withheld).

15. Erect a TV or radio aerial or satellite receiver.

16. Leave or permit to be parked anything which causes an obstruction in or to any approach road or path to the property.

17. Use a washing machine or dishwasher when not in the property. *[If it leaks, you want your tenants to be there so they can do something about it!]*

18. Use the common entrance hall for purposes other than for quiet and peaceful entry.

19. Leave any item in the common hallway.

20. Allow anyone else to use the address of the property as a postal address.

The tenant **must**:

1. Notify the landlord promptly by phone and then in writing of any defect or disrepair in the property or to the fixtures and fittings or to smoke or carbon-monoxide detectors.

2. Advise the landlord of anything that could lead to a claim being made on insurance arranged on the property. In particular, to notify the landlord if the property will be left vacant for more than fourteen days. *[If unoccupied, you*

need to know so you can advise the insurance company. Where unoccupied, the premiums may increase.]

3. Notify the landlord of any change in work, home and mobile telephone numbers. *[You need to be able to contact him!]*

4. Forward all mail addressed to the landlord or to "the owner", as soon as reasonably possible, to the landlord's home address.

5. Open and forward any mail addressed to "the occupier" that is relevant to the landlord and advise the landlord of the receipt of any notice, contact or complaint from a local authority, corporation, neighbour or any other body.

6. Whenever the property is left unattended, to lock all windows and doors properly.

7. Ensure that the common hallway areas are kept in a clean and tidy condition. Where damage to the common areas is caused by tenants or their visitors to pay to the landlord the costs of making good. *[Where the lease says that the occupiers of a group of flats must take turns to clean common areas then your tenants must do this so it should be included as a clause in the agreement.]*

8. Permit the landlord, his agent or the managing agent by appointment (but at any time in the case of emergency) to come onto the property for the purposes of carrying out and completing structural repairs, decorative improvements or to examine the state and condition of the property.

9. Permit the landlord or his agent, provided that reasonable notice has been given, within the last forty days of the tenancy to view the property with prospective occupiers, valuers, surveyors or buyers.

10. Use only the allocated refuse store bins. *[Don't forget to tell them where the communal refuse bins are kept.]*

11. Take reasonable precautions to prevent frost damage. If the property is going to be empty overnight or for more than twelve hours in cold weather, enough heating must be left on to prevent the water system freezing.

12. Keep all lights, smoke alarms, carbon monoxide detectors and bulbs in working order and replace all fuses, bulbs and fluorescent tubes when necessary.

13. Clean the refrigerator and defrost it when necessary and arrange and pay for cleaning the windows every six months.

14. Use only the allocated parking space (where applicable) for the parking of one motor car or motorbike, the vehicle to have a current road fund licence.

15. Keep any allocated gardens in a neat, tidy and well maintained condition. *[You must give him the necessary tools to do this!]*

16. Adequately heat and ventilate the property and wipe down surfaces to stop the build-up of mould growth.

17. Take reasonable precautions to keep the premises free of infestation by vermin, rodents, fleas or ants. Where any such infestation is due to the action or inaction of the tenants, the tenants to be responsible for appropriate cleaning and fumigating costs and for the costs of removing such infestation.

18. At the end of the tenancy:

(a) Remove all personal items from the property and, where necessary, make arrangements with the council to have any unwanted large items removed. Any personal items belonging to the tenant which are not removed after fourteen days' written notice has been given may be sold within one month, with the residual value returned to the tenant, but with costs associated with their removal deducted from the deposit.

(b) If the carpets have been badly soiled, arrange for and pay (at the tenant's own expense) the cost of hot water extraction steam carpet cleaning – this work to be carried out by a professional carpet cleaning company. *[Only include this clause if the property was steam cleaned at the start. For some reason, even the nicest tenants are remarkably resistant to getting this done!]*

(c) Return all keys to the property to the landlord.

(d) Properly clean the property.

The landlord **will**:

1. Allow the tenant to hold and enjoy the property for as long as the tenant performs his obligations under this agreement.

2. Insure the property and the items listed on the inventory, and arrange for any damage caused by an insured risk to be remedied as soon as possible.

3. Keep in good repair the structure and exterior of the property and the installations for the supply of water (including heating and hot water), electricity, gas and sanitation and the fixtures and fittings (including mechanical and electrical items) included in the inventory.

Diplomatic immunity

The tenant cannot claim diplomatic immunity under any aspect of this agreement.

Rent review

If the landlord agrees to extend the tenancy beyond the fixed term, the rent amount will be adjusted annually by the landlord giving at least two months' notice.

Agent

Any person other than the tenant, who pays the rent due to the landlord, shall be deemed to have made such payments as agent for and on behalf of the tenant.

Notices

The address at which the tenant may serve notices on the landlord is **INSERT YOUR ADDRESS**.*[It's a legal requirement to state your address or that of your agent which must be in the UK.]* Any notices or other documents shall be served upon the tenant by either being left at the property or being sent to the tenant at the property by first-class or recorded-delivery post.

Should the tenancy be extended beyond the end of the initial term, the notice period required from the tenant to end the tenancy is one month.

Data Protection

The landlord or his agent may share details about the tenant's performance of obligations under this agreement with credit-reference agencies for referencing purposes and rental decisions and with utility providers, council tax, housing-benefit departments and mortgage lenders to help prevent dishonesty and for occasional debt tracing and fraud prevention.

Making rent payments

Payments are to be made to the landlord's account at **INSERT YOUR BANK NAME, BRANCH ADDRESS, SORT CODE AND THE NAME AND NUMBER OF YOUR ACCOUNT**.

Inventory

The landlord does not have facilities to store any items that the tenant does not require.

Fixtures, fittings, furnishings and effects must be left in the same place and condition at the end of the tenancy as they were at the start.

Tenants are to pay for the washing (including ironing) of all linen and for the washing and cleaning (including ironing) of all blankets and curtains which have been soiled during the tenancy.

LIST ALL ITEMS ON INVENTORY

[For each item on the inventory, the condition, make and model number should be noted and whether operating instructions have

been provided. Describe the condition of carpets, curtains, walls and windows with any marks or flaws noted. Include a statement that the items in the inventory are all in an immaculate condition unless the inventory notes to the contrary.

The tenant should initial, against the description of each item and for the number of keys received. It is recommended that all landlords appoint an independent inventory clerk to carry out the inventory and a schedule of condition at check-in and at move-out. This should include close up and far away time-dated photos and ideally a video. It is best if the same clerk does both check-in and check-out inventories.]

I have read and understood this agreement and have been given 1) a copy of the current ten-year energy performance certificate (EPC) for the property, 2) a copy of the current 12-month gas safety certificate for this property, and 3) a copy of the document called "How to Rent". I also have been shown that the smoke and carbon monoxide alarms work properly. Signatures of tenant(s) including guarantors (if a guarantor has been used).

_____

_____

[If you use a guarantor add the following statement which should be signed by the guarantor and witnessed and signed by an independent third party:]

I hereby guarantee to **INSERT YOUR NAME** that in return for you granting the above tenancy to **INSERT TENANT'S NAME(S)**, I will pay rent to you in the event of failure of **INSERT TENANT'S NAME(S)** to pay it and will make good to you any losses, costs or expenses that you incur as a result of failure of **INSERT TENANT'S NAME(S)** to observe any aspect of the tenancy agreement. *[For subsequent rent increases, you will need to get the guarantor's signature, suitably independently witnessed, agreeing to the new amount.]*

Appendix 2
Useful Contacts

Chapter 2

National Landlords Association
22-26 Albert Embankment,
London, SE1 7TJ
Tel: 020 7840 8900
www.landlords.org.uk

Residential Landlords
Association 1 Roebuck Lane,
Sale, Manchester, M33 7SY
Tel: 0845 666 5000
www.rla.org.uk

Scottish Association for
Landlords
Hopetoun Gate, 8b McDonald
Road, Edinburgh, EH7 4LZ
Tel: 0131 564 0100
www.scottishlandlords.com

Landlords' Association for
Northern Ireland
197 Lisburn Road, Belfast,
BT9 7EJ
Tel: 028 9082 7033
www.lani.org.uk

Chapter 3

The following are good websites
for local information. On
all these sites you can obtain
information for the specific
postcode you are buying into.

www.homecheck.co.uk
Offers reports on the risk of
flooding, subsidence, radon,
coal mining, landslip, landfill
sites, air quality and pollution.
www.hometrack.co.uk
(0845 013 2350)
and www.rightmove.co.uk
Are good for information on
house prices and trends.

www.rightmove.co.uk
Is a very easy site to use with a
lot of functionality and useful
information and you can chart
houses prices for different
types of properties in a specific
postcode over time.

www.environment-agency.
gov.uk/homeandleisure/
floods/31650.aspx
(03708 506 506)
Has flood maps by postcodes.

www.home.co.uk is a very
usable site with very up to date
asking price and selling price
trend information right down
to postcode level.

www.hmrc.gov.uk
This is the Inland Revenue's
website.

www.communities.gov.uk
(030 3444 0000)
Has lots of useful data on a
wide variety of things such
as house prices, rents and
regeneration initiatives.

Land Registry
www.landregistry.gov.uk

Association of Residential
Managing Agents (ARMA)
www.arma.org.uk
(020 7978 2607)

Leasehold Advisory Service
www.lease-advice.org
(020 7383 9800)
Companies House
www.companieshouse.gov.uk
(0303 1234 500)
Website giving information
on upcoming auctions:
www.eigroup.co.uk

Chapter 5
Royal Institute of British
Architects
www.riba.org
(020 7580 5533)

Royal Institution of
Chartered Surveyors
www.rics.org
(024 7686 8555)

Gas Safe Register
(0800 408 5500)
www.gassaferegister.co.uk

The Chartered Institute
of Plumbing and Heating
Engineering (IPHE)
www.ciphe.org.uk
(01708 472 791)

The Association of Plumbing
and Heating Contractors
(APHC)
www.aphc.co.uk
(0121 711 5030)

National Inspection Council
for Electrical Installation
Contracting www.niceic.org.uk
(0870 013 0382)
Electrical Contractors'
Association (ECA)
www.eca.co.uk
(020 7313 4800)

Chapter 7
Royal Mail
www.royalmail.com
(0845 774 0740)

Chapter 8
For IPHE, APHC – see
Chapter 5 above.
For ARMA see Chapter 3
above.

Energy Saving Trust
www.est.co.uk
(0300 123 1234)
England 020 7222 0101
Wales 029 2046 8340
Scotland 0131 555 7900

Northern Ireland
028 9072 6006

www.boilers.co.uk
The Energy Saving Trust's
website offers useful help
including a range of grants that
may be available.
With the site boilers.co.uk,
you can type in what your
specific needs are, size of home,
energy source, etc, and the site
will come up with suggestions
starting with the most efficient
model and information on grant
availability.

For Land Registry – see
Chapter 3 above.

Oyez Stationers
www.oyezforms.co.uk

www.landlordzone.co.uk
(0845 260 4420)

www.landlordlaw.co.uk

www.lettingfocus.com – my
own website with a regularly
updated blog

Chapter 9

For Oyez Stationers,
see Chapter 8 above.

Courts Service
www.hmcourts-service.gov.uk

Chapter 10

Inland Revenue (HMRC)
www.hmrc.gov.uk

Index

abroad *see* overseas property

accelerated possession procedure 193, 205–6, 207, 215, 216

access to the property 216

accidental damage insurance 112, 114, 166

accreditation schemes 110, 197–8

administration 24, 26, 115–16 *see also* management

advertising 34, 140–7, 167

architects 97, 98, 251

assured shorthold tenancies (AST) 65, 74, 117–18, 120–4

  agreement 120–4, 258–68

  deposits 123

  early-vacating tenants 122

  ending a tenancy 184–92, 202–3

  eviction *see* eviction

  fixed terms 118, 120, 121–2, 184, 185, 202–3

  guarantors 121

  monthly periodic tenancy 120, 122, 203

  more than one tenant 120–1

  rent reviews 123

  unfair terms 121

assured tenancies (AT) 65, 118, 194–5, 216

auction, buying at 62–9

  completion 67

  deposits 64, 67

  finance 68

  guide prices 64

  "hawking" 68

  paperwork 65–6

  pre-auction offers to buy 68

  reserve prices 63, 64, 67, 68

  viewing a property 66

auction, selling at 221

bad debts 33, 229 *see also* rent, arrears

bailiffs 210, 212, 215

bank loans *see* loans

bank statements 154, 156, 157, 159, 162

bank status enquiries 161–2
banker's drafts 168
base-rate tracker mortgages
    83
bathrooms 100–1, 108
below market value (BMV)
    properties 23, 72–7
    sourcers 73
boilers 176, 178–9
bridging loans 68, 73–4,
    87–9
    closed bridges 89
    open bridges 89
building regulations 66,
    98–9
Building Regulations
    Approval Certificate 99
building society drafts 168
building surveyors 97–8
building work 93–9
    architects 97, 98
    cash payments 96
    contracts 95–6
    detailed specifications 67,
    93–4, 95
    estimates 93
    finding a good builder 93,
    94–5
    fixed quotes 67, 90, 93
    planning permission 96, 98
    snagging 95
    timescale 95
    trade accounts 96

VAT 96
    see also tradesmen
buildings insurance 32, 33,
    112–13, 114
buy-to-let mortgage see
    mortgages
buying a property see finding
    and buying a property
buying agents 22, 56, 58,
    60–1
buying clubs see syndicates
"buying for income" 45
"buying for yield" 45

"cap and collar" mortgages
    81
capital allowances 227,
    232–3
capital gains tax (CGT) 39,
    40, 55, 218, 225, 229,
    232–8, 239, 241, 243, 255
    annual exemption 231–2,
    237–8
    calculation 232–8
    principal private residence
    (PPR) exemption 234–6,
    238, 241, 242
    private letting relief (PLR)
    exemption 231, 234–6,
    237
    rates of 237–8
capital growth 29, 39–40, 41,
    45, 46, 57, 236

calculation 39–40
carbon-monoxide detectors
    105, 124, 263, 265, 268
carpeting 100
cash buyers 71
co-mortgages 80
commonhold 51–2
communal hallways 51, 192
communication skills 24
company lets 118–19, 163–4
    company tenancies
        118–19
    management of 164
    references 163–4
competition, checking out 30
completion statements 92
condensation 127, 180, 181
contents insurance 33, 104,
    166
conveyancers 91
    auction-experienced 64,
        66
conveyancing 89–92
    leasehold properties 91
    Scotland 90
corporation tax 225, 231
costs of total investment
    35–8, 39
council tax 31, 116, 195–6
County Court Judgments
    (CCJs) 82, 160, 208, 209
credit reference checks
    159–61

credit scores 82, 160
crowdfunding 26, 76
curtains and fittings 99

damp 54, 126, 180–1, 200
death of a tenant 213
decoration see furnishings
    and decoration
demand for rental
    accommodation 19–20,
    21
demographic trends 46
deposits:
    amount of 151
    assured shorthold tenancies
        (AST) 123
    payment of 168
    property purchase 80, 92
    return of 186, 187, 189,
        190, 191, 193–5
    see also tenancy deposit
        schemes
derelict properties 47, 86
development finance 87–8
diplomatic immunity 119,
    164, 266
disability adaptations 111–12
discounted mortgages 82
dishwashers 127
disputes see problem
    neighbours; problem
    tenants
"distressed sales" 63, 72, 73

drainage 125, 126, 180

economic downturns 21, 27
electrical problems 181
electrical safety regulations
    105–6, 181
electricity fuse boards 70
emergencies 113, 124, 125,
    126, 127, 169, 175, 176,
    177
  insurance cover 113, 127,
    177
  see also House Guide
employer references 154–7
empty homes 77
ending a tenancy 184–92
  belongings, abandoned
    192
  cleaning 192
  giving notice 184–6
  inventory checks 190
  return of deposit 186, 187,
    188, 189, 190, 191
  Section 21 notices 184–5,
    186, 193, 202–3, 205
Energy Performance
    Certificates (EPCs) 32,
    35, 92, 106–7, 123, 137,
    179, 186, 197, 268
energy saving schemes
    107
Enterprise Investment
    Schemes 239, 244

estate agents 68, 70
  online agents 222
  relationships with 43
  selling property through
    219–21
European Economic Area
    (EEA) holiday lets
    239–40, 246
eviction 34, 119, 202–5
  assured shorthold tenancies
    (AST) 118
  assured tenancies (AT)
    216
  court action *see* possession
    proceedings
  discretionary grounds for
    202, 204
  holiday lets 120
  mandatory grounds for
    202–4
  possession proceedings
    205–7
  Rent Act tenants 118,
    210–11
  serving a notice 202–3
  squatters 210–11
  unlawful 185
ex-council properties 45–6,
    85
ex-government housing 63
Exchange with Delayed
    Completion (EDC) 76
extractor fans 127, 180, 181

"fair rent" 118
finance *see* loans; mortgages
finding a good tenant
129–68
advertising 34, 140–7
gut feeling 162–3
references 153–61
screening 26, 147–53
specifying the type of
tenant 145–6
see also letting agents;
referencing
finding and buying a
property 41–77
buying at auction 62–9
buying below market value
(BMV) 72–7
"buying for
yield"/"buying for
income" 45
choosing the right kind of
property 44–7
leasehold/freehold 47–52
local information 21,
42–3
location 41–4
negotiation 70–2
new or old 53–4
new-build and off-plan
54–62
pre-purchase checklist
69–70
fire safety:

smoke detectors 106, 127,
181
soft furnishings 104–5
flats:
above shops 45, 85
basement and ground-
floor flats 47
buying at auction 66
communal hallways 51,
192
conversions 51, 180
ex-council flats 46
floor plans 60
insurance 112, 114
leasehold 47–52
managing agents 177, 178,
180
"mansion type" blocks 46
mortgages 49, 86
new-build 55–6, 57, 59,
61
paperwork, managing
196–7
problem neighbours 182,
183
service charges 32, 46, 47,
49, 51, 58
short lets 116
water leaks 126, 128, 148,
176–8, 180, 183–4
Flips for Free 76
flood risk areas 86, 115
flooring 100

foreign nationals, letting to 119, 160–1

forwarding addresses 189, 191, 195

friends, letting to 129–30

furnishings and decoration 99–104, 133, 144–5, 152, 221
  fully furnished lets 104
  legal regulations 104–5
  quality 33, 41, 99
  replacement costs 33
  wear-and-tear tax allowance 229

garden maintenance 101–2, 200

gas appliances 33, 105, 175, 177

gas leaks 126

gas safety certificate 123, 186, 268

gas shut-off valve 127, 128

Google Street View 43

Green Deal 107

ground rent 32, 47, 49

guarantors 121, 123, 154, 160, 162, 163, 164, 167, 200

harassment 155, 212–13

"hawking" 68

head lease schemes 168

heating 177, 178–9

High Court enforcement 209

history of residential property letting 16–17

HMOs *see* Houses in Multiple Occupation (HMOs)

holiday lets 117, 142, 204, 239–44
  abroad 239–40, 246–7, 249–50
  European Economic Area (EEA) 239–40, 246–7
  loans and mortgages 247
  longer-term tenants 246–7
  running costs 247, 249
  tax treatment 239–41, 248

Home Information Packs (HIPs) 222

House Guide 117, 124–8, 166, 169, 174, 176, 200

house prices 20, 21, 23, 27, 46

house shares 164 *see also* Houses in Multiple Occupation (HMOs)

house-building programme 19

Houses in Multiple
    Occupation (HMOs) 86,
    107–11, 112, 113, 123,
    164, 197
  conversion to 110
  management 173
  mortgages 109
Housing Association Leasing
    Schemes (HALS) 131
housing associations 130
Housing Health and Safety
    Rating System (HHSRS)
    108, 111
housing supply 19, 46
housing-benefit tenants 13,
    20, 110, 131, 145, 154,
    162, 191
  management of 170–2,
    200–1
  overpayment claims 171,
    191, 214
  problems with 165, 214
"How to Rent" document
    124, 186, 268

identity fraud 116
illegal activities, tenants' 212
income *see* yield
income tax 39, 55, 84, 218,
    226–30
  deductible expenses 27–8,
    227–30
  rates of 230

inheritance tax 225
inspection visits 172, 174,
    190
insurance 112–15
  accidental damage
    insurance 112, 114,
    166
  appliance cover 181
  auction properties 64, 67
  buildings insurance 32, 33,
    112–13, 114
  claims 114
  contents insurance 33,
    104, 166
  emergency assistance
    feature 113, 127, 177
  empty properties 31
  excesses, standard 114
  exclusions 113
  flats 112, 114
  flood risk areas 115
  leasehold properties 32
  overseas property 252–3
  premiums 33
  public and employer's
    liability insurance
    112–13
  rent guarantee insurance
    113–14
  tenancy deposit protection
    33, 34, 138, 193–5
  tenant default 33
  water damage 126

interest-only mortgages
83–4
inventories 133–4, 151, 166,
187, 188, 189, 190
inventory clerks 133–4, 166,
190, 194
investment clubs 22
investment, sensible limits of
26–8

"jet to let" 246–57
Joint Venture deals 23, 76

kerb appeal 101
kitchens 100
Land and Building
Transaction Tax 241
Land Registry 47, 89, 159
landlords:
accreditation schemes 110,
197–8
negative associations 17
organisations 34–5, 112,
133, 185, 197–8, 203,
207, 228
registration (Scotland and
Wales) 34
successful landlords 22–6
leafleting 47, 72
leaks see water damage
leaseback schemes 250
Leasehold Advisory Service
52

leasehold properties 47–52
buying the freehold 47
checking the lease 49–50
commonhold 51–2
conveyancing 91
extending the lease 49
ground rent 32, 49
management 48–50, 52
mortgages 49
service charges 32, 46, 47,
49, 51
see also flats
leaving day 190
legal expenses 34
letting agents 131–9, 168
chancers 147
contracts 137–8
deposits, handling 137,
173, 195
drawbacks 134–6
fees 32, 119, 128, 135–6
fidelity bonding schemes
138, 173
finding a good agent
136–9
management of 172–4
management services 32,
172–4, 176
ombudsman schemes 138,
173
online agents 134, 141
relationships with 24, 43,
172–4

role and services 26, 32, 129, 131–6

tenant charges 133, 151

LIBOR rates 87

licence to occupy 119–20

licensing schemes 34, 107–10, 197

limited companies 255–6

listed properties 54

loans 27, 84

  bridging loans 68, 73–4, 87–9

  foreign properties 252

  tax deductible 27–8, 227–8, 243

  see also mortgages

local housing allowance (LHA) 171, 214

local knowledge 21, 42–3

location 41–3, 143

locks, changing 69, 206

lodgers 119–20

London Rental Standard 110

losses, rental 230, 237, 239

maintenance:

  by letting agents 172–3

  costs 33

  "Home Emergencies" contracts 177

  House Guide 117, 124–8

  legal obligations 175

  management 175–82

  minor repairs 124

  tax-deductible costs 227, 243

malicious damage 113, 114, 155

management:

  deposits see tenancy deposit schemes

  ending a tenancy 184–92

  of letting agents 172–4

  maintenance 175–82

  paperwork 196–7

  problem neighbours 182–4

  tenants 169–72

  utilities and council tax 195–6

manholes 70, 180

meter readings 116, 166, 189, 190, 191, 196, 261

migrant workers 19, 44

mixed tenure developments 59

mortgage brokers 84, 252

mortgage fraud 75–6

Mortgage Market Review 79

mortgages 37, 78–92

  additional advances 85

  ancillary charges 79

  application fees 80

  base-rate tracker mortgages 83

blanket restrictions 79, 86
"cap and collar" mortgages 81
co-mortgages 80
discounted mortgages 82
early redemption penalties 82–3
ex-council properties 46
fixed-rate mortgages 81
flats 50, 86
Houses in Multiple Occupation (HMOs) 109
interest rates 38, 82, 84
interest-only mortgages 83–4
leasehold properties 49
loan to value 80
new-build schemes 56
one-off capital repayments 85
"rent to interest" restriction 80
repayment mortgages 83, 84
self-certificated mortgages 84
surveys 80–1
tax deductible 227–8
valuation reports 54, 81
variable-rate mortgages 82
move-in day 165–6

National Insurance Contributions 225, 242, 243
National Insurance numbers 162
National Landlords Association 35
neighbours, problem 182–4
new-build properties 23, 55–62
   city centres 54–5, 57
   discounts 59, 61
   flats 57
   guarantee schemes 61
   guaranteed rental yields 59
   "mixed tenure" developments 59
   mortgages 57
   off-plan schemes 23, 55–6, 58, 61
   snags 53, 68
   sweeteners 59
   tenants' ghettos 57, 59
   valuation 56
"next-day remortgages" 73–4
nil cash flow situations 84–5
   see also void periods
notice, giving 184–5, 186

off-plan schemes 23, 55, 56, 58, 59
   back-to-back sales 55, 61

goodwill deposits 55

opportunity costs 37

overseas property investment
246–57
exchange rates 252
finance 252
holiday homes 249–50
holiday lets 231, 238,
239–40, 246–8
insurance 252–3
off-plan schemes 23
tax treatment 255–7
where and what to buy
253–4

own home:
letting out 85, 119–20,
204, 242
lodgers 119–20
re-occupation 204,
210–11

painting 101, 200

paperwork, managing 24, 26,
196–7

parking facilities 46, 58, 152

pensions, and property
investment, compared 18

periodic tenancies 120, 122,
203

pest problems 181–2

pets 168

planning permission 54, 66,
98, 110

portfolio diversification 46,
246–57

possession proceedings 119,
155, 205–7, 213, 217
accelerated possession
193, 205–6
normal possession 206–7
online applications 216
possession orders 185,
202, 204, 206, 211, 215
using a solicitor 207

premium rents 31, 102, 118,
170

privacy, tenants' 103, 191–2

Private Sector Leasing
Schemes (PSLS) 131

probate sales 62, 64–5

problem neighbours 182–4

problem tenants 34, 155,
169, 199–217
claims for money owed
155, 206–10, 212–13,
214
death of a tenant 213
harassment, avoidance of
155, 212–13
housing benefit/local
housing allowance
problems 214–17
managing problems
199–200
squatters 210–11
see also eviction

proof-of-posting certificates 186, 205

property development 243–4

property funds 20, 27
  exit fees 27

property investment companies 25, 239–40, 255–6

Property Lease Options 76–7

property shows 197

Protected Intending Occupier (PIO) 210–11

public and employer's liability insurance 112–13

quantity surveyors 97

Rachmanism 16, 17

Real Estate Investment Trusts (REITS) 20, 244

referencing 136, 146, 153–63, 212
  bank statements 154, 156, 157, 159, 162
  bank status enquiries 161–2
  company lets 164
  credit reference checks 159–61, 209
  employer references 154–7

guarantors 121

house shares 164

landlords (tenants' references) 191

previous landlord references 157–9

proof of identity 159

self-employed people 154

verifying references 156, 157, 158–9

work permits 161

regeneration areas 42, 59, 75

regulatory costs 34

relocation agents 119

remortgages 73–4, 88–9, 227–8, 243

rent 20, 26, 142, 147
  arrears 170–1, 200, 201, 202, 203–4, 205, 206, 209, 214
  late payment of 169, 200, 201, 204
  reductions and waivers 175–6
  rent guarantee insurance 113–14
  reviews 123
  setting a rent 30–1, 133
  standing orders 166, 169
  unpaid rent 33, 34, 155

Rent Act tenancies 16, 63, 65, 118, 211

Rent to Rent schemes 76

rent-a-room scheme 241
RentSmart Wales 110, 138
repairs *see* maintenance
repayment mortgages 84
repossessions 62, 65, 68
reservation fees 165, 166, 168
Residential Landlords Association 35
Rightmove 34, 42–3, 58, 102, 133, 134, 137, 140, 219
  Price Comparison Report 58
"Right to Rent" 161
risk 28
rogue landlords 109
rollover relief 239
running costs 29, 32–5, 37
  advertising 34
  general maintenance 33–4
  ground rent 32
  insurance premiums 33
  landlords' organisation fees 34–5
  legal and other regulatory expenses 34
  letting agency fees 32
  personal costs 35
  replacement fixtures and fittings 33
  service charges 32

Sale and Rent Back (SARB) 74
Scotland:
  conveyancing 90
  gas safety regulations 105
  Houses in Multiple Occupation (HMOs) 108
  selling property 222
  short assured tenancy 117
  stamp duty land tax 241
  tenancy information pack 117
screening tenants 23, 147–50
sealed bids 71
seasonality of the rental market 141–2, 167
Section 8 notices 203, 204, 205, 213, 214, 215
Section 21 notices 109, 175, 184, 185, 186, 193, 202, 203, 205, 214, 215, 260
Seed Enterprise Investment Schemes 239
selective licensing schemes 109
Self Invested Personal Pension Schemes (SIPPS) 244
self-certificated mortgages 84
self-employed tenants 154–5, 225, 243

selling property 218–23
    at auction 221
    costs 218
    Home Information Packs
        (HIPs) 222
    Scotland 222
    selling it yourself 221–2
    through an estate agent
        219–21
    timing the sale 218–19
seminars, property investment
    22, 23, 197
service charges 32, 47, 49,
    51–2
    ex-council properties 46
    new-build schemes 58
set-up costs 37
shared ownership schemes
    60
short assured tenancy
    (Scotland) 117
showers 97, 101, 126, 148,
    176
sitting tenants 63, 118
small claims procedure 94,
    207–8
smoke detectors 106, 127,
    181
social housing tenants 19, 25,
    59–60, 130–1
social media 162
soft furnishings regulations
    104–5

solicitors 55, 213, 217, 251
squatters 192
    eviction 210–11
stamp duty land tax 225,
    233, 241–4, 256
stock market, and property
    investment, compared 18
stop valve (stop cock) 70,
    125, 126, 127 128, 180
structural engineers 98
students 19, 110, 113, 140–1,
    142, 160, 162, 167, 200,
    257
subletting 206
subsidence 63, 64, 67, 98,
    114
surrender 201
surveys:
    auction properties 66
    building surveyors 97–8
    full structural surveys 54,
        81
    quantity surveyors 97
    structural surveyors 97
    valuation reports 54, 78
syndicates 22, 23, 56, 58,
    60–1, 244

tax 224–45
    double tax relief 256
    holiday lets 239–40
    interest, tax relief on
        230–2

managing paperwork 196–7

non-UK residents 225, 256

overseas property 255–7

rent-a-room scheme 241

SIPPS, syndicates and REITS 244–5

tax returns 225–6 *see also* capital gains tax (CGT); corporation tax; income tax; inheritance tax; National Insurance Contributions; stamp duty land tax

tenancies

ending a tenancy 184–92

see also assured shorthold tenancies (AST); assured tenancies (AT); company tenancies; Rent Act tenancies; short assured tenancy (Scotland)

tenancy agreements 34, 117–28, 133, 166

draft copies 166

sample agreement (Assured Shorthold Tenancy) 258–68

tenancy deposit schemes 35, 118, 137, 193–5

custodial schemes 193, 194

dispute-resolution procedures 193, 194, 208

insurance-based schemes 34–5, 137, 193–5

tenancy information pack (Scotland) 117

tenants:

eviction *see* eviction

letting to friends 129–30

management of 169–72

relationships with 24

see also company lets; finding a good tenant; holiday lets; housing-benefit tenants; social housing tenants; students

time-share schemes 250

To Let boards 192

tracing agents 216, 217

tracker mortgages 83

tradesmen:

emergency call-outs 127, 175

legal action against 94

relationships with 24, 175

service-level agreements 175

trade body membership 93

see also building work

trading losses 230, 237

transport facilities 43, 144, 149

tumble driers 181

Universal Credit 165, 170–1, 200–1
unlet properties *see* void periods
utility bills 116, 159, 195–6

valuation reports 54, 81
variable-rate mortgages 82
viewings 103, 143, 147–53
    tenants' privacy 103, 191–2
void periods 26, 31, 134, 136, 153, 167, 170
    council tax 31
    insurance 31
    property security 191, 222

washing machines 127, 145, 181

water damage 124, 125, 126, 128, 176, 178
    damage to other properties 124, 125, 148, 178, 179
water stop valves 70, 125, 126, 127, 180
white goods 100, 102, 145, 174, 181
    appliance cover 181
work permits 161

yield 29–30, 38, 39, 41, 46
    "buying for yield" 45
    calculation 30, 35–40
    effect of voids on 31
    guaranteed rental yields 59
    net yield 37, 38, 39, 46

Zoopla 34, 134, 140, 219